Praise for
The Power of I Am

"I love this book! *The Power of I Am* will touch your soul and challenge you to awaken from the mass trance that holds millions in the bondage of poverty thinking."

—KEN D. FOSTER, author of *Ask and You Will Succeed;* CEO, Shared Vision Network

"John Maxwell Taylor empowers us to maintain our true identity amidst the madness of a world in transition. It is a wake up call to all who do not wish to be a part of the negativity that drives this mass hypnosis."

—JOAN GATTUSO, author of the bestselling *A Course in Love, A Course in Life*

"To whom much is given, much is expected. John Maxwell Taylor has been given much and is a beautiful conduit for its flow."

—ERIC BUTTERWORTH, author of *Spiritual Economics: The Principles and Process of True Prosperity* and *Discover the Power Within You: A Guide to the Unexplored Depths Within*

THE POWER OF I AM

Creating a New World of Enlightened Personal Interaction

JOHN MAXWELL TAYLOR

Foreword by Peter A. Levine, Ph.D.

Frog,
Ltd.

Published by Frog, Ltd.

Frog, Ltd. books are distributed by
North Atlantic Books
P.O. Box 12327
Berkeley, California 94712

Cover and book design by Suzanne Albertson
Printed in the United States of America

ISBN 1-58394-142-8

For Emily

Acknowledgments

Special thanks to: Betse Bernstein, Carina Tinozzi, Barbara Goodman, Rikki Mundhenke, Lisa Joy Riordan, Peter Levine, Jason and Michelle Taylor, and James Slatic.

I would also like to thank Winn Kalmon for her superb editing, as well as the whole team at North Atlantic Books/Frog, Ltd.

Contents

Foreword

In my work helping people recover from the effects of trauma, I have observed that the shocks to the system life sometimes delivers can have a numbing effect on our ability to feel fully alive. Through a series of practices and psychological induction processes, I help individuals regain a "sensed/felt" connection with themselves. This recovery of feeling is an essential key in attaining personal wholeness and freedom from neurosis.

John Maxwell Taylor's work, as outlined in this book, also encourages a return to wholeness, but from a different yet complementary approach. He proposes that the energy in a stressful and potentially demoralizing social situation can be converted "on the spot" into a powerful source of clarity and self-transformation. As in my own work, the accent is on the recovery of sensation and the reestablishment of active consciousness as opposed to passive reactivity. John practices what he preaches in the thick of what he refers to as the "improvisational theater" of everyday life.

My first experience of John was when I saw him performing his award-winning twenty-character, one-man-play *Forever Jung* on the life of famed psychologist Carl Gustav Jung. From my own background in Jungian psychology, I was able to clearly recognize that he had captured not only the essence of Jung, but also many of his associates, including Sigmund Freud. Compacting the essential incidents of Jung's life, his inner explorations, and interactions with his wife, mistress, and a host of dream figures into a two-hour performance must have been a daunting experience. But John apparently thrived on it in a poetic and dazzling performance.

When I asked him how he managed to stay so energized on stage, he replied that he was practicing "divided attention" throughout the show. Further inquiry revealed that this meant he consciously kept a continuous "sensed/felt" connection with his body throughout his performance. This way he could place 50 percent of his attention upon the audience and 50 percent upon experiencing the totality of himself on stage during the experience of acting.

"The play is naturally word and idea heavy," John told me. "If I were to stay in my head the audience would perhaps find it wearing. But as an actor I have learned to feel my body and my emotions to the same degree that I am mentally active on stage. This automatically puts the audience in touch with their bodies and their feelings. The words and ideas then fall into a collective audience mind which is like a still pool, a well of mental receptivity."

Later, as I got to know John personally, I found that this is how he approaches all of life. For him, as for Shakespeare, "all the world's a stage," even for ordinary social interactions. This does not mean that he is a "drama king," constantly overacting in public and stirring up scenarios of human confrontation. On the contrary, most of the time he comes across as a rather private person with a quiet, focused demeanor. Yet when he speaks about that which is meaningful to him, one finds oneself placing clear attention upon him and what he is saying. One senses that something is going on inside him. He emits a sense of "presence" that commands attention and respect. And this internal, yet outwardly expressive, state seems to be in a condition of constant regeneration. Indeed, I was so taken by this work that I took a few individual coaching sessions, which greatly enhanced my capacity to speak comfortably in front of large audiences.

In this book you will find the thoughts and ideas, key tools and techniques, and perceptions that John uses, not just on stage but in daily life. He knows how to transform potentially negative, disturbing, and disruptive social situations into a regenerative healing power, in the moment, amidst real-world situations. Before we can transform the world at large, or anyone else, we must first know how to remain centered within ourselves amidst interpersonal friction and even conflict. Without friction, or the play between positive and negative forces, the human race would never have discovered fire or electricity, learned to make heat at will, or light our streets and homes. To create a better world, a more enlightened world, as John proposes, we must first enlighten ourselves as individuals. From that place of self-illumination, we can then extend to others the option to join us in the light, if they so choose. If they do not wish to, at the very least, we ourselves shall be able to travel through the world in an illuminated manner. By doing this, not only shall we see clearly where we are going; we shall also be blazing a trail that future generations, with perhaps a more innate predisposition toward the truth than at present, may choose to follow.

The Power of I AM shows us the way and, happily, it is highly entertaining and a rattling good read. Enjoy your journey with John Maxwell Taylor. I can assure you that you are in very good hands.

Peter A. Levine, Ph.D.

Author of *Waking the Tiger: Healing Trauma* (North Atlantic Books, 1997) and *Healing Trauma: A Pioneering Program for Restoring the Wisdom of Your Body* (Sounds True Book/CD, 2005)

CHAPTER ONE

Standing Strong in a Stressful World

Personal Authority through *I AM* Awareness

Have you ever walked down the street, seen a stranger coming toward you, and intuitively felt you should give that person a wide berth? Something about the person activates an inner avoidance mechanism. Instinctively, you draw into yourself as he or she passes by.

At such times there may be more at stake than simply guarding your social identity. You could be preventing yourself from being drained by a static energy exchange with someone who might be inharmonious to your soul. This book is about *consciously* activating within ourselves a force of energy that will render us immune to disturbing external influences. It will give you the power to move through the chaos of our modern world with a sense of spiritual authority, inner strength, and personal security.

The source of this power is rooted in the core of your own being. It is the *I AM* intelligence that lets you know that you exist and are alive. By learning to draw on this energy at will in the midst of your daily affairs, you can stay centered in any social situation.

Being spiritual does not mean that we should be social pushovers. We all have a right to be strong and to project to the world a quality of self that commands respect and ensures that we be treated with dignity. Inner peace does not mean that we become externally passive. To do so can place our well-being at risk, as a story from India illustrates.

The Snake That Wouldn't Hiss

In a village close by the Ganges, the inhabitants were being terrorized by an aggressive snake. Whenever anyone ventured outside the compound, the snake would rush forward and attack. All attempts to capture the creature failed and the villagers lived in a constant state of fear and watchfulness.

One day a wandering holy man came into the village. Sensing an air of tension and seeing the worried faces of the inhabitants, he inquired as to the source of their trouble.

"Our lives are being made miserable by a wretched snake that delights in terrorizing us," said the head of the village. "Please help us. We are at our wits' end."

The holy man went into the jungle and found the snake sunning itself outside the hole in the ground it called home. Recognizing the highly spiritual nature of its visitor, the snake listened respectfully as the holy man spoke on behalf of the villagers.

"You cannot go around terrorizing people," he said. "This is India, the birthplace of Mahatma Gandhi and nonviolence. You must mend your ways. I shall give you a mantra, a sacred word that you are to meditate upon as you try to feel compassion in your heart for all beings. Cease to attack the villagers and anyone else. In a year I will return and will expect to find you greatly changed for the better."

The snake, not wishing to disobey a holy man, bowed reverentially and retired to its hole in the ground to contemplate peacefulness.

In due time the holy man returned to the village and found everyone living in a state of contentment. No longer troubled by the snake, the people's lives had become serene. But when the holy man went to check on the snake, he found it in a pitiful condition, lying helplessly outside its hole, cut and bruised from nose to tail.

"Why, snake," said the sage. "What happened to you?"

"It's your fault," hissed the reptile very weakly. "I did as you requested and practiced nonviolence. But when the villagers found out that I was harmless they beat me with sticks. Now every day the children come and throw rocks at me. Look at the state I am in. My life is miserable and it's all your fault."

"You foolish snake," said the holy man. "I told you not to bite. I didn't tell you not to *hiss!*"

Deep down we want to believe the best about other people. Like the snake, we try to be loving and cooperative. Yet we all know what it feels like to have our acts of kindness misused and abused. The mature spiritual individual recognizes that getting along with others requires a clear view of human nature in all its manifestations, the benign and the unpleasant. And such a person also knows when and how to hiss if necessary.

The Power of *I AM* to Transform Life When Under Pressure

Many people today are becoming increasingly aware that they are souls living in human form. In previous eras, those who sought connection with higher intelligence used to withdraw from the world to monasteries, ashrams, and retreats. Now human evolution requires that we find our spiritual selves in the midst of modern life with all its tension, stress, and contradictions. By learning to convert every day the static electricity of social confusion into a high-voltage charge of positive energy that can increase our consciousness, we can greatly hasten our spiritual development. And through the example of the suprapositive energy that emanates from us as we cultivate a sensed and felt awareness of *I AM* in, through, and around us, we heal the world as we move through it.

The personality of every human being is like a city populated by thousands of people who call themselves "I." But they are all imposters. One "I" will emerge from our brains for a few seconds to speak through our voice and then be gone to be followed by another a few seconds later. One little "I" will write a check and all the rest will have to pay for it. A group of them will decide to go on a diet on Thursday night. But when we awaken the next morning, another group of these imposters who say "I" have occupied our brains during the night. They know nothing about a diet and make us eat what they want. What *we* want is to have a permanent sense of ourselves. To make decisions and stick to them. To say "I" and know that this is who we really are because it is the *I AM* at the core of our being directing our thoughts, words, actions, and intentions.

By immersing ourselves in the presence of *I AM,* that which is real within ourselves in an age of stress, fear, and uncertainty, we can maintain ourselves amidst the madness. We can then use the energy generated by the friction of having to deal with people trapped in the ego-driven, collective, contemporary nightmare-dream they perceive as "reality," to awaken ourselves from the mass trance that holds millions in slavery. Every time people are rude, unfriendly, devious, self-interested, or aggressive toward us, they are actually doing us a favor. If, instead of buying into the particular dream/delusion they are projecting onto us and forgetting who we are, we practice *self-remembering,* in that moment we cease to be hypnotized by our own reactivity. We become *proactive.* The power and presence of *I AM* steps forward into our consciousness and fills body, mind, and emotions with an incredible sense of power and well-being. Then we can say and do anything we want with a sense of self-certainty that commands respect and places external situations in our favor.

We can "eat" stressful situations alive and convert potentially negative static energy into fuel for life. The dramas caused by the struggle between shadow and light, or ignorance and reason are very real in our world and must be handled realistically. How we personally respond to pressure in the school of life is supremely important. We are constantly tested by circumstance to see what level of *consciousness, conscience,* and *behavior* we will operate from in the face of difficulty.

Can we be kind and loving, or will we fold up and run away, or get angry when someone turns on us? Do we have the ability to speak our truth in the face of miscomprehension and grow from the experience? Or will we become filled with self-doubt and a sense of inferiority? At what level does our capacity for total forgiveness collide with our pragmatism or desire for revenge? Can we cancel all debts and respond firmly, yet without personal animosity, to someone who is behaving toward us in an inappropriate manner? These are large questions. We answer them by how we live day by day.

What I have observed in myself is that when I apply the techniques you are going to learn in this book in the face of interpersonal difficulty, I experience an immediate shift in consciousness. First, my energy levels increase exponentially and this seems to cause a fusion of my spirit, or soul if you will, and my human self. I become highly focused and purposeful, and suddenly know who and what I am at a level far beyond any self-conceptions I normally entertain when identified with my personality structure. It's as if my value suddenly increases on some cosmic stock exchange and I feel connected with an unfolding pattern much greater than my usual self-conceptions. A sense of *I* emerges that seems linked to an eternal process. This *I* has watched from behind the scenes through all the changes my human, ever shifting personality-identity has gone through. I recognize this *I* by a certain inner taste and remembrance of its having appeared before at various crisis times in my life, such as when I was rushed to a hospital for an appendectomy at the age of six. It has also emerged each time I fell in love and its advent has shown me that the love I was feeling was the true nature of this *I* and therefore of mine. It is the *I* of the *I AM,* the eternal substance behind all life.

Since *I AM* is the underlying substratum of myself, the core of my own being, it is also the underlying reality of everyone I meet, including the rude, the ignorant, the ill-mannered, and the misbehaved. People behaving badly have forgotten the presence of *I AM* within them. When I remember and connect with it in myself while they try to force their ego-based agendas on me, *I AM* floods my being and looks at them through my eyes. This *looking* carries with it a certain unusual energy that represents a higher order of intelligence, as if a world above were looking at a less coherent world below. The atmosphere generated by this process is palpable and can create some dramatic shifts during friction-laden interpersonal encounters. The appearance of *I AM* gives pause to psychological bullies who want to turn the happy dream of life we were meant to live into a neurotic arena. Such individuals want to cause friction so they can inflate their egos at the expense of those who want to live in peace and harmony.

I AM puts clever words in my mouth. It turns the tables on troublemakers and defangs energy vampires as it empowers my personal self to be awake and unaffected by antisocial craziness. So we are not talking about escaping to some otherworldly dimension when harassed by life. Instead, we bring a higher intelligence to bear on the everyday situations we encounter in the real world. By aligning ourselves with and allowing a flow through us, of that which we all are, beyond the illusions of apparent separation from each other, we teach by example and personal demonstration. This process is one of the highest forms of compassion because it is practically effective. It changes things around us. At the same time, it advances our personal evolution because to act in such a manner, we have to become inwardly more conscious while dealing with external pressure. And all real growth is based on expanding consciousness.

Self-Assertion versus Aggression

George Bernard Shaw once said, "If the Christians want to redeem anybody they had better start looking a bit more redeemed." I believe this holds true for people who are aligning their lives with the emerging global sense of a new spirituality. If trying to live in congruence with the values of higher consciousness is so great, then the results ought to be visible in all areas of our lives. They should be readily apparent to other people through our right behavior, personal strength, and *self-mastery.* This includes being able to stand up for ourselves in conflict situations, without abandoning our spiritual values, or hiding behind them out of personal weakness.

No one likes to be pushed around, and the desire to assert our will is always going to come out one way or another. Spiritually inclined individuals who cannot address difficult issues directly, as they arise, often fall back on passive-aggressive behavior. Those who can be assertive, when self-assertion is called for, stand a far better chance of resolving the tensions of the moment, as they are happening. *Self-assertion* should not be confused with *aggression,* which is often ego-driven and seeks to wound or devalue the other person. The difference between "hissing" and "biting" is that when we bite (an action stemming from the desire to wound), the venom we inject into another person poisons us also. Hissing, on the other hand, can be seen as a bit of conscious playacting, deliberately assuming a particular type of behavior to let people know they are not to mess with you.

Truly successful human beings develop a set of skills that enable them to negotiate all aspects of interpersonal experience. These are people who live from a positive state of mind and have an abundance of life energy. They know how to maintain their sense of self in the face of difficult interpersonal transactions. Unlike the snake, they may not even need to hiss. The high-voltage energy of their integrity speaks loudly in a nonverbal manner. It automatically dissuades others from interfering with them.

Walking Like a Dragon: The Power of Inner Strength

In ancient Japan, the greatest Samurai warrior had his sword made by the best swordmaker in the land. He hardly ever had to draw it. Such was the beauty and balance of the instrument that it radiated a power others could feel, even when it was sheathed. Its mere presence at his side spoke volumes, and troublemakers seldom dared to accost him. The beauty of the energy that radiates from a truly balanced spiritual person is similar to that of the Samurai warrior's sword. It is a force field that automatically discourages others from messing with us—and it can be consciously cultivated by anyone, using the methods in this book. Such power serves as a living demonstration to others of our personal integrity through right behavior. It naturally commands respect from them.

In the following pages you will find many insights, stories, and techniques to empower your life with this type of magnetism. In addition to serving as a protective field of energy, the electrifying qualities arising from such high levels of personal power make us magnetically attractive to others. People naturally seek social interaction with high-energy individuals, in the hope of becoming energized by association with them. When we have strong life energy, we automatically exert an invigorating influence upon those who are capable of receiving a positive charge from us. We must also know how to draw on that power when dealing with negative people, particularly with egotists who seek to manipulate or control us.

When we allow ourselves to be adversely affected by negative people and situations, we actually *leak* life energy. As our personal magnetism weakens, our innate sense of who we are flies away from us. Under the influence of disturbed emotions it becomes hard to think straight. Our hands, arms, and legs may shake, while the stomach does flip-flops and irregular breathing makes our speech shallow and ineffective. Temporarily dispossessed from ourselves, we are vulnerable to personal invasion by the disruptive aspects of the unconscious side of human nature.

Some people try to escape from this syndrome by adopting a facade of habitually aggressive behavior. Others place emotional armor around themselves, withholding their feelings and refusing to let anyone in. But erecting barriers as a way of life can be very draining. And no matter how tough we try to act, someone will always show up who knows where to find our weaknesses and play upon them.

The Clash of the Amazon Coworkers

My friend Jayne is quite an intimidating figure. She stands six foot one in stocking feet and has a three-inch pile of hair on top of her head that raises her to six foot four. With a rather loud voice, a forward manner, and an inclination to "tell it like it is," she hardly comes across as a pushover in any situation. But the last time I visited Jayne in Florida, she told me that her life was being made miserable by a challenging coworker.

"This woman drives me nuts," Jayne informed me, between snatches of toast and coffee one morning, as she bustled to get ready for another day at the office. "Her name is Regina. It used to be a pleasure going to work. Now I have to force myself to eat a decent breakfast. The thought that I'm going to be seeing *her* in a few minutes sticks in my throat."

"What exactly is it about this woman that gets your goat?" I inquired, surprised that anyone could disturb my seemingly powerful friend.

"Regina! The name says it all. She's got a queen complex and acts like she's better than everyone else!" snapped Jayne, momentarily going bug-eyed as she flushed with anger.

"Especially you?" I volunteered.

"Exactly!" Coffee slopped over the table as Jayne enthusiastically slammed down her cup in agreement. Then, realizing she had walked into a self-created trap, she slumped visibly as the real weight of her dilemma hit home. "I don't know what it is. I just seem to lose myself when confronted by her. It's like I don't know who I am anymore. I stumble over my words and can't get my point across. The more I flounder, the smugger she gets. It's as if she knows she's throwing me off and gets a kick out of it. And she always manages to get the last word in before she flounces off."

"Let's talk about it tonight after dinner," I offered, as Jayne grabbed her purse and headed for the door. "She could be an energy vampire. I have a few techniques that might help you deal with the situation."

"Anything," said Jayne, sighing and shaking her head. "I'm ready to try anything."

That evening, we picked up our conversation. "Regina enjoys the feeling of power that comes from robbing you of your identity," I volunteered. "And you are *letting her take it!*"

"But why does she do it?" Jayne lamented. "And why do I let it happen?"

"Probably because you don't want her to think that she is superior to you! So you try to act in a superior manner toward *her* to prove that she's not."

"All right," said Jayne, shifting around in her chair, not without a trace of wariness. "I can accept that. But what should I do?"

"You need to find a way to connect with who she really is. Get beneath the surface. Is there anything about her that you *do* like?"

An awkward silence filled the room. Then Jayne's lower lip started to quiver slightly. Tears appeared in her eyes and trickled slowly down her cheeks.

"I do like her," she said softly, in a quavering voice. "Or I did when I first met her. But she doesn't seem to like me. I tried to be friends but she pushed me away. And it hurt."

"I'm willing to bet she likes you too," I suggested gently. "But neither of you can get past your ego stuff. We have to find a way for you to see the best in her—to get beneath the surface and really connect with her at the deepest level. Is Regina left-handed or right-handed?"

"Right . . . I think," she replied, looking puzzled. "What's that got to do with it?"

"Well, try looking mainly into her left eye when you speak with her. It will help you to make a harmonious connection."

"Why is that?" said Jayne, her face brightening as she rubbed the traces of tears from her cheeks. "What's so special about her left eye?"

Seeing *I* to Eye

"One eye of a person reflects his or her real, or *essential,* nature—who that person really is," I continued. "It's what people were born with, as opposed to what they have picked up from life. Babies are nothing *but* essence. They are pure energy filled with positive emotion and life potential. That *essential* part of us usually remains visible to a degree in one particular eye of a person throughout his or her life. I call this the *essence eye.* The other eye reflects that person's life experiences. It seems to be wired into the brain in such a way that you can see the personal history on display there. That's what I call the *personality eye.*"

"You mean that's where we can see the good, the bad, and the ugly?" asked Jayne, with a mock shudder.

"Generally speaking, if you look in someone's essence eye, he or she will be open and responsive to you. However, when you look into the personality eye, the connection you feel with that person will vary according to his or her type, mood, or the situation you are in. It can be particularly dangerous when personalities clash and things are starting to boil over."

"You mean looking in the wrong eye at the wrong moment might really set somebody off?" laughed Jayne. "Regina and I glare at each other all the time. I bet we're doing the personality eye thing without knowing it. So what's the answer?"

"You might start by looking more into her essence eye. That way you stand a chance of connecting with her better instincts. You might even see her soul."

"I don't think she has one," said Jayne with a wry smirk, momentarily reverting to her feisty self.

"Now Jayne, be nice," I cautioned playfully and then suggested she settle comfortably into a chair, let go, and relax. "We're going to sit here quietly and look at each other in a sort of detached, meditative way. And I want you to gaze into my left eye. I'm right-handed, so my essence eye is the left one. You are also right-handed. So as I look at you, I am directing my attention to your left eye to connect with who you really are."

A feeling of softness started to pervade the room. The fading light outside seemed to infuse an extra sense of peace into the warm Florida evening.

"There now," I continued reassuringly. "That feels nice, doesn't it?"

"Uh huh," nodded Jayne, obviously enjoying the chance to relax. Then her mind kicked in. "But how do you know if someone is right-handed or left-handed?"

"Don't go into your head," I suggested gently. "We'll get to that later. Let's just work on Regina, who we already know is right-handed. So to establish a feeling of trust with her, try to look more often into her left eye—her essence eye—the way I'm looking at you right now. As we look at each other, there is no barrier between us, is there? We both seem very open to each other, right?"

As she responded to my guidance, the beauty of the Jayne beneath the tough exterior was becoming increasingly apparent to me. Something luminescent seemed to be shining through her skin, softly erasing the tensions from her face. She didn't know it but the *I AM* in her was stirring as an energetic presence.

"Yes, we do. I feel really comfortable with you right now," she said softly. "But this term *essence eye* sounds a bit vague to me. I'm still not sure I know what it means."

"We don't have to define essence at this stage. It's not something you think about so much as something you see, or sense intuitively. I'm going to teach you how to see it in yourself and in other people, and bring out the best in them. I assume you like the feeling of peace and connection that we are experiencing together?"

"Sure"

"It makes you trust me?"

Jayne nodded, smiling.

"Then for the moment, let's call your essence eye your *trust eye*."

Again we slipped into the enveloping friendly silence. A few more moments passed comfortingly, then a sudden cloud of irritation crossed Jayne's face. The signs of her *I AM* vanished. She wriggled in her seat and a hard, tense look possessed her face as she dropped back down into false personality and unconsciousness.

"Wait a minute!" she snapped. "We're supposed to be talking about dealing with Regina at the office here. I have tried to make nice with her and it doesn't work. When I do, she looks at me with contempt and makes me feel like a weakling for trying. She's not going to sit around like this and have 'trust eye' feel-good sessions with *me!*"

Jayne's energy switch took me by surprise and I lost connection with the *I AM* presence in, through, and around myself.

"No, of course she isn't," I managed to reply calmly. "You are going to have to *earn* her trust gradually. I'm not suggesting that you suddenly start staring at her, following her optically around the room like the periscope on a submarine. Just be natural. In your ordinary conversations with Regina, make sure you glance into her essence eye once in a while. When you do, be sure to send her a good feeling. That will do for a start."

Putting a Troublemaker on "Pause"

"And what about when she starts acting like a bitch?" Still unable to get away from her automatic reactions, thinking of the unpleasant aspects of Regina again stirred Jayne's aggressive side to even greater insanity. She glared my way as if I had metamorphosed into Regina, fully projecting her work-related annoyance onto me. But I was not about to receive it. A living demonstration was called for. Now was the time to teach Jayne something, while protecting myself at the same time.

"If she is being uncooperative, you don't have to become a doormat," I said. "When she won't 'get real' and relate to you in a cooperative, mutually honoring manner, you can serve notice on her that you are someone who is not to be messed with. Like this. . . ."

I deliberately broke eye contact with Jayne. Turning my head to look out the window, I began placing my attention upon my own body, rather than on her. First I dropped down mentally into my feet, and as I did so, they began to tingle with energy. Then an electrical current ran quickly up my legs, filling me with a solid sense of connection with them. Next my hands started to tingle and vibrate in a similar manner. The sensation moved through my arms and then into my chest and stomach until a powerful feeling of being centered pervaded me entirely. I was back in the *I AM* presence. Still looking out the window, I said to Jayne, "When Regina gets testy with you, you can look into her personality eye. Like this. . . ."

Slowly I turned my head back toward Jayne. Directing my attention from *my* personality eye, I gazed into her right eye, *her* personality eye. My attitude was detached yet firm. While giving the impression that I was not to be trifled with, I was not projecting hostility toward her. Nevertheless, the unspoken underlying message was "You'd better not start with me. I'm onto you."

Jayne's eyes widened like saucers. Her spikey hairdo seemed to stand even more erect on her head than usual.

"Oh my God," she cried out. "There's no way I'm going to mess with you." By now she was practically jumping up and down in her seat with excitement. "I'm locking the doors. You can't leave. Tell me *more*. Now! Immediately!"

Establishing Rapport: The Subliminal Connection

I went on to explain that when I meet people for the first time, I make it a point to look into their essence eye as we shake hands. This creates an immediate rapport and a sense of friendly acceptance. On the other hand, when people are being difficult, I may need to signal that I am not about to be bothered by the negative stuff they are putting out. In such a case, I look into their personality eye in a manner that lets *them* know that *I* know they are out of integrity. In a nonverbal form, I am conveying to them, with a look, that I can see they are coming from false personality and being run by their past programming. The virus-ridden software acquired from previous dysfunctional moments with other people is temporarily running their present-moment behavior. Their past history is causing them to act like a malfunctioning computer in the here and now!

When I initiate this process, something seems to register in other people subliminally that they are letting themselves down. It's as if their higher self becomes embarrassed for them. The *I AM* in me sees the *I AM* in them and observes our personalities either behaving like idiots, or getting it together and cooperating. In a place beyond momentary reactivity, somewhere between the personality level and *I AM,* these distraught individuals sense that they are not being true to their highest potential. Nine times out of ten a miraculous shift occurs. They start to behave in a more noble, expansive, and cooperative manner. The better part of their human nature comes out and assumes command of their behavior.

Regina and Jayne had a strange interpersonal chemistry that caused my friend to lose all sense of herself during confrontations. As most of us do when someone is behaving in a troublesome manner toward us, she misplaced her own identity. During the few days of my visit, I taught Jayne ways to strengthen her sense of self under pressure. I shared with her specific valuable techniques for getting out of her head and remaining grounded in her body when friction occurred. She learned to see *personality* and *essence* in her *own* eyes while standing in front of the mirror. Then I showed her how to spot these qualities in everyone she meets, including Regina. Additionally, she learned various techniques for not overreacting or taking the bait when deliberately provoked. Finally, she realized that when she became identified with her negative reactions she fell asleep, that is, forgot who she was and behaved like a program-run idiot. Through *self-remembering,* the opposite of self-forgetful reactivity, she was able to start creating a connection with *I AM* and feel a presence greater than her ego when she felt attacked. Eventually, with daily practice "on the job," Jayne was able to transform the situation that had been causing her so much distress, uplifting her coworker in the process.

Using Interpersonal Tension to Create Consciousness

We live in an age of rudeness, characterized by the put-down and aggressive antisocial behavior. Some of the games people play, unconsciously or otherwise, revolve around trying to make others look or feel foolish. Since the unconscious shifting of power from one person to another involves a gain or loss of energy, one of our first tasks is to prevent ourselves leaking life force as we deal with others. This is crucial for all who want to live in the present moment, fully empowered. It is doubly imperative for anyone who wishes to develop *I AM* consciousness in a world where spirituality is largely an undervalued commodity.

I have trained myself not to shrink from the possibility of conflict or friction. Now I know how to connect with and absorb a positive charge of energy from the surrounding atmosphere when people are being obnoxious. They are usually totally unaware that I am powering up with life while they disenfranchise themselves in front of me. You might say I am eating the energy behind the negative situation and converting it into food for my soul. I have this down to such an art that now, when I see a troublemaker coming at me, my first reaction is "Oh good, here comes lunch."

Many people today are seekers of higher consciousness, a state of being beyond the dullness of mundane perception. But to maintain our spiritual sensibility, we must be able to remain steady in the midst of the upheavals of ordinary life. A few seconds of negative emotional reactivity can burn up much of the vital energy our bodies need to run optimally. Even a momentary loss of life force can be spiritually catastrophic because when we are physically drained, we *feel* disconnected from our souls. Higher consciousness manifests most succinctly through a sound, socially connected body, stable emotions, and a clear mind. Application of the rule "feet on the earth, head in the heavens" was never more needed than now. Collectively and individually, we can no longer afford to live in such a way that our spirits are allergic to our bodies and our personal lives.

For those wishing to exist in harmony with their souls and other people, the ability to consciously invoke *I AM* awareness is essential. Under the barrage of friction arising from disorderly encounters with individuals who are not interested in higher consciousness, we can easily get thrown off center. *But the underlying dynamic of stressful encounters can be transformed into a source of high-voltage spiritual current for our personal empowerment. With the right tools and techniques, interpersonal friction can be used to catapult us into awareness of I AM at the moment of tension.*

When we know how to neutralize the negative forces we are dealing with in others, we can draw a supercharge of energy from the surrounding atmosphere into ourselves. Then, instead of feeling weak and helpless in the face of difficulties, we actually *increase* and become filled with power and strength. The *I* of the *I AM* automatically appears. By absorbing and putting into practice the principles described in this book, you can empower yourself at will, anytime, anywhere. As you gain in proficiency, universal forces will line up around you. They will back your stand for coherence and stability in a world gone mad and continually reinforce and rebuild your life energy, even when you are asleep at night.

Many of us work out our unresolved tensions through dreams and nightmares, tossing and turning in our sleep. The psychic pressure we fail to convert into useful energy during the day can arise to haunt us nocturnally. Successfully transmuting stress energy into fuel for the soul and higher consciousness, *at the moment of difficulty,* frees us from a nightly traffic jam of unprocessed daily trauma. Therefore we sleep more deeply and awaken with renewed life energy, confident that we can deal effectively with problems as they arise the next day.

Energy Is Our Daily Bread

Life *is* energy and energy is the source of all power. The person who knows how to gather, conserve, and recycle his or her own energetic resources becomes a natural leader. Such individuals radiate a positive charge into the atmosphere around them. They have a *high level of being* and personal magnetism, a constant and true underlying sense of who they really are. What is your level of being? It is the atomic weight of who you are. The amount of air you displace when you walk in a room, the sum total of all your life experiences, everything you know and understand about life, converted into the force field of energy that surrounds and emanates from you.

Individuals with a *low level of being* have difficulty being effective because they fail to make a lasting impression upon others. Lacking sufficient amounts of life energy, they are often lethargic in their movements and their voices tend to be monotonous. They seem to be out of sync with themselves and separated from the positive forces of nature. When you look into the eyes of such a person, you get a sense that there is nobody home.

People with a *high level of being* appear to shine from within. Their eyes are usually bright and they tend to have good, erect posture. Their movements are fluid, their speech is musical and involving, and they possess a basic attitude that seems to affirm the value of existence. As a result, life conspires to support them with good fortune.

Because such individuals are personally magnetic, they are able to attract to themselves the people, events, opportunities, and circumstances that allow them to advance in life. This happens because they are fulfilling one of creation's most basic laws: *Your level of being attracts your life.* Attraction depends on magnetism and fortunately anyone can become magnetic at will. No matter how many times you feel you have failed to fulfill your potential and allowed people or circumstances to limit you, you can turn that around by embracing the following principle: *Change your level of being and you automatically change your life.*

Self-Mastery + Personal Integrity + Magnetic Attraction = Success!

The tools and techniques employed in cultivating *I AM* consciousness naturally raise and enhance one's level of being. In the following pages, through insights and stories, along with processes and practices, you will be led gradually to an understanding of how to experience *I AM* for yourself in the midst of everyday situations. You will learn how to stand unshaken when people are behaving badly toward you and how to not get caught up in your own negative thoughts and reactions. As we travel together, you will gradually feel a new sense of great possibility arising within you.

Like any journey, the destination is reached only when we actually get there. The experience of *I AM* cannot be made to appear by prizing a concept off the printed page. You have to work for it by letting yourself follow the text of this book in whatever unexpected directions it takes, practicing with the tools and implementing the techniques. While reading, forget what you know and abandon expectations. There is an energy in these pages that is far deeper than the words and cannot be grasped with the ordinary intellect. Let the words fall into your mind without thinking about them and the *I AM* in you will hear them and wake up. "It" will read through you and you will see the result in your life.

As you start putting what you learn into practice, you will become more personally magnetic. Your power to influence others will appear as a natural attribute and your soul will shine through your personality. Old fears and insecurities will start to melt away and you will notice how your life seems to become more orderly. Opportunities to advance in career and relationships will start presenting themselves with increased frequency.

More people will want to be friends with you and look to you for advice and stability. The reason for this is simple: You are putting yourself in harmony with nature and society at a much higher level than that on which most people function.

To successfully negotiate the complex world in which we live, we must seize the supreme advantage that comes from governing our reactions and behavior in social situations. By living as an example of what a human being *can and should be,* we honor our days with health, prosperity, and happiness. As more and more individuals learn to live from such a place, the world will be healed, one life at a time. Your participation in this process is already underway. The ideas you are being exposed to in these pages synthesize and redefine the principles of ancient knowledge in highly practical, modern forms. Together they represent a call to personal heroism that can be ignored *only* by making an agreement with oneself to remain asleep in the consensus trance.

George Bernard Shaw once described the planet earth as "the lunatic asylum of the galaxy." Looking around at the world today, who can disagree? By becoming a source of coherence in a world of socially interactive chaos, you will be demonstrating the emerging model of the new man or woman. Tomorrow belongs to the human prototype of the future, the spiritually endowed man or woman who is arising from the chaos of a world in transition. The first step to becoming such an individual in the social arena is to become master of our reactions to life and circumstance. Then the forces of evolution that are driving our planet forward to greater intelligence will naturally fill us with power and strength. Synchronistic opportunities and a sense of order become magically apparent, even amidst mass confusion. They can arise naturally out of the most complex circumstances to enhance our growth as expanding instruments for the good of humanity.

To be able to maintain the citadel of evolving consciousness in the face of ill-treatment by others is a real measure of the spiritually evolved man and woman. Such people define the true meaning of success—not as a goal to be reached, or a dream to be attained, but as a *sensed reality* of their value as human beings, here and now in the present moment. By successfully responding to the daily challenges of life, they convert negativity into a force for good through their inner peace, self-awareness, and ongoing personal harmony. Such people are centers of clarity in an age of chaos. As you develop a living awareness of *I AM,* a sense of self that does not rise or fall with the constant changes of fortune and circumstance, you will become like them. And the powerful results of your practice will help you to bring yourself and your true gifts to the world.

CHAPTER TWO

Getting Real in an Unreal World

The Rude Waiter and the Enlightened Woman

Our planet has great need of inner *and* outer peacemakers if we are to ever have global harmony. Being an instrument of peace and coherence is an effective way of blessing yourself, for life always seeks to create harmony out of apparent chaos. The wrong image of a pacifist is of someone who takes the line of least resistance. But being peaceful within does not require that we become *outwardly* passive. The most powerful response we can make under pressure is to take charge of our emotional reactions, and then speak with authoritative calm and certainty.

My friend Kimberly, who lives in California, is five feet four inches tall and dresses with quiet elegance. She comports herself with dignity at all times. A few years ago we met for afternoon tea at a La Jolla restaurant with ocean views. Shortly after we had sat down, a waiter across the room saw us and started heading toward our table. Watching him advance on us, Kimberly rolled her eyes heavenward and sighed resignedly.

"Oh dear. Not *that* waiter. I've had him before and he's a troublemaker. He always tries to create a disturbance."

Before I could comment, he was upon us. "Hi, my name is Brian. I'm your waiter," he announced pleasantly enough as he handed us two menus. "We have some specials today. They are . . ." and he launched into his memorized list of culinary delights.

"We'd just like some tea, please," said Kimberly, handing the menus back to the waiter. His face fell considerably as the prospect of a large tip faded. He gave us a mixed look of contempt and irritation and paraded off to execute our request.

A few minutes later he came back holding a wooden box containing tea bags. He opened the lid and extended it across the table toward Kimberly and me so that we could examine the contents. We leaned across the table toward the box and peered at the gaily colored assortment of various herbal tea sachets. Suddenly, without warning, our host slammed the box lid in our faces.

So unexpected and startling was this move that Kimberly and I jerked back to an upright position as if we had heard a shot.

"Oooops. Sorry," said the waiter with a smug grin, before slowly raising the lid to once more display the contents of his treasure chest.

Again we leaned toward it to make our selections. I was about to say, "I'll take Chamomile," figuring anything calming to the nerves would be good right now, when *slam!!!* Once more the lid snapped shut a few inches from our noses. I felt Kimberly gather and focus her energy as she slowly sat up and leaned back in her chair. She then looked up at the waiter's face, her pretty yet powerful eyes holding his attention in a headlock. Then she spoke, softly, and yet with great purpose.

"You know, that's twice you've slammed that box lid in our faces. I have to tell you, if it happens again, you will awaken something in me that you'll find very unpleasant."

The waiter's mouth dropped open like a fish and his eyes widened in disbelief. For a moment he stared at Kimberly as if she were a visitor from another world. Then he slowly and politely raised the lid for a third time. And kept it open. He also served us with courtesy, respect, and attention during the rest of our time there.

By not reacting in kind, calling the manager, or bad-mouthing the man, Kimberly created a space for transformation to occur. She invited the waiter to let go of a program that was running him and he moved to a higher level of behavior. Her demeanor was firm and direct and brooked no opposition. And it produced threefold results: the passive aggressor became a gentleman; I had the pleasure of seeing a woman I admire take charge of the situation in an exemplary manner; and Kimberly got to increase her energy levels and sense of self.

Action, Reaction, and Our Overloaded Brains

The trick in such situations is to remain inwardly unshaken when friction occurs. While not denying what is happening, we simultaneously size up the situation for what it is and shift ourselves to a state of grounded *nonreactivity*. At the core of each moment of interpersonal tension lies a vortex of pure energy. It is there to be tapped by the individual who remains centered in the midst of conflict.

By staying coherent, we cause the energy contained in the atoms and molecules that make up our bodies to vibrate with vivid intelligence. We become more than we would be if we went with a desire to fly off the handle and resist evil with evil. Instead of getting lost in the maze of ego-driven human entanglements, we escape the madness by redirecting our attention. We invoke the presence of our souls and our spiritual energy and quickly find ourselves again, recentered, *more present and more powerful than we were before the trouble started.* And we can speak our truth more coherently because our sense of self-identity now exists *at a higher level of being than it would have if we had been overpowered by reactivity.*

No one respects an individual who "loses it" under pressure and becomes flushed and irrational while blurting out wild emotional statements. But everyone respects the person who can maintain the power to reason and act with personal authority in the face of social tension. There's an old saying: "He that masters himself is greater than he who takes a city." The "city" that we must take, as the world presses ever more deeply into international, social, and interpersonal complexity, is the citadel of our own consciousness, our sense of who we are. To let other people or circumstances rob us of our selfhood is the real modern tragedy—not the fall of nations or the stock market.

In his book *The User Illusion,* a runaway best seller in Europe, Danish author Tor Nørretranders cites some interesting information on how our brains work. During any given second, eleven million bits of information stimulate our senses. Our brains must then try to process that information. Unfortunately, our gray matter is only capable of accurately processing sixteen of those eleven million bits. However, our *bodies* are receiving and sometimes even *storing* the jumbled information from the rest of the eleven million bits. As human social interactions daily become more complex, is it any wonder we can make less and less sense of life?

Not only must we endeavor to figure out our personal entanglements, we are also required to absorb the download of terrifying local and global impressions from the news media. The central nervous system, responding to the brain's attempts to make sense of a world in chaos, sends signals that activate fight-or-flight responses in our bodies. This produces states of almost constant stress. Too much pressure is affecting everyone. For those who wish to not only survive but also thrive, acquiring a whole new set of social navigation skills is imperative.

Some people try to deal with mounting tensions through spiritual practices such as Yoga, Tai Chi, meditation, and so on. These are positive tools and can put us into a peaceful place in the safety of our own home. However, a common complaint of people who practice some form of inwardly renewing discipline is that they cannot hang on to the aftereffects of their spiritual harvesting. They lose it when confronted by real-world pressures.

I understand this phenomenon because I passed through it myself on my own spiritual journey. After twenty years of deep daily meditation, I was still unable to maintain my inner peace throughout the day in the face of chaotic situations. I might do very well until, say, 11:15 a.m., when something would happen to scatter my inner peace and personal harmony to the winds. Then I discovered the principles that enabled me to cultivate the power of *I AM* consciousness.

The Warrior Princess and Me

At the time I was five years into a relationship with a woman who loved to start arguments. Don't ask me why I would ever get myself into such a situation in the first place. Attraction is apparently blinding and places a halo of imaginary attraction around the object of our desires. For seven years I was well and truly hooked. The recipient of my amorous projections was five foot two with eyes of blue, an angel face, and a taste for battle that would have made General Patton proud. When we rented a video, she always wanted to watch war movies. She told me, some years after we parted, that what she missed most about our relationship was the conflict!

If we want to be strong, we must learn how to wrestle with the strong. I have to admit that working out with my willful female warrior developed my socially interactive spiritual muscles to a high degree. Our relationship was a perpetual judo mat on which I was constantly called into question and challenged by my beloved. She seemed to get a kick out of seeing if she could "throw" me. When I was able to hold on to my sense of self and not get tossed about psychologically and emotionally, her love and respect for me multiplied. If she threw me, we both suffered because she lost respect for me. From this I learned that one of the things a woman wants most from a man is that he maintain his dignity, sense of presence, and rationality when she is being unreasonable.

Socrates was once asked why he stayed married to his wife Xanthippe, who was a nagging shrew of colossal proportions. He replied that by bearing her unreasonableness at home without flinching, any troublemaker he encountered outside the domicile was a lightweight by comparison and troubled him not.

I used to remember this when dealing with my own romantic comedy of terrors and tell myself that, like Socrates, I was working out with the "Xanthippe principle." In retrospect I see with absolute clarity how perfect this situation was for my growth. How it strengthened and made a man of me. I "graduated" when my "goat" became "ungettable." Instead of taking the bait, overreacting and *forgetting myself* when challenged by my love, I did the opposite: I learned to use the pressure to snap out of reactivity, come to, and *remember myself.* Each time I was able to do this effectively I could feel the presence of my soul, in and around me. As the months passed and I became more or less permanently capable of initiating this shift at will, I became more and more freed from the disturbing influences of my personal Xanthippe. Eventually the spell of romantic projection was broken, releasing both of us to move on to new lessons and growth experiences with other people.

How did I affect this transformation of myself? How did I go from being someone who would always let his goat get got and lose his inner peace, into someone who could stand tall and grow even stronger under pressure? In the following pages I will share the secrets, tools, and techniques that I have now used countless times over the years in many situations. You too will learn how to emerge victorious from encounters with verbal bullies, emotional abusers, passive-aggressive manipulators, energy vampires, and egomaniacs. Not by plowing them under, but by rising to the heights and strengths of your own individual character and true sense of self-worth.

For example, imagine going home to visit your relatives and not reverting back to old modes of behavior around them that you outgrew long ago. Wouldn't you like to avoid being put in the box of their perceptions of who and what you are now, based on who it was they thought you were back then? Wouldn't it be nice to have them really see you as you are now—and all this without making them wrong? You can. It is easy when you know where to find the right gears and levers inside yourself and how to pull the right ones at the right moment.

It's All Relative: Dealing with Family and the Push-Button Past

In 1996 I went back to the UK to visit my relatives for the first time in twenty-three years. My mother and sister, who live in North Wales, had been to the United States to visit me. But this return trip to my native shores would be a proving ground. I wanted to see whether I could remain true to myself and not get caught in old childhood patterns of reaction to their limited perceptions of me. I was particularly interested in how I would respond to the negative aspects of my mother's personality. Russian philosopher P. D. Ouspensky said that "an English education consists in the acquisition of a good set of negative attitudes." This was certainly brought home to me when, after arriving in Wales, I picked up the phone at my sister's house to let my mother know I was in town.

"Hi, Mom. I'm here." My voice bounced with a positive transcontinental ring, if not an American accent.

"Oh yes. That's nice," said my mother, briefly affirmative before flipping to a negative mode of operation. "Come on over. We'll have a good moan."

Moaning and complaining is a time-honored British pastime, almost a national right. It can manifest as grievance against a universe in which the weather, or an unreliable bus service, is seen as a cosmic conspiracy designed to personally annoy. This sanctions the questionable joys of justifiable irritation and the right to complain.

One afternoon I was trapped with my mother in a parked car, waiting for my son to return from a shopping expedition. Suddenly she started to play what I call her "psychological violin." This is her instrument of lamenting reproach against what she personally considers to be the slings and arrows of outrageous fortune. Although she knows many tunes, they are mostly variations on the theme of "if only," unfinished symphonies about past missed opportunities. As her litany of roads not taken began to sound forth, I could feel my spirits sinking into the concrete of the street upon which the car was parked. Then my inner alarm started ringing, reminding me to practice the techniques I use to induce *I AM* consciousness.

Mom and I were sitting half turned toward each other in our car seats. She was holding contact with me through her personality eye. Occasionally it would flicker witheringly, as her tale touched on some sore psychological point of remembered past annoyance.

The first thing was to break eye contact. So I turned away and looked out the side window of the car for a few moments. As I did so, I scanned my own body (the technique I described earlier when helping Jayne put her coworker on "Pause"). This took me out of my head and away from automatic mental-emotional reactions and started to fill me with *presence* and *centering*. A sense of great calm swept through me. My emotional reactions switched from agitated to neutral, then to positive, as my body took on a feeling of great solidity. Then I slowly turned my head and looked into my mother's personality eye from an inner place of gathered personal attentiveness.

As soon as I looked at her, the moaning flow of words ground to a halt in mid-sentence. An atmosphere of absolute stillness filled the car. Her essence eye grew huge. For a moment I thought that her soul was actually going to speak to me. Then her ego kicked back in. Her personality eye squinted at me like Clint Eastwood and she hissed through her teeth, "Stop trying to hypnotize me!"

I wanted to laugh but managed to contain myself. "Mother, I'm not trying to hypnotize you," I said, mentally completing the rest of sentence for myself: *"I'm preventing myself being hypnotized into past reactive patterns by you!"*

And I succeeded. The spell was indeed broken. The sinking feeling so familiar from childhood in the face of my mother's negativity was gone. Instead I felt doubly charged up with energy and my normal, present-day sense of myself.

That evening, back at my sister's house, I was helping her make a salad for dinner when my mother wandered into the kitchen and began to go on negatively about something. I could practically see my sister's knees buckle as she stood at the sink washing celery. I live in California, six thousand miles from the moaning, but my sister gets it on a daily basis, so she is particularly vulnerable.

Recapturing the state of gathered personal attention that I had generated for myself earlier, in the car, I engaged my mother in some inconsequential chitchat. By deflecting her attention elsewhere than her "moaning," while *remembering myself,* I was able to free all three of us from its negative de-energizing effects. As my mother left the kitchen in a relatively happy frame of mind, my sister approached me, bearing an upraised stick of celery in her hand. With a look of awe on her face she tapped me lightly with the vegetable on each shoulder, saying, "I dub you

Sir Invincible." It was attainment of every British schoolboy's dream—knighthood at last.

I should point out that my mother is actually a very spiritual person and can be most charming when she desires. But she too has her mechanical programming and, as with most people, it tends to come out around those with whom she is most familiar. As I was leaving Wales to return to the States, the last thing she said to me was, "Are you pleased with us?" A rather touching remark, I thought. I was able to answer "Yes, of course." Being an intelligent woman, my mother had quickly picked up on the fact that moaning and groaning around me was not going to work anymore. After the two initial confrontations she had behaved like an angel for the rest of the visit.

Quick Recovery and Energy Generation

We can train ourselves to avoid catching the static energy fallout from difficult social situations and the psycho-emotional indigestion that follows it. By so doing we can save the best of ourselves for the simple joy of feeling alive and self-empowered.

When someone launches a verbal attack in our direction—a family member, a coworker, even a stranger—we may still experience a moment of feeling unsettled. But that sensation of moving off center can be used as an alarm signal. By immediately applying *self-remembering* and other techniques within ourselves *and* toward the external situation, we can quickly realign ourselves. *Almost miraculously, we become stronger than we were before the trouble started.* Dynamic protocols like self-remembering or sensing and feeling can quickly induce in us a degree of *I AM* consciousness. As we gradually become more and more skillful in our practice, the greater will be the degree of our ability to feel the presence of *I AM* inside, around, and through us. Without the dynamics of social friction we would perhaps not feel compelled to make the effort. Therefore those who verbally attack us are actually doing us a favor. They force us to wake up and realign.

Morihei Ueshiba, the founder of Aikido, said, "It is not that I don't get thrown off. I recover so quickly you don't notice I was away." In the process of returning to center, we become self-empowered as our adversaries *disempower* themselves without any help from us! In fact, when we harmonize ourselves in the face of chaos and disruption, extra life energy is generated as we realign ourselves into a state of wholeness. We do not *take* energy from others. We simply refuse to accept delivery of their negativity, and in the process transform the energy they are throwing away into something we can use to raise the level of being of both of us.

We are not trying to control other people by forcing our will upon them. We are redirecting the flow of energy between them and ourselves. While practicing external noncooperation with individuals who are being abusive to us, we can be secretly working to help them. When people become identified with their mechanical programming, they are actually lost to themselves. Our positive way of dealing with the situation invites them to self-reclamation on a higher level than their automatic unconscious behavior. Often an angry outburst is really a cry for help from people who cannot manage to control their impulse to be disruptive for themselves.

Negative behavioral patterns are hard to deal with because when they are active, they seem to possess the person who is playing host to them. The rational self almost disappears. The person loses objectivity and cannot accurately see what it is he or she is actually saying and doing because *unconscious forces beyond his or her control are in charge.* What we are unable to see about ourselves cannot be controlled. However, when we go unconscious, others are always quick to catch on. That is why people often turn away to hide a half smile when someone loses it in public. Heated arguments always appear ridiculous to bystanders because they can clearly see that two supposedly intelligent beings are behaving like idiots. What is really happening is that *their automatic programming has temporarily turned them into automatons!*

Attack of the Clones: The Machines Are Among Us!

No one likes to think of themselves as an automaton, yet reactive behavior almost always makes us go unconscious. But there is hope. Carl Jung said, "One does not become conscious by imagining figures of light, but by making the darkness conscious." To do this we must be able to step aside from our programming and see it for exactly what it is: nothing but *mechanical, automatic, preprogrammed behavior.* We have to be able to separate from our reactivity, to stand aside and observe it as clearly as a bystander who impartially observes someone else. No one wants to feel or behave like a machine. Seeing mechanical behavior in ourselves when it is acting up is the first step to self-mastery. When you can actually observe reactive behavior in yourself *as it is happening,* in that moment you are *not* your programming. *You are that which is doing the looking!*

By freeing ourselves from knee-jerk reactions and not getting drawn into combat with others, we create a breathing space where empowerment can occur. Not just for us. We also do it for those who are behaving antagonistically toward us. Our centered state offers them a field of energy greater than the limitations of their right-or-wrong, black-or-white arguments or aggressions. Again, we invoke this state by applying the tools and techniques *to ourselves* in the moment of tension. The instant we become behaviorally nonreactive, we grow in size. Our consciousness expands and our spiritual strength multiplies exponentially. The people who are arguing with us may feel this shift and start relating to us in a completely different manner. If they persist in remaining obtuse and obnoxious, they only harm themselves, not us.

Choice of behavior is only possible when a transformational space exists between people. To create this space we must step back in consciousness from our automatic reactions, even as our buttons are being pushed. We create and become an *observing I* that sees our programming in operation as an impartial observer. From that place of objectivity, it is easy to observe that people attacking us are lost to themselves. A sense of compassion arises when we see that the person before us has ceased to exist as a rational human being.

If your computer suddenly went mad and started printing out obscenities directed at you personally, you wouldn't pick up a hammer and smash it to bits. You would simply say "Oh dear, it's got a virus" and see what you could do to correct the malfunction. When people are abusive toward us, we might say that they too have a virus. They have become possessed by their programming and have lost their sense of self. Through finding *our* sense of self in the face of such onslaughts, by *self-remembering* (as opposed to losing it and forgetting ourselves), we can help those who are out of sorts reconnect with themselves. In this manner we are blessing our enemies, doing good to those endeavoring to revile and abuse us. Like Mahatma Gandhi, the great pioneer of nonviolent passive resistance, we are exposing them to a higher energy than the one they are using to try and destroy our peace of mind.

Put-Down Artists and "Little Murders"

Perhaps you think using the term "enemy" to describe social troublemakers is excessive. But Maya Angelou said in an Oprah interview, "Make no mistake, these people are after your life." She described the cutting, cruel, put-down remarks that now pass for legal verbal currency as "little murders," a term coined by cartoonist Jules Feiffer. The "life" abusive people are after is *our life energy,* our "daily bread," the power that infuses our bodies, minds, and emotions and animates our very existence.

Though all living forms possess life energy, it is found most abundantly in a person who cultivates a positive, open approach to life and to self. The more energy we have, the more conscious we are, and vice versa. Those who don't have enough of these twin blessings will try to steal it, unconsciously or deliberately, from those who have them in abundance. To do this they must first destabilize the high-life-energy person by making him or her switch from a positive current to a negative state, mentally, emotionally, and/or physically. This process is often initiated through verbal and behavioral cruelty.

To maintain a high state of consciousness when faced with personal abuse is a very high form of love, completely devoid of false sentiment. It is a love that holds a field for the possibility of personal transformation for both parties. Essentially this is where the power of *I AM* consciousness lies. Love *is* stronger than evil. But in order to work its transforming effects, it must be able to flow through an individual who is grounded and rooted in the power of a sense of self. The practices you are learning will help you to develop a secure identity that does not change as you stand in the flow of Nørretranders's eleven million bits of information per second. Holding such awareness, not just for self but also for others, especially when they appear to be working against us, is *true conscious love.* It is a doorway to the highest potential of human development.

Both courage and compassion are required in order to stay centered and be able to help oneself and another. We also need understanding and mastery of special principles, tools, and techniques, such as the ones in this book. The processes described in the following chapters lead to deep levels of connection with our selves. Through their application, we can learn to hold on to our personal and spiritual identity in the face of potential disruption.

The Courage to Love

Gandhi said that "love is not for cowards." Without a grounding base of individual power and self-management, the energy of love will quickly dissipate. The subtleties of our spiritual nature are easily extinguished in the ether by human restlessness, cruelty, and the density of gross perceptions of life. Power without love quickly becomes manipulative and self-serving. Love without power lacks the force to transform adversity into victory. The power that we need is sovereignty over ourselves, mastery over the mechanical forces of life that keep the human race collectively tied to the dark side of the unconscious mind.

What you are studying is a system that offers definite means of self-mastery to be applied in both private and social contexts. Simply reading the information in this book, acquiring a new set of concepts and more information, will be of little help on the chaotic battlefield of daily life. Concepts can certainly change our outlook on life. But if our knowledge simply remains in our heads, the reality of our personal interactions with people and the world around us will go on as before. *Lasting change happens when what we know with our heads becomes anchored in our bodies and our behavior.* It comes when our inner connection has the power to affect the real world, to change our *external* experience of life. In short, our *truth* must become an *organic part of who and what we are.*

The tools and techniques for personal transformation outlined in these pages work best if approached and applied with a sense of fun and adventure. Then we can easily turn life into a psychological gymnasium where we daily develop our spiritual muscles. You need never be bored again, by any person or any situation. Every encounter, benign or friction filled, is an opportunity to inwardly practice techniques to develop your spiritual strength, sense of personal power, and well-being.

A Time for Spiritual Heroism

In my workshops I have taught thousands of people to free themselves from the debilitating influence of personal insecurity in the socially confused times in which we live. Transforming ourselves and the world with the energy of higher consciousness is heroic duty, a cosmic imperative from which there can be no retreat. In order to survive as a race, those who understand this are now being asked to stand firm in the face of the massive odds of historic human ignorance. No longer can we afford to live simply for ourselves. The pressure and peril of the times in which we are living call for heroic consciousness and quiet individual heroism.

There is a wonderful moment in the film *Zulu,* which is based on a true incident. The scene is South Africa in 1879. One hundred and twenty Welsh soldiers have been detailed to build a bridge over a river. The company is composed of men who are engineers rather than line soldiers. A few days earlier, 25,000 Zulus inflicted a crushing defeat on the British Army, wiping out more than a thousand men at the Battle of Isandhlwana.

Fired up with success, they advance upon Roarke's Drift, a mission near where the Welshmen are constructing the bridge. The men suddenly find themselves surrounded by four thousand magnificent Zulu warriors and hastily set up a defensive perimeter around the mission.

As the soldiers in their scarlet tunics stand in thin lines, rifles at the ready, and the spear- and shield-brandishing hordes advance upon them, one young soldier is obviously afraid. Noticing this, an old experienced sergeant-major standing behind him whispers reassuringly, "Steady, lad."

Shaking with fear, the boy says, "But why, Sarge. Why us?"

Still looking straight ahead at the advancing enemy, the older man says softly, in a fatherly manner, "Because we're 'ere, lad. Ain't nobody else, just us."

We too may sometimes wonder, as we face the chaos and dangers in the world today "Why *us?* What are *we* doing here?"

Perhaps there are some mysteries that can only be answered in eternity. But one thing is certain. We who are choosing to live in higher consciousness and embody spiritual values *are* here and I believe we are meant to stay. Those who wish to be the servants of a higher vision of life have a right to be heard and seen in the darkness. And we have a right to deflect from ourselves the unpleasant behavior of people caught in old patterns of negativity and self-limitation. Those who can teach a higher, more spiritual way of life, by attitude and example, are the hope of the planet and the future. We may be few in number to stand firm in the face of global chaos, but we *are* here. For now there may be "nobody else, just us." And yet we are backed up by the visionary energy of long-term planetary renewal and hope for a new humanity based on evolved consciousness.

"A man convinced against his will, is of the same opinion still," goes an old saying. But when we can *change ourselves at will,* anywhere, anytime, even in the most trying circumstances, we change others by our living example. And by extension we change the world the only way it can ever be changed, one life at a time.

The insights, tools, and techniques you are about to explore have been tested for many years in the crucible of my own life experience. Properly applied, they will give you the power and sense of security you have always longed for in your social interactions. You will be able to bring out the best in others with a mere look, or a change of attitude within yourself.

You can be a true peacemaker, someone who achieves positive results not by aggressive confrontation, but by shifting your consciousness to higher levels in the face of difficulty. In the following pages you will not only discover ways to move through the societal madness unscathed. You will learn how to become a prototype of the emerging new man and woman, a living embodiment of the very best the twenty-first century has to offer.

CHAPTER THREE

Body-Centered Spirituality

Lost in a World of Talking Heads

A large percentage of the people we encounter every day are suffering from a debilitating collective disease and don't even know it. Once I point out to you the physical manifestations of this malady, you are going to see it in almost everyone you meet. You may even find you are suffering from it yourself. But please don't be alarmed. It is quickly curable. In fact, you are holding the key to its remedy in your hands right now. What is this illness? Simply that as a race we human beings have become stuck in our cerebral processes! We have lost a natural, organic connection with our bodies and have turned into walking, talking, obsessive-compulsive, non-stop-thinking *heads!*

This is about as far away as one can get from *I AM* consciousness, which requires that we be fully present in our *bodies* at all times.

In simpler eras, when people lived closer to nature, it is likely that they thought less and were more in touch with their bodies and the earth. They were also probably connected with simple positive emotions in a far healthier way than most of us today. Under the torrential bombardment of verbal and visual information from the media, cell phones, the Internet, and so on, we overspend huge amounts of mental energy trying to process the unmanageable verbal downloads and canned visual images. More than sixty years ago Carl Jung wrote, "The world has sold its soul for a mass of disconnected facts." Modern men and women have become the heirs of Jung's prescient analysis. Top-heavy with internal word processing, we have lost our natural center of gravity. To reclaim ourselves we need to get out of our heads, back into our bodies, and into our lives.

When presenting my workshop "Living from I AM Consciousness," I begin by demonstrating what it feels like when we are confronted by people who are stuck in their heads. I ask the participants to observe that my body is fully relaxed as I stand before them and that I am fully present in it. Therefore as I speak, my voice seems to rise up from deep in my belly. It issues from my mouth in a relaxed way that inspires confidence in those hearing it. As I move around the stage, my body works as a unified whole, not as a head that is dragging a body along with it.

To show the difference between being head-centered and body-centered, I tell participants that I will deliberately put myself in my head. Turning my back to them, I bring my attention from my body to my head by doing some mental arithmetic in an effortful way. Within seconds I feel disconnected from my body and become centered in the overload in the brain. Then I turn to face my audience and address them again, this time as a talking head, and say, "I am here today to speak to you about how the universe works from a mathematical point of view."

Instantly, a series of moans will issue forth. Some people make the sign of the cross at me with their fingers, as if to ward off a vampire. Others look nauseous. The sense of relief is palpable when I demonstrate a return to *whole body awareness*. This I accomplish by coming out of my head and dropping into full body sensation, scanning down mentally into my chest, stomach, arms, legs, and feet.

I once performed this demonstration at a class in a private home. A large dog was lying sprawled on a rug a few feet in front of me. When I went into my head and did the bit about explaining the universe mathematically, the dog leapt to its feet, howled, and ran out of the room! If an animal can tell when we are not in touch with ourselves, what effect are we having on other *people* when we are in our heads? And what effect are *they* having on *us* when they are in theirs?

Getting Out of Your Head and Into Your Life

During one of my workshops in Texas I wanted to make this point clear. I called for a volunteer from the audience and a lanky gentleman in his mid-forties rose to his feet.

"Why do they always have to be taller than me?" I joked with the audience as he made his way onto the stage to stand uncomfortably beside me. Asked to introduce himself, he told us his name was Joe and that he worked in the electronics industry.

"Joe," I said, looking up at the wrinkled furrows piled on his forehead and the worry lines around his eyes, "I would like you to say the word 'I,' as if in reference to yourself."

The folds of skin covering the front of Joe's cranium moved up and down like an accordion as he went into his head to try to find his sense of identity. Then, with obvious discomfort at being in front of people, he managed to emit a reedy, thin, wavering sound.

"Iiiiiiiieeee."

"And point to where that sound comes from, please. Indicate the place where the sound seems to originate in your body."

Joe raised his hand uncertainly until finally, a wobbly finger was pointing to his head. The audience murmured knowingly, perhaps wondering if they too would sound like that in his place.

"Do you like that sound? Does it feel like you?" I asked.

"No," mumbled Joe sheepishly. "Not really."

I turned my attention from Joe to the audience. "The sound of our voice reflects where our attention is placed within ourselves. I'm five foot six inches tall and yet I have a deep, resonant voice. When I speak I feel as if the sound arises from the depths of my stomach. It then moves up, *through* my chest and throat, and comes out of my mouth in an easy, comfortable manner. I speak with what we might call a *body voice.*"

Glancing over at Joe, I saw that he was still wrestling with his discomfort at being on public display. His hands were clasped in front of his genitals, a sure sign that he habitually suffered from "fig leaf" consciousness.

No Sexuality = No Power

An individual's sense of psychological disconnection with his or her sexuality often manifests in public as physical covering up. In his perennial classic, *Think and Grow Rich,* Napoleon Hill pointed out that successful people often have a strong natural connection with their sexual selves. He devoted an entire chapter to the "transmutation of sex energy," claiming that our innate creative forces can be used to awaken the dormant genius in all of us. Joe's lack of connection with his own vital power manifested in his personal demeanor. The way he stood, moved, and spoke telegraphed a sense of personal weakness and lack of self-confidence.

"Would you like to speak with a body voice?" I asked him. "A voice that reflects your deepest strength and a feeling of who you really are at your best?"

"Sure!" Joe's eyes brightened at the prospect and his body seemed to relax a little.

"Then, first of all, I want you to uncross your hands. Let them just hang loosely by your sides."

As Joe did this, I walked across the stage to a point some ten feet away and then turned to look at him. I had already figured out that he was right-handed. The hand he chose to point to his head when asked to identify the reedy "I" sound it had made had been the right one. This meant his essence eye, which reflected his essential self, was his left eye.

"Now, Joe," I went on, as reassuringly as possible, "I want you to just keep looking into my left eye and try to become aware of your feet mentally. Drop all of your attention down into your feet. Just observe me in a detached way and let your mind scan your toes and feet at the same time. Feel the weight of them and the pressure of your shoes around them."

I felt a shift in Joe as he did as requested. Even a minor replacement of attention in ourselves can bring instant change. For the first time since Joe walked on stage, I felt that we were not looking at a walking, thinking, talking head.

"Perhaps your feet feel warm, or heavier, or more solid," I continued.

"Maybe there's a tingling sensation gathering in and around them?"

"Tingling," said Joe softly, while nodding slightly. "Like an electrical current."

"That's good," I encouraged him. "That tingling is *life energy*. It is the electricity of your own body. Now let that sensation move up both legs as far as the knees. Can you do that?"

"It went by itself as soon as you said that." A grin was spreading across Joe's face.

The Power of Presence

I continued leading Joe through the process until he had an awareness of tingling energy in his legs, hands, and arms. The audience was perfectly still, as if holding its breath. A tremendous presence was starting to radiate from both of us up there on the stage. It began to expand outward to fill the room as Joe and I continued looking at each other, all the while mentally feeling the tingling sensation in our arms and legs.

"All right, Joe, well done." I wanted to keep him feeling safe as we moved toward an even deeper experience. "While holding on to the feeling you have gathered in your arms and legs, close your eyes and imagine that your head just disappeared. Pretend that above your shoulders there is nothing but empty space—vastness—the universe perhaps. But still keep the awareness of your arms and legs."

As Joe followed my request, the remaining tension left his face. The furrows on his forehead vanished. A thick atmosphere of peace seemed to surround him.

"Now let your attention drop like a stone, down from where your head was into your belly," I continued. "Let it come to rest behind the navel. Imagine that your head has reappeared, but that now it's inside your stomach. Visualize that you are actually looking down on your own head."

As Joe did this, I could sense a change in the entire room. He was getting out of his habitual stuck-in-the-head syndrome and becoming *body conscious*. And the audience was automatically *replicating his state*.

An audience always mirrors the state of a speaker on stage. If he is fearful, they will be uneasy. If he is boring, they will be bored. The secret of success in public speaking is to be completely relaxed, stay in the moment, and be body-centered. When audience members look at someone who is in his or her head, they immediately start tuning that person out. Nobody wants to sit and look at someone who subconsciously reflects our own sense of overload. We want to get away from that person, mentally and physically. We try to avoid him or her, even in our internal reactions, and so we disconnect. The more Joe relaxed into himself, the more he normalized the room. Those watching him now felt open and sympathetic toward him.

"How does that feel?" I asked him.

"There's a sense of power growing in my stomach. The more I focus down there the stronger it gets. I like it a lot."

"Then turn to face the audience, still keeping relaxed attention on your arms and legs and feeling the power in the stomach."

Joe did as I requested, carefully, as if he did not wish to spill a drop of his gathered awareness.

"Very good. We're almost there. So with your center of attention still gathered behind your navel, when I count three, I want you to open your eyes and say 'I' again—but this time *from the depths of your being*. Are you ready? One . . . two . . . three."

A deep resonant sound seemed to stir inside Joe, as if drawn from an ancient well of strength and silence. It rose up from his belly and issued effortlessly from his throat and mouth.

"I."

Several members of the audience gasped and then the entire room reverberated with applause. Joe had been transformed, at least temporarily, from a talking head into a powerful man with a *body voice*. He was filled with personal power, energy, and presence.

Joe Gets Authentic

I asked Joe to tell us about his home and his family and he did so in a coherent, flowing manner. When he described his wife and children, the audience seemed moved by his now obvious warm feelings for those he loved. He had gone from being head-centered and fearful in public to being someone who could express his affectionate side before strangers. I indicated to Joe that he could leave the stage and reclaim his seat in the auditorium. But he wasn't done yet.

"I want to say something more."

He was like a different person, relaxed and confident. Now that Joe had tasted his power in public, I couldn't get him off the stage.

"This feels very familiar. It's like I remember this state—this feeling of being connected with myself. I've found something I already had, but somehow misplaced."

"That something is *you,* Joe!" I assured him. "And it's bigger than the Joe who is always changing and feels insecure at different times throughout the day. You just *remembered yourself.* Instead of speaking from a fraction of yourself, from some weak little sense of "I," you spoke from an awareness of real *I,* the underlying power you have always been and always will be. And you did it in front of people. Instead of hiding out, you connected with an authentic sense of your own aliveness and demonstrated it in front of others. And you did it by getting out of your head and into your body. Congratulations!"

As he left the stage to another warm round of applause, Joe was still smiling and still relaxed. He had gotten out of his head and into his life. What he had experienced was not true *I AM* consciousness but a precursor. Deep inside himself, something had stirred. It was as if the true reality of his being, the *I* slumbering for so long, stirred in its sleep, yawned, and stretched toward waking up. The first step had been taken.

Living in the "Zone"

One of the initial major keys to successfully developing full-blown *I AM* consciousness over time consists of keeping our center of gravity out of our head and in the center of our body. Otherwise we live vicariously, as an idea of ourselves, rather than an experience we can feel. This does not mean we forget how to think. Rather, we replace automatic, unconscious thinking with directed attention on a continual, underlying, sensed perception of our own aliveness. And we use the power of the mind to observe and govern our reactions to other people and external events. Instead of playing host to internal gossip columnists, chattering away inside our heads about smallness, the mind becomes a director of energy throughout the body. By gathering and focusing our life force in, through, and around our bodies, we become whole and powerfully effective in society.

Perhaps you are beginning to see new possibilities for personal success in a world where so many people are on automatic pilot. To live in the head is to be asleep, to walk through life as an artifact in the collective trance. So many people are busy having a conceptualized experience of life that they never really connect with anything "out there." To be *proactive* rather than simply *reactive* in society, one must be in flow with the world as a dynamic process of serial opportunity, a living continuum that is constantly reordering circumstance and events in our favor. Nature wants us to win. Life wants us to win. We lose when our three instruments of expression—our bodies, minds, and emotions—do not work together as a team. When we are in a state of incomplete connection, we expend too much energy in wrong directions to fully grasp the possible fortune life wishes to place in our arms.

Excellence is best achieved by using our physical, mental, and emotional equipment in an optimal way. People recognize this quality even if they cannot demonstrate it themselves. That is why they leap to their feet and applaud the miraculous touchdown, gaze in wonder as the dancer performs a ballet to perfection, or feel chills when an opera singer hits and holds the high note. The champions are the ones who can enter the "zone" at will, to stay focused and relaxed during the moments crucial to victory.

In the realm of arguments and interpersonal social friction, the fully grounded, body-centered individual always has the advantage. To be in the head is to be top-heavy. A tree that is not firmly rooted in the ground is easily blown over. People who are in their heads may be clever with words. During an argument they may throw facts and figures at us with machine-gun-like rapidity. Those who are disconnected from their feelings are often masters of sarcasm, the cruel put-down, and the pointed remark. But when their personal emotions get stirred up, they become irrational, lose objectivity, and start to bluster. Their mental dexterity and power to reason accurately fly away like leaves in a gale and the tree of their sense of self-identity can easily be uprooted.

The Way They Walk and Talk—Movie Stars and Body Awareness

Did you know that the way people walk reveals where their *center of gravity* lies? Most men tend to lead with their heads down, leaning forward, as if mentally butting their way through the world. But not all men—Clint Eastwood, for example, walks leaning slightly backward with his pelvis tilted forward, leading with his crotch. Neither mode is natural, although Clint's stalking momentum probably accounts for the sexual attention he has apparently gotten most of his life.

Today, many successful movie actors are all talking head and no body. Next time you watch Robert De Niro, notice that most of his energy emanates from his head. The force coming through his face is very intense and works for him, given that he often plays intimidating characters. De Niro is certainly an accomplished and versatile thespian. But it appears to me that he is not happily situated in his body. Oscar winner Sean Penn acts completely with his head. When called upon to express emotions, his face contorts wildly, as if his brain is an instrument of feeling and not thought. This type of actor can be draining and emotionally disturbing to watch. Looking at someone who is head-centered makes *us* head-centered, whether we are aware of it or not.

Modern actors are often required to embody psychological dysfunction and the corresponding physical disconnection that stems from mental abnormality. In our stressed-out age, many people relate to characters that represent or embody an out-of-whack human condition. Disturbed energy is what they experience themselves as a reality in their daily lives. Therefore they easily identify with the troubled characters they see on the screen. They want to see reflections of life as they know it, *even if what they are seeing is technically abnormal!* To people stuck in their heads, other talking-thinking heads come across as normal human beings. Dysfunction is thus celebrated as the yardstick of reality and a "good" actor is now judged by how abnormally normal he or she can appear.

Real Men Don't Act—They Embody

The great Japanese actor Toshiro Mifune is one of my favorites, someone with whom I can identify. Mifune's whole body is employed in his acting. Watching him move is an invigorating, normalizing experience. It relaxes my being, takes me out of my head, and grounds me in my body. He is a classic body-centered actor. In Japanese Samurai films such as Akira Kurosawa's *The Seven Samurai,* one can observe how Mifune walks with a sense of gathered presence. His central focus is easily observable as being in the belly, a placement of energy that can work just as well for modern Westerners as it can for Shaolin monks and Samurai warriors.

Perhaps you recall the on-screen presence of the late James Coburn when he appeared in *The Magnificent Seven,* which was a remake of the *The Seven Samurai* transferred to the American West.

In an interview, Coburn said he was thrilled to be asked to play the very character he had most related to in the original film. "I saw *The Seven Samurai* twelve days in a row when it played in Los Angeles at a theater on La Brea that specialized in Japanese movies," recalled Coburn. "I loved the character who goes into the woods alone, stands in the rain, and practices drawing his sword. He had such focus and presence. I thought 'I want to be the first actor to embody that presence in an American film.' And I got that role in *The Magnificent Seven*."

The image that comes to mind when one thinks of James Coburn is gathered energy, focus, and presence. Oddly enough Akira Kurosawa, recognized worldwide as one of the great film directors of all time, was himself influenced by the classic westerns of American director John Ford. Toshiro Mifune, the actor most closely associated with Kurasawa's great films, is regarded as the John Wayne of Japan.

The two men move in a completely different manner, reflective of the societies in which they grew up. Mifune has gathered belly energy, a relaxed yet intensely focused persona, and a walk that borders on a swagger. Wayne has a casual energy and a loose, swaying gait, reflective of relaxed American amiability tempered with toughness. On screen at least, both men emit a sense that they are not to be trifled with. Whatever one may think of such cultural icons as role models, both have one undeniable quality in common: they exude and emit *presence,* a force field that jumps of the screen, as it also did, according to most accounts, in their off-screen lives.

Presence, Energy, and the Body Connection

Presence is a supreme protection mechanism. We can learn to walk unscathed through our confused world of talking-thinking heads and live continually in a state of body-centered presence. As we progress, we shall explore some simple techniques for attaining and maintaining high levels of body-centered energy and presence.

Presence and energy are intimately connected. They feed each other and give us a strong sense of self-identity. When you know who you are as a presence, you emit an energy field stronger than personality—your own or other people's. Surrounded by such a force, any man or woman, even a child, can automatically command respect.

Your body wants you! It wants your love and your kind attention. By taking command of our brains and using them to maintain a full body connection while we think, speak, do, talk, play sports, make love, and so on, we constantly energize our own sense of being truly alive. People who possess a full connection with their bodies, minds, and emotions are rare in this world. If instead of just reading this book, you adopt, practice, and implement the tools and techniques suggested, you will see great changes in the way others respond and react to you. By learning to be fully connected with yourself, you can become that rarest of human beings: a whole person who moves through the world in touch with all the powers nature intends us to have. You will exemplify personal confidence and presence. The energy of success will radiate from you as a protective force field, even as it magnetizes your personality to bring the highest good into your life.

As you implement these strategies, you may find yourself being tested by those who think they know you best. Friends and relatives often want us to remain trapped in their limiting perceptions of who and what they think we are. But as you persist in your self-reclamation, they will come to love and respect you as a living demonstration of their own forgotten wholeness.

Strategies of the Energy-Seeking Egotist

In everyday life, we continually encounter people who are low on life energy and try to power themselves up at the expense of others. In the worst cases we may be dealing with energy vampires, those who seek to directly empower themselves by stealing energy from us. We shall address this phenomenon in depth in a separate chapter. For now let us understand that for people to take energy from us they must first make us negative. Energy will only travel along a like current—the same level of intelligence. If you are *up* and others are *down,* they will have to bring you down to their level to get charged up from you.

The underlying reason people start arguments is that they wish to relieve themselves of their negative charge. They want to replace it with your positive current. To do so they must first get your attention and will do this by trying to push your buttons. Button pushing can take many forms. Here is a short list, to which you can add your own observations:

Ignoring you (stealing energy by withholding attention)
Looking superior (making you feel inferior)
Using "you" statements (for example, "*You* did this to me")
Making you wrong (in tandem with the "you" statements)
Accusing you of saying this or that (when you probably didn't)
Denying that they said what they did say
Bullying and intimidating by walk, stance, or look
Conveying an attitude of contempt for you
Shaming and blaming
Sighing heavily (as if you are a burden)
Refusing to make eye contact
Staring in a hostile manner
Repeating exactly what they just said (implying that you are too
    stupid to get it)
Telling negative, disgusting, or morbid stories
Adopting a reproachful tone of voice or manner
Lamenting about injustice
Giving a statement of accounts (past and present wrongs)
Putting out a "heavy" atmosphere or vibe
Looking around the room when you are talking
Interrupting
Speaking in a loud voice
Speaking with a robotic, disinterested voice on the phone

Reading the list, you probably thought of people you know who have run their negative energy on you. Unfortunately, unless we know how to neutralize the disturbing effects of others upon us, we may become emotionally paralyzed, even speechless, or start babbling like fools before them.

Becoming Process-Oriented (Not Outcome-Oriented)

With the right tools, techniques, and training, it is easy to turn the tables on those who purvey abusive behavior. We can become even stronger than our seeming adversaries and "eat" their negativity in the face of difficulty by transforming it into a positive charge of energy we can use.

However, we are not looking to simply manipulate other people to our advantage. Rather, our attention is on maintaining our sense of self, building up our presence and energy while relaxing down into the situation. In this manner we grow larger while they either join us in reconciliation, or stay stuck in their self-created limitation. Or disappear down the bathtub hole around which their consciousness swirls in confusion when the plug of their ego has been pulled.

The social advantage naturally switches our direction as a result of finding and strengthening our connection with ourselves while under pressure. The energy we generate in this manner causes other people to either shift into harmony with us, or fall out of connection with their ego-driven will to abuse us. In other words, we get out of the way and they disenfranchise themselves.

Talking heads are always *outcome-*, not *process*-oriented. This position makes them nervous, worried, insecure, fearful, overly aggressive, grasping, greedy, needy, and therefore manipulative. If they don't easily get their way, they can quickly turn negative, verbally abusive, and start pushing others around. Or they may use passive-aggressive behavior to try and get the upper hand. All this can be very draining to our well-being. The energy put out by people in such a state actually poisons them. Our task is to make sure that they don't poison us!

Primarily it is in our best interests to avoid confrontational situations with disturbed people. But since it is hard to move through life without encountering fractious scenarios, we must find ways to stay focused in the face of disruption. This means we must connect with forces inside us that are deeper, stronger, and more powerful than the level of personality interactions upon which arguments are based.

Conscious Acting and the Games People Play

You may be required to speak forcefully in response to verbally abusive behavior. But you will be able to do it without a sense of personal disruption or self-violation. This is what I call *conscious acting,* as opposed to unconscious *reacting.* Pull this off, and you will not only *not* leak energy, you will gain in courage, strength, and personal power as a result of the conflict situation. The atoms of your body will be charged up with a life-affirming energy. Again, nature wants harmony above all things. She will support you in times of stress with an influx of coherence in an attempt to stabilize a perturbation in the order of things.

No one respects a human being that behaves like a machine. What irritates us and arouses our contempt for other people is their mechanical behavior. Subliminally it reminds us that we ourselves often behave like automatons, the slaves of our reactions and social conditioning. Unfortunately, tricking other people into exposing their reactive sensitivity is a sadistic social game many people enjoy. Today the power-play struggles that ceaselessly sway back and forth in social interactions often revolve around trying to trigger other people's reactive weaknesses through put-downs.

The cruel, personally insulting remark, disguised as humor, has become as omnipresent in TV sitcoms as it is now in life. In this "game," people on the receiving end are not supposed to show by the least indication that they have been hurt. If they do, the out for the perpetrators will be the ubiquitous "just kidding," which puts *them* in the power position. The hidden message is:

I have the ability to hurt you, therefore I am more powerful than you. If you accuse me of doing this, I will say that you are too sensitive and your weakness shows by the fact that you can't take it. If you were really smart or cool, you would come back with a better put-down of me. Since you can't, I am obviously the one with the power to control your reactions. Therefore you are inferior to me.

Individuals who perpetrate such crimes, the previously mentioned "little murders," are simply trying to stand tall by cutting off the heads of others. Their neurotic behavior is usually a reflexive compensation mechanism triggered by an inferiority complex.

Presence and the Soul for Superior Protection

The way to neutralize the paralyzing effect of this type of behavior is to throw our attention on something within us more powerful than our human reactivity and sensitivity to hurt. Before focusing on the external challenge, we first become body sensate. This act invokes self-remembering, which in turn allows the presence of *I AM* to permeate us to some degree. When we are under verbal attack by another person, a swarm of reactive impulses try to tell us that each one of them is *I*. These little imposters seek to express anger, annoyance, or some knee-jerk outburst in the name of our ego. The more strongly we can switch our sense of identity from them to the reality of our being, *the I of the I AM,* the less we will be gripped by false personality.

True personality is our personhood acting in alignment with and as a representative of the soul. *False personality* is our personhood acting out in the world when aligned with the inauthentic aspects of ego disassociated from the soul.

When we experience the higher aspects of ourselves, we feel it as *presence.* In prayerful moments of peace or meditation, or even in moments of great personal stress, something extraordinary can start to emanate in, through, and around us. At such times we seem to be standing in a field of power that is greater than ourselves, a quality of being that brings about a natural centering. Then our human faculties spring into alignment with ease, clarity, and grace. Knowing how to invoke this state at will, anytime, anywhere, even in the midst of an argument, is the key to living the extraordinary life.

The exemplary individual knows how to enter, sustain, and maintain a connection with presence in difficult social situations. Without the friction that goes with interpersonal tension, the great forces of good inside us remain dormant. But these latent powers can be trained to emerge to reinforce us when we are faced with potential disruption. They can help us hold the field of higher consciousness within ourselves when others are being difficult, or even going temporarily mad.

Not all people will feel the immediate effect of the blessing that is available to them, through you, when their own soul connection is being usurped by their disturbed personal reactions. *But you will feel it, as the presence, peace, power, and strength of your own true nature.*

No matter how spiritual we become, it is imperative that we remain capable of dealing with real-world situations in the most practical terms. One of the funniest sights I ever saw was a nun trying to start a stick-shift car that was parked on a hill. Spirituality should not be incapacitating. Perceptions of higher consciousness should not turn us into "bliss bunnies."

A "Bliss Bunny" Almost Meets Her Doom

I sometimes meet people who tell me they don't really want to be here on this planet. Invariably they feel they are so spiritually sensitive that the dense vibrations of our confused world disturb their equilibrium, so they would simply rather not be here.

Five minutes from where I live in Encinitas, California, there is a beautiful cliff-top hermitage with gardens that overlook the Pacific. Built in the 1930s by Paramahansa Yogananda, author of the spiritual classic *Autobiography of a Yogi,* the hermitage is a place of great serenity and high energy. Visitors from around the world enjoy strolling through this idyllic setting. Tourists of all nationalities mingle peacefully with enlightenment wannabes who sit meditating quietly in secluded nooks and arbors. The natural setting and power of the place also makes it attractive to "bliss bunnies."

Such an individual is a local middle-aged woman who occasionally floats through the gardens on a perfumed cloud with a look of otherworldly distraction upon her face. Over the years I have been engaged in conversation by this person and been regaled with tales of her disenchantment with life on this plane of existence. One glorious morning I saw her coming toward me on the cliff top. The prospect of being subjected to her litany of complaints against "this world" caused me to groan inwardly. For a moment my legs wanted to run away. But I decided to go on the offensive instead by being super positive.

"Good morning," I sang out. "Isn't this a beautiful day?"

"I suppose so," she sighed wearily, obviously irked to be faced with such positivism about life. "But I can't wait to be *up there*." Her eyes flickered toward the heavens with a look of pained longing.

"What's the matter?" I retorted, feigning surprise, as if I had never heard this song of otherworldly melancholia before. "Don't you like life?"

"Oh, it's all right." She shrugged, as if seeking to rid herself of a burden. Then her face brightened somewhat as she leaned into me and whispered conspiratorially. "But I've been told that when the earth shifts on its axis in 2011, I won't be here to see it. Isn't that wonderful?"

We were still standing on the cliff top, the dazzling Pacific pounding on the rocks a hundred feet below. A sudden thrilling urge swept through me as I thought "I could give her a push right now and put her out of her misery!" Instead, I looked into her personality eye and, appropriating a line from Tolstoy, said, "As far as I'm concerned, if you don't love life, you don't love God."

She stared at me for a second with a mixture of pity and contempt. Then she turned on her heel and swept away, delivering a parting put-down over her shoulder, "Well, in that case...."

She left me with the distinct feeling that further conversation with such a life-affirming Philistine as myself might expose her to thought contamination.

As I looked out across the sun-dancing ocean to the horizon, I smiled, thankful to see nature spread out glitteringly before me, expansively inviting me to enjoy life.

Looking the World in the Eye

In *Julius Caesar,* Shakespeare advises us to "Set death in one eye and honor in the other and look upon both indifferently."

The world may be full of dualities, inconsistencies, and betrayal. Sometimes we may find it all a bit too much. And yet the earth is still a wonderful place to be. There is no need to run away from it and use our spirituality as a crutch. Shouldn't spiritually minded people be fully capable of looking the world and those we meet fully in the eye? To be able to work with the behavior of others by seeing what comes from personality and what comes from the soul is a great gift. All we know of love, we learn from one another. Not only are the eyes the windows of the soul, they are the library of a person's character. We penetrate the deepest mystery of another person by accepting and working with both the light *and* the shadows we see written there.

In the next chapter I shall more fully unveil the mystery of the eyes. You will be introduced to many practical suggestions, such as how to look at people so that they feel fully seen by you. We Shall embark on an in-depth exploration of how to go deeply into spotting the difference between *essence* and *personality.* You will be learning in clear, practical terms *when* to look into *which* eye of every person you meet and bring out the best in people whenever possible.

We shall also study ways to *avoid* making eye contact and soaking up another person's negativity. Wouldn't you like to know how to prevent angry outbursts from exploding in your face with just a look? Or get an aggressive person to back off without saying a word? We can all benefit from being able to establish favorable eye contact when shaking hands with a prospective employer or a customer. And how about being able to check prospective lovers for compatibility through their eyes, or keep the kids in order with just a glance?

These are highly practical, even necessary tools and they will enhance your life the minute you start to apply them. Still unconvinced? They can even keep you out of traffic school or having your auto insurance premium raised. Let me tell you about the time I talked a California motorcycle cop out of giving me a ticket by looking into his essence eye.

CHAPTER FOUR

Exploring the Eye-to-Eye Differential

How I Dehypnotized a Cop and Got Away with It

Twilight was descending on San Diego as I moved with the flow of traffic toward my date for the evening. Suddenly, my mood of happy anticipation was disrupted by the flashing lights and wailing siren of a motorcycle cop. He pulled alongside and signaled me to move over onto the hard shoulder, clambered off his machine, and swaggered toward my car.

"You were doing seventy," he said in a gruff voice, peering down at me from behind his shades. "Let me see your license and insurance."

"Sorry, officer. I guess I was just following the flow of traffic." I smiled up at him stiffly as I handed him the documents, wondering if there was actually a living soul behind the tight-lipped, inscrutable mask. The poor guy was zipped into his "I'm a cop" persona tighter than the uniform he was wearing. He scrutinized my papers with an air of distaste, as if willing them to transform into instruments of my damnation. As he did so, I made a few more half-hearted verbal attempts to connect with him. But he wasn't buying.

"I'm gonna give you a ticket," he announced finally and strolled back to his motorbike to write his curse on my insurance record.

I sat there, feeling deflated. This was meant to be wonderful evening, full of romance and excitement. What went wrong? Why should this stranger be allowed to disrupt my happiness and send me on my way feeling deflated and humiliated? Then I *remembered to remember myself.* Instantly, there was a huge energy shift as I quickly came back into ownership of my destiny.

"This won't do," I thought. "I'm not going to accept it. I was happy and now I am not because this guy is interfering with my well-being. He's supposed to be a *peace officer* but I'm letting his attitude rob me of *my inner peace.* He may be in the right and maybe he ought to give me a ticket. But he is being unfriendly and now that I'm remembering myself, I shall get him to treat me as a human being and not a statistic."

I got out of my car and walked back up the hill to where he stood by his motorcycle, pen poised in his right hand about to make the first fatal stroke. "Aha. He's right handed," I noted to myself. "So his essence eye will be the left one!"

"Officer, I'd like to talk to you for a moment," I said, calmly now, feeling that my confidence had returned.

"Okay," he said, trying to hide his surprise behind a mask of languorous indifference.

"And might I ask you to remove your sunglasses. I like to see who I am talking to." This bit of brinksmanship worked in my favor. He slowly raised his right hand and took off the shades.

"Gotcha," I thought, feeling a harmonizing power flow through me as I looked into his left (essence) eye for a spark of something real. For a second there was nothing but blankness. Then suddenly, in the depths of the pupil, his spirit ignited and shone out toward me with a look of transpersonal recognition. *His* essence was looking at *my* essence. In that moment, I knew this man and he knew me. And I knew beyond a doubt that I was going to reach him.

"Officer," I said, in a calm voice. "I realize that you have one of the most difficult jobs in the world. But you have the opportunity to do something wonderful here this evening."

I thought his eyes were going to fall out of his head. His mouth dropped open in momentary amazement, but he quickly recovered and said, "What would happen if I bought this line from everyone?"

"It's not a line," I continued, now willing his humanity to look at me through both his eyes. "And I'm not just an everyone. I'm a unique human being like yourself. I'm trying to connect with you on a level where we share a common sense of humanity. Most of the people out there tonight on the freeway are probably tired, stressed out, and in a negative frame of mind. If you let me go, I'll be in a *positive* frame of mind ... so I'll be a force for good in the world this evening."

He looked at me in amazement, his head jerking back slightly from the shock. Then a curious smirk started to play across his lips, as if he were at odds with his own desire to smile. Finally, the impulse got the better of him and he gave me a full-on grin. Then he handed my license back to me, shaking his head slightly as if disbelieving what he was doing and said, "What do you do for a living?"

An impish side of my nature rose up gleefully inside me. I wanted to say, "Well, actually, I'm a professional hypnotist!" but wisely managed to resist the temptation. Apart from blowing my chances of escape, it would not have been true. I am *not* a hypnotist. Never have been and never will be. But I am a *dehypnotist*. I specialize in helping myself and other people escape from their personal self-hypnosis and the terrifying sleep of the collective social trance.

After a few courteous closing remarks to the agent of the law, who I now thought of as an "officer" and not just a "cop," I was on my way, free and feeling elated. I had reclaimed my power and sense of self. Now I *was* a force for good in the world and would remain so for the rest of the evening. As I drove along, I felt harmoniously disposed toward everyone else on the freeway, especially the police.

The rest of the evening with my date went great, by the way. Dehypnotizing myself from entering a state of self-forgetfulness and personal weakness with the officer had put me in an awakened state that lasted for hours. I didn't need to check my hair and my teeth and do positive self-talk to boost my confidence. I was *self-confidence itself*, connected with that place within all of us that knows no sense of shortcomings.

All the time during the improvisational theater with the officer, I had kept doing certain internal exercises, maintaining an essential connection in myself that would pull forth a corresponding state in him. Then, in the midst of our interaction, I saw his soul wake up. It came out just about the time I got to the word "humanity." His official sense of his personal self was probably worn out from holding up "the mask" day after day. For an instant, something real was alive inside him. And he was grateful to me without knowing why.

How and Why the Magic Worked

Why did he change his mind? Was it the words I used? The result of *my* connecting with *his* humanity? Or did I just play with his sense of reality? All three were involved, but on the simplest level, I got the man to mirror me. By mastering my sense of personal disruption at his intervention in my life, I was able to pull a few particular levers inside my psyche, change my reactions, and draw forth power from a high source of transformational energy. If I had stayed paralyzed by his "I'm gonna give you a ticket" attitude, I would have been lost to myself and to him. But as I dehypnotized myself from the power of an authority figure's ability to put me into a state of compliance, my adversary became dehypnotized from his habitual, self-induced attitudes. This allowed him to come into alignment with my wish to be free. The words I used were important. But they were carefully chosen and spoken from a place of inner peace and strength.

When the officer first pulled me over, my organism went into fight-or-flight reactions, lowering my immune system and rendering my personality ineffectual. Wishing to recover from this, I restabilized myself by focusing my attention on my arms and legs. This disconnected me from the reactivity of fear in my heart, lungs, and adrenal glands and steadied me in my body. And from this arose a *remembered sense of self* that quickly restored me to personal authority over my reactions. Having attained focus through the techniques, I then got out of the car and went to work on the situation with the officer.

I looked into his essence eye while feeling the presence of my own essence all around me and his essence around him. He let me go because of what I became for him—a mirror in which to see and experience the submerged spark of reality that lies just beneath the surface of our social personalities.

Essence as a Barometer of Personal Evolution

While it is true that the essence eye can allow us to catch a glimpse of the spiritual side of people, not everyone manifests that part of their nature to the same degree. Life is like a group of schools in which people are on different tracks and in various grades of learning. When we speak of essence, this does not indicate the soul per se, but the soul's potential and ability to express through someone. This is dependent upon that individual's degree of transparency—his or her ability to let the power of I AM pass through self into the world. Therefore we may say that essence is the blueprint code of personal and spiritual potential. The fusion of these two into one expression is a major goal of spiritual development in a lifetime. Our souls may be equal before God as originally created. But in the affairs of men and women, variability of essence connection and its external expression is an unpredictable spin on the roulette wheel of personal evolution.

Sometimes we may look into a person's essence eye and get no sense of response. It's like dialing a wrong number, expecting someone you know to pick up and getting an alien being on the line instead. This is due to the fact that the person you are looking at is deeply asleep and the subjective personal self is all that person knows. In some cases, looking into people's essence eye may produce a look of contempt toward you because you are trying to embody and reach that which they have failed to connect with in themselves. This can be very apparent in some teenage boys as they swing between arrogance and insecurity. Seeking to create a social persona that mirrors the collective disillusionment of their peers, they may look at you with a dead essence eye. Such a look stems from an unconscious attempt to reject love, which they are equating with weakness. If you encounter this syndrome, look into their right eye at once and they will back down and treat you with respect.

The "dead eye" image also leaps out at us from movie posters with head shots of characters who are supposed to be hard and tough. Hannibal Lecter, the cannibalistic maniac in *The Silence of the Lambs,* is an example of this type. Still shots of Anthony Hopkins for the movie and its sequels sometimes showed his essence eye as a black hole, as if the entire socket were a well of death. Essence is connected to the higher centers of intelligence in a human being. Gangsta Rap, on the other hand, is plugged directly into the dark side of the unconscious mind. Essence cannot embody qualities of nonbeing and departs when an individual tries to behave in an inhumane manner.

Hopefully, you will not be meeting too many people like that. But suppose you are talking to someone and suddenly that person's essence eye goes dead. You can be sure he or she is connecting down line into the collective primal past of the human race. Another way to look at it is that such a person's reptilian brain just got active. In such cases, avoid essence eye contact altogether.

How much connection you can make with people's essence eye is indicative of the degree of spiritual development they have attained. We need to know who and what we are dealing with as we encounter a multitude of psychological types each day. Seeing the degree of spiritual openness, or lack of it, can be extremely helpful in negotiating our interpersonal social transactions successfully.

The Essence and Personality Eye Differential

The social advantages we can derive from being able to actually see that the eyes of a person reflect two aspects of their nature are tremendous.

Most people have no idea that one eye reveals their essence—their unique spirit—while the other eye carries a record of their human strengths and weaknesses. From birth to death, the *essence* eye carries the blueprint of what we are at the core of ourselves before it manifests outwardly as personality. The other eye reflects the personality characteristics we have acquired from life. Our hopes, fears, sorrows, and the many pains of existence—registered, remembered, and codified in the brain—are on display in the *personality* eye. The word "personality" derives from the Greek word persona, which means mask. For this reason I call the eye that reflects our connection with worldly experience the personality eye. You can see the difference between these two eyes in yourself right now.

Mirror, Mirror on the Wall, Which Is the Real Me, After All?

Go to the mirror and look at your face. Observe your eyes dispassionately, as if you are looking at another person, someone you've never seen before. Be sure to wear a blank expression and don't smile. *When we smile, essence comes out of both eyes.* When someone is smiling we cannot see the eye-to-eye differential. That is why a smile is such an asset. It is a great tool for bringing out the best in people and making a good connection right off the bat.

So, now, *without smiling,* if you are *right-handed,* take your *right hand* and cover the *right eye* with it. Then look dispassionately into the *left* eye. Does it appear clear and open to you? Is there a spiritual quality about it? Does it look childlike, hopeful, optimistic, and somewhat innocent in spite of past unpleasant experiences? You may have a sense that you are gazing off into infinity, or looking at something that has been touched by the eternal. This is your essence eye.

If you are *left-handed,* instead of covering the *right eye* with your *right hand,* take your *left hand* and cover up the *left eye.* Now you will only be able to see your essence eye. Again, it should appear innocent, guileless, agenda-free, and so on, just as in the description above for right-handed people. Simply put, for left-handed people the eye difference is reversed. Let me repeat the formula clearly:

If you are right-handed, your essence eye is the left eye.

If you are left-handed, your essence eye is the right eye.

Now change hands and cover up the eye that was exposed previously. This means that right-handed people will cover up their left or essence eye and be looking into the right eye—their personality eye.

Left-handed people will be covering the right eye with the right hand and looking into the left eye—their personality eye.

Do you see a difference from the essence eye? Practice until you can. Compared with the essence eye, the personality eye may seem heavier, duller, perhaps a little sad. Maybe you can see and feel pain there? Remember to have no judgment. You are simply conducting an experiment. So just look dispassionately and see what is in the mirror.

Next, cover and uncover both eyes in succession several times and familiarize yourself with the differences. As you do this, the difference should become clearly visible to you.

Interestingly most male homosexuals and some lesbians have a reversal of the essence and personality eyes. What this translates to is that if you are right-handed and homosexual, your essence will be in your right eye, as if you were a left-handed person. If you are left-handed, your essence will be in your left eye, as if you were a right-handed individual.

Study Faces in Magazines

One way to quickly familiarize yourself with the eye-to-eye differential is to look at faces in popular magazines like *People* and *US*. Look for photos in which the person is facing the camera and then cover up one of his or her eyes with your thumb. Try to get a feeling for whether you are seeing essence or personality. Since you have no way of knowing if the person you are looking at is right- or left-handed, this is a good way to develop your intuition.

Now cover up the other eye with your thumb and see what kind of a take you get on the eye that is now visible. Remember that in the essence eye, you are more likely to sense and see innocence, clarity, a certain air of detachment, perhaps even a touch of spirituality. You will probably feel quite comfortable as you observe an essence eye. When you switch to the personality eye, a slight feeling of discomfort may arise. Or you may have an "Oh my God" moment as you see the huge discrepancy between who this individual is as a person and who he or she is as a spiritual being.

Don't try this exercise with fashion models in advertising shots. Often the eyes in such photos are digitally altered to make both eyes look the same. You can check this out for yourself simply from curiosity, but you will not see a difference. So this type of shot is no good for training purposes.

Dealing with Authority Figures

Sometimes we have to deal with authority figures whose sense of self-identity comes from who they think they are in their own little world of power. Police officers, court judges, customs officials—anyone who can directly affect your life for good or ill must be handled very carefully. If you stare such people down by looking intently into the personality eye, they may get resentful and make life difficult for you. For safety's sake and for making a smooth connection, when in doubt, simply look into the essence eye.

My own experience with people who have any form of public authority is that if you see them as they think they are, or as they think they should be in your view, things will go smoothly. But if you see through the mask and spot the underlying insecurities, they will disconnect from you rapidly and things could go badly for you. This phenomenon may be found in anyone who receives a lot of attention from others and holds a decision-making position.

How *Not* to Look Someone in the Eye

The maxim to remember is this simple definition of an egotist: *He thinks he is who he thinks he is!* So don't rock the boat by letting such individuals sense that you *don't* think they are who they think they are. Here is a super technique to prevent creating difficult moments with people whose good will you may need.

Eye contact is usually a sign that we are willing to be fully engaged with another person. When this is not desirable for some reason and we are in a situation where it might be disadvantageous to give the impression we are avoiding eye contact, we can *look into the white of the eye and not the pupil.*

Thoughts transmit from one mind to another through open contact with the colored center of the eye, the iris. You know this from the experience of gazing romantically into someone's eyes. If we consciously choose not to look into the pupil, but into the white area surrounding the iris, we are not likely to be accused of ignoring someone. We are still looking into his or her eyes. But at the same time, we are not going to make the other person uncomfortable, or pick up a load of negative or intimidation energy.

When implementing this technique, be sure to blink frequently and naturally. Let your eyes move around quite freely from one part of the white of the other person's eyes to another. Move your attention casually from the corner to close to the pupil but always without ever making real eye contact. Obviously, while doing this, it does not matter which eye we are looking at. The whites of the eyes have no doorway into either the personality or the essence of an individual but are simply the neutral zone of the eyes.

I know of an order of nuns who receive instruction to look only into the whites of the eyes of any man they may be required to speak with during the course of a day. In this manner, they are not likely to get locked on to the energy of a male-female interaction that can emanate from personality eyes and forget their calling.

This technique can be applied by members of either sex. Suppose someone is coming on to you with advances you do not wish to encourage. Here you have a subtle way to detach and not get drawn into an uncomfortable situation.

It is also useful if we meet people who have low self-confidence and seem shy or insecure before us. To let them off the hook, saving them from embarrassment and discomfort, we can look into the whites of their eyes. Then they will start to settle down. When they sense that they are not going to be personally scrutinized, we can then look into their essence eye and see if they are willing to connect with us at a soul level. Personality can often be uncomfortable while essence remains unaffected.

Include Feeling and Intuition

Be sure to keep in mind that sensing the difference between the two eyes is not just something you see, as I mentioned before. *It is something you feel!* Use your intuition! When you look into another person's essence eye, there is generally a feeling of connection at once. He or she will probably smile back and look at you in an open, trusting manner. There are variations to this experience and we will cover them shortly.

Conversely, personality eye contact often puts you at variance with the other person, creating a sense of mistrust, or even hostility. Since you can't walk up to people and start off by saying, "Excuse me, are you left-handed, right-handed, or gay?" it is best to get a clear sense of the eye-to-eye differential by experience over time. Once you *know* what *essence* feels like, you will be able to find it easily. If you look for it in a person's left eye and *don't* see it, then look quickly into the other eye. Perhaps that individual is left-handed. In that case, a look into the right eye should cause the essence to show up.

Don't Stare at People

Sometimes, at workshops where I have explained the eye-to-eye differential, I see people during the break staring at each other, one eye bulging forward with Cyclops-like intensity. Others approach one another like jewelers squinting through a lens to check a stone for flaws or value. When I catch this going on, I always caution them, "Don't stare at one another. Be casual and behave normally."

It is very important not to give any visual clues that we are operating from a system of social interaction that is out of the ordinary. Outwardly we should appear relaxed in our behavior toward others. So remember . . . *no staring!*

At all times be as casual as possible while you let your eyes take in every aspect of other people. Notice their hair, nose, ears, clothing, stance, and so on. An occasional direct, but *nonstaring,* look into the essence eye is more than enough to reassure people that you and they share a common essentiality. Each time you do this you are letting them know that you have really seen them and are open to being *fully seen by them.* When you are not looking into people's essence eye, nonchalantly look at their nose or their hair, or some other neutral aspect of their face. Glance away to take in the room and let your eyes convey that you have a wide interest in what is going on around you. In other words, be everything a natural person should be.

The Shadow and the Personality Eye

Most people respond well to being seen in the essence eye. But the personality eye is the home of the shadow—the hidden, unacknowledged side of an individual. Even if people do not know that they have a resident shadow side to their personality, *it* knows and *does not like to be seen!* Carl Jung wrote extensively about this hidden side of human nature and how we project the aspects of ourselves that we don't like onto other people. The classic, oft-quoted example is how the Nazis projected their shadow self onto the Jews. To get rid of what they could not accept as a reflection of something in themselves, they tried to remove an entire race from the face of the earth.

The shadow is a shape shifter—it takes many forms, like Proteus, the fantastic metamorphosing creature from Greek myths. When the shadow gets stirred up in an argument and starts acting out through someone, it may hiss at you like a serpent one minute and roar like a lion the next. The shadow does not like to be made wrong and will initiate arguments to make the other person wrong at the drop of a hat. Only in very rare cases of seriously disturbed individuals does the shadow appear in the essence eye. Its habitual domain is the personality eye.

To successfully deal with people on a social level, we must be able to look fearlessly and with wisdom into their personality eye. By using our knowledge of the separate nature of the two eyes, we can take a measure of any person. We can look dispassionately to see if a person is someone with whom we wish to transact and involve our natural energy. With a little practical experience in the field, you will soon be able to look into anyone's personality eye and make an accurate character assessment in a second or two. Then you can move back to the essence eye and safety before the other person becomes uncomfortable with the fact that you might be seeing human weaknesses in his or her personality eye.

If ever you look into someone's essence eye, hoping to bring out their best qualities, and he or she looks at you with contempt, switch to the personality eye at once. People who are habitually vain and egotistical generally have no time for the qualities of essence in themselves. Therefore it is futile to expect them to recognize and value essence in you. Such types regard kindness, gentleness, or compassion as signs of human weakness. Should you see an open disregard, a smirk, or a sneer coming at you to make you feel that you are a weakling, you are honor bound not to take delivery of that self-devaluing projection.

Usually what will happen is that as soon as you switch from the essence eye to the personality eye, the smirk will fade. The other party may suddenly exhibit insecurity or even fear. At that moment, look back into their essence eye and they will probably seem relieved and start to behave nicely toward you. Like all bullies, once you confront them, such types will generally back down. Standing up to them for courtesy and right behavior's sake helps both you and them. You get to exercise conscious control over yourself and become strong in the face of potential disruption. And they get a chance to conduct themselves at a higher level of human connection, instead of simply acting out their delusions of self-importance before you.

The sidebar outlines some key tips for handling people who might present disruption and difficulty for you.

Key Tips to Remember

#1. Dealing with "the man." Never look a police officer in the personality eye. Police recruits are trained to make suspicion their second nature. They learn to always be on the lookout for visual cues that will alert them to troublesome individuals. If you look into their personality eye you will see that suspicion—perhaps also the fear and tension that goes with the job. If they sense that you are seeing their human insecurity, they may become slightly paranoid and compensate by questioning and probing you in an unfriendly manner. Try to figure out quickly which is their essence eye. Sometimes you can do this by checking out which hand they are using to write with, or which side their gun is on. When you do make contact, focus mainly on the essence eye, but remember not to stare. Be as casual and relaxed as possible.

#2. Meeting a prospective employer. When personality eyes meet, anything can happen. Suppose you walk into a job interview, shake hands with your prospective employer, and your personality eyes meet. You are feeling nervous about the interview. The other person senses you are not comfortable but has no idea why. This creates a sense of misconnection that he or she reads as "this person doesn't like me."

You cannot know in advance whether the person you are meeting is left- or right-handed. Here's how to tell: If you look into one eye and people immediately look away, when they look back at you, try to connect with them through the other eye. When the gaze is steady and noncombative, you are most likely locked on to their essence. Send acceptance to them while you are both connected and they will probably smile at you.

#3. Smiling and essence work together. Looking into the essence eye will usually elicit a responsive smile. Personalities differ widely in their style, character, likes and dislikes, and so on. Essence shares a common bond. We are all born in essence and when essence connects, even with total strangers, a common bond can be quickly established.

#4. When we smile, essence comes out of both eyes. If you want people to really like you, try and get them to smile at you by making an essence eye connection. Then quickly make that sense of essence migrate into the personality eye. This can be accomplished more easily if you back yourself up with a complimentary remark about the other person. An appropriate joke can help also. Be friendly. Get their personality eye to light up with essence and you are home free. When essence comes out of both eyes of people, they will really see you because you are seeing them. And they will like you.

#5. Tips for making sales. When trying to make a sale, first and foremost address the essence eye. Again, don't stare. Be casual, normal, and friendly, but be sure to make lots of essence connection. From time to time, do make a quick check of the personality eye and see if it is coming into agreement and alignment with you. You can also check there *briefly* for signs of real or feigned interest. If the personality eye is lit up, radiating a high degree of interest and is steady as it looks at you, you know you are getting close. When you close the sale, you will notice that the personality eye is now in full agreement with you and may even have a look of essence eye (trust and openness) about it.

#6. Tips for buying. If you are buying something, spend more time checking out the personality eye. Watch for shiftiness on the salesperson's part—or excessive staring, as if willing you to submit. If a salesperson's attitude is too pushy, or you feel you are getting drawn in against your will, looking in the whites of the eyes will help create some distance. In short, make salespeople come to you. They want to relieve you of your hard-earned cash. Get them to work for it and prove to you that they are worthy of your respect along with your money.

#7. Dealing with people who don't value and respect essence. If you look in someone's essence eye and get a feeling that there is "nobody home," don't push it. These people may be so out of touch with their own essence that they are incapable of responding to yours. This is often the case with egotists, who consider authentic connection with others to be weakness. If you look in people's essence eye and they return your gaze with contempt, look away at once. It is no use trying to reach someone who places no value on friendliness and compassion and who sees these virtues as signs that you are their inferior because they habitually mistake goodness for weakness.

#8. Avoid the essence dead. On very rare occasions you may meet people who have made behavioral life choices of such abnormality that their essence has basically shut down. If you look for essence and find only a black hole, a cold void that makes you shudder, don't look into either eye of such people. Get away from them as quickly as you can. Such people could even be potential or actual criminal lunatics and therefore highly dangerous to your health and safety.

Consciously Creating First Impressions

When you meet people for the first time, look into their left eye to see if you can connect with their essence. Let us assume that the world is predominantly geared to the right-handed person. We can practice looking for essence in the left eye until we are so familiar with how this feels, that if we don't get locked on to it straight away, we can easily switch to the other eye and find essence there.

This simple type of awareness puts people at ease immediately. When I look in people's essence eye while shaking hands, they almost always smile back at me. Conversely, if we look into the personality eye on meeting people for the first time, we might cause them to feel defensive by seeing the fears and insecurities reflected there. All people have personality traits they may not even be consciously aware of. Better, therefore, to extend the possibility of an essence connection to one and all initially and see if they can receive it graciously. In a sense, it is the ultimate act of courtesy to let someone know you are meeting in open friendship on the highest level. Your unspoken message is that you want to connect, soul to soul.

Since the common denominator for all of us is that we are spiritual beings, when we can consciously connect with people at an essence level, they won't need their habitual defenses. Essence eye connection relaxes people. Personality eye contact can make them defensive. *Know the difference by feeling the vibratory connection of receptivity flowing between you and another.* And again, don't stare. Simply integrate this "seeing awareness" into your natural style of behavior.

Enlightening the World through Personal Interaction

To walk through the world in a trance is to be like a robot. Who wants to be a machine driven by automatic impulses of thought, distorted feeling, and physical reaction?

The positive results of a conscious life should make us invulnerable to the confused, negative energy of hatred and rage that is polluting civilization. Outmoded realities, patterns of human behavior that are not expansive and in alignment with the highest evolutionary thrust of this planet, cannot stand. The earth is a conscious being. Each day the energy field of this planet grows stronger in its will to produce a conscious humanity. All who resist and are not in alignment with this emergence will feel that energy thrust toward enlightened consciousness as personal and international tension. This is the reason for the current global conflict. Outmoded patterns of thought and behavior are resisting the change to the all-encompassing wholeness and compassion of a one-world vision.

The greatest revolution the earth has ever known is happening right now. Millions are seeing for the first time, collectively, what saints and sages have perceived: that the essential nature of a human being is Divine Energy. To be fully part of this emerging vision, those who would be the pioneers of a better global destiny must build a new reality through personal demonstration.

We must be able to sense, and connect with, that Divine Energy in every person we encounter, whether they "get" what we are doing or not. Even if they are behaving toward us in the most outrageous manner, we must not go unconscious ourselves and respond from dysfunction. This does not mean that we become doormats. It may be that through our words and behavior we must forcefully let them know we are not taking delivery of any offensiveness toward us. But we can do this with no personal animosity, desire for revenge, or urge to personally wound. By entering a state of connection with the presence and the power of *I AM,* we can make a connection with the *I AM* in others.

Sometimes when we do this, the static energy of personality conflict falls away to be superseded by more enlightened communication. The world suddenly changes and is created anew at a higher level, if only for a moment. It has become more conscious, in and through us, and we are more enlightened than we were before. Instead of going into the collective trance, falling asleep in reactive behavior, we awakened and held the field for someone else to interact with us at a higher level of consciousness.

Maya and the Illusion of "Reality"

In the next chapter we shall explore seven questions we must ask ourselves if we wish to live a fully conscious life. We shall also study the pervasive nature of the sleep that grips those we must deal with each day. The ancient sages of India called the illusion of atoms and molecules masquerading as solid matter Maya, the cosmic illusion. To be identified with Maya as the sole reality is to be *in delusion*. It is essential to understand the hypnotic power this force has over all of us. I have seen through the great trance with my own eyes, via a conscious experience that was transmitted to me by a great female yogi from India in 1970. I know exactly the nature of the illusions we are dealing with and I want to transmit the essence of that experience to you.

Once we see how Maya grips and motivates the other players in the game of life around us, we can then sway the illusion to cooperate with our human-divine will. No matter what is going on around us, we can always be crystallizing our soul awareness through *conscious participation* in the cosmic dance. As an active agent for harmony and reconciliation, you will become a conduit for a higher intelligence to enter the lives of those who are still in the caught in the Maya-induced trance. And you will be rewarded for your efforts.

Jesus said, "The harvest is plentiful but the laborers are few." He also said, "The laborer is worthy of his hire." Undertake this work and you shall have your reward. Life will reshape itself around your intention. You will find your material needs met with greater ease so that you can constantly increase in effective daily expression of these principles. You will establish a higher connection than the flow of benign circumstance than ever before. People, places, and synchronistic events will align with your intention. An all-knowing intelligence will back you all the way as a force for good in the world.

CHAPTER FIVE

Staying Conscious in a World of Sleep

Seven Questions for a Conscious Life

The following seven questions are an essential prerequisite to living a conscious life.

1. Do I want to turn lead into gold from the everyday circumstances of life?
2. Am I willing to extract from life an extraordinary energy, a force, and a power that most people have no contact with or knowledge of?
3. Can I accept that by accessing this power I will become responsible for it and in my behavior toward others, seek to bring out the best in them whenever possible?
4. Do I understand that practicing these techniques will not allow me to live like a sleepwalker in the collective trance?
5. Realizing that other people will sometimes misunderstand my actions and judge me according to their level of sleep, will I not use my power to harm them, even in my thoughts?
6. Can I embrace that as I create a sense of presence in and around me, my level of being will increase and unprecedented degrees of good and abundance will naturally flow into my life?
7. Understanding the above, do I now accept that I am willing to be awake in the great cosmic dream and act as a conscious force for good in the universe?

A World of Sleeping Machines

I hope you answered these questions in the affirmative. If not, you are in big trouble, because you have already read too much to go back into the collective trance and sleep with the same comfort others enjoy. Characterizing the human race as a bunch of sleepwalking zombies may well be the final frontier of political incorrectness. But suppose life really is but a dream through which we merrily row our boats of self-delusion? And what if Jesus' "sleep not, for no one knows the hour when the Son of Man comes" is not simply an ancient little homily, but a dire warning not to let death catch us with our evolutionary pants down?

The world's scriptures are loaded with sleep references. And Plato's "watchers in the cave" allegory is a direct metaphor of how we mistake shadow illusions for reality. Mystics and seers of all times and places, those who have experienced moments of true seeing, testify that the world we see is an illusion. They *know* we are all dreamers caught up in its seeming reality. From their expanded viewpoint, the sleepwalking state of the human race is readily observable. And this type of perception is apparently transmittable from someone who has it to one who does not. I know because I have experienced this phenomenon directly for myself.

A Hindu Guru Comes to Town

In 1970, I was privileged to get a transmitted bounce from the consciousness of an Indian sage who was visiting various spiritual groups in England. I had recently returned from America, where I had learned to meditate using the techniques given by Paramahansa Yogananda and his Self Realization Fellowship. Now I was living in Leicester, a Roman founded town in the Midlands, the contemporary fame of which derives from producing a super-abundance of socks. Not finding many aspiring yogis with whom to meditate in the sock capital of the world, I was delighted to discover an ad in the local paper announcing that a certain Sri Shyama Mataji from India was going to be giving "darshan" on Saturday afternoon and all were welcome. *Darshan* is a word that means the holy sight of a sacred person. Simply being in the presence of an enlightened individual can cauterize negative seed tendencies lodged in the student's brain. The teacher can then subtly redirect the spiritual aspirant to higher levels of enlightenment.

Desirous of getting *"darshanized,"* I betook myself to the address in the ad on Saturday afternoon and found myself knocking on a door in the Hindu-Pakistani area of Leicester. When it opened to admit me, I was ushered into a small house filled with dark faces and black eyes, which stared at me in either curiosity, surprise, or contempt. My little white ass was moved through the throng to the kitchen where Sri Shyama Mataji herself was busy stirring a large pan full of some curried lentil concoction being prepared for her devotees. I immediately took this to be a favorable sign. Enlightened or not, the yogi woman was not above rolling up her sleeves and getting down to the nitty-gritty with the pots and pans. When she saw me, the sage stopped stirring and advanced upon me with intensely scrutinizing eyes. They were extremely luminous and I felt as if the record of my life was being probed by some cosmological radar system. She seemed to be ferreting out my imperfections and arranging them for assessment alongside my possibilities for good.

The varied reactions of those who had first witnessed my arrival now fell into watchful, expectant silence. Wide-eyed and curious, they observed their teacher's unusually intense interest in me. Finally, she asked me in her own tongue if I would like to eat. Not understanding a word, I gaped at her like a fool until someone grabbed a plate, ladled a helping of curried lentil whatever and chapati onto it, and thrust the offering into my hand. I quickly shoveled some of the food into my mouth to cover my confusion. And found it to be delicious. My visible delight at the splendid taste broke the ice and laughter dissolved cultural differences into an afternoon of fun and spiritual exploration.

Mataji Zaps Me Awake

After everyone had eaten, some of the women present, dressed in beautiful traditional costumes, performed what I assumed were sacred dances, in which a strange blend of spiritual-erotic content was readily observable. Then Shyama Mataji indicated that I and a few of her devotees were to follow her upstairs. I did so and was ushered into a special room that had been set aside as a shrine for meditation and prayer. We all sat cross-legged on the floor and the sage chanted for a while. Then we meditated. When this ended, a period of questions and answers followed, again in a language I did not understand.

Sitting next to me was a bright-eyed young woman who spoke English and she tried to give me the gist of what was being said. At one point she leaned over to me, whispering conspiratorially, "You see that statue of Lord Krishna on the altar. She puts food out for it and then the statue comes to life, gets down from the altar, and eats the food. When you see that, *then* you will believe in God!"

I looked at the statue of Krishna, who was, as usual, playing his flute, and saw no indication that he was about to get hungry and mobile. Being perhaps a bit of a pompous spiritual ass in those days, I whispered back in answer to my informant's confidence, "I don't need to see miracles to believe in God," which produced a shrug of indifference from her. Apparently she was not surprised that a foreign wannabe yogi would fail to see the relevance of a miraculous manifestation.

I was jerked back to reality by the voice of the interpreter conveying Mataji's words to me. "Mataji says you have very good karma from past lives. She will pay your way to India. You will be her guest and live in her ashram where you will shave your head and chant to Krishna all day long."

A chorus of ooohs and aaahs filled the room as the other attendees smiled in either awe or envy at my great good fortune. I was busy running my fingers through my hair to make sure it had not been miraculously removed already by Lord Krishna.

"You have until tomorrow to decide," continued the interpreter. "Now you can go. But first you can touch her feet and she will give you her blessing."

I knew that reverent contact with the feet of an enlightened being can transmit a subtle current of energy to another person. Whether or not this Mataji was such a transmitter, I had no way of knowing. But I liked the lady and had been sensing a powerful magnetic force of energy about her since our eyes first met. So I unlocked my stiff legs, crossed the room, and, kneeling before her, placed my hands on her feet. Instantly I felt a huge current of energy surging into my hands from the contact. It ran up my arms and poured into my body with an electrifying power. I looked up into her eyes and she put her hands on my head to give me a final blessing. Now I became really blissed out. I could hardly move but somehow managed to get to my feet, back out of the room, and, after much genuflecting and *Namaste* (the God in me bows to the God in you), made it to the street. But it was not the same reality I had left behind when I knocked on the door and entered Little India two hours previously.

The City of Sleeping People

Whatever strange force Mataji had transmitted to me had obviously created major perceptual shifts in my brain, for now I found myself staring at a city populated by sleepwalkers. In every direction I turned my gaze, everyone seemed to be moving through the world on automatic pilot. I observed them in shock and disbelief. Before seeing Mataji, I had been like them. *Now I was an awakened stranger in a city of human automatons.* People were being moved in their courses by some form of invisible radar system that turned them left or right, shifting their limbs and opening their mouths. They spoke to each other as if in a dream and were even driving their cars in a trance.

A few hours earlier I had walked the same streets thinking I was awake and accepting the normal appearance of things as a matter of fact. Now I observed that the brick walls of the houses were alive with a radiant energy that was drunk with the bliss of its existence. Even the road and the paved sidewalk upon which I stood emanated an extraordinary aliveness. I wanted to laugh out loud with joy. I could perceive directly that the seemingly inert matter of creation was actually vibrant with the bliss of a great consciousness that was holding "reality" in its apparently substantial form. The joke was that the so-called inanimate world of objects and things I had hitherto taken as fixed and immutable was actually more alive than the sleepwalking people moving through it. I decided to walk the three miles back to my home in my consciousness and savor the experience while it lasted.

As I moved, I could see that my own body was in fact being operated by some universally rooted process that was guiding every minute aspect of my life and the lives of all people. I was not actually walking at all. Something was moving through my form, *making it move*. Normally I would have thought it was I myself who was doing the walking. But now I could perceive that all my thoughts and actions, like those of everyone on the street, were being executed by a superior force. This higher intelligence was running directive waves of magnetism through my body and theirs. It turned our bodies hither and yon through invisible currents of energy, as a radio-controlled model toy is guided by the person operating the remote unit. I had always assumed that what I thought of as I myself was calling the shots. But apparently our so-called free will is a case of misplaced identity. The *real* "Doer" of everything is a force inside each person far greater than our minds can conceive. "It" is the active quality and we human beings simply *the effect of the doing*.

As I continued home, this perception grew exponentially. I began to feel myself as this "doing" force, inside the walls of the houses, the sidewalk, and even the street. No longer limited to my particular physical body, I was simply moving over the vastness of my own great periphery, which now extended in and through matter in all directions. And the nature of this vastness was absolute bliss and joy.

I See That My Mother and Sister Are Asleep

As I neared home, I saw my mother and sister walking on the other side of the street, heading for the grocery store with their shopping baskets. Amazingly, they didn't see me, even though I was heading in the opposite direction in plain view. I reached our house and went inside. When they came home from their shopping expedition half an hour later, I found myself conversing with two people who were technically asleep. Everything my mother and sister said and did was completely automatic. They cooked the dinner and set the table in a trance, as if the world around them was in fact simply the material creation it always appeared to be. When we sat to eat, our dinner conversation took place in a dream they took for reality. The scary part was that as soon as I started to get caught up in their moaning about their various problems or ramblings or projections about this illusory world of theirs, *I too began to fall asleep.*

Now I clearly saw that we are self-hypnotized and our supposedly meaningful "social interactions" consist largely of placing our particular imaginings about life into other people's heads. And we invite equally sleeping partners' phantasmagoria to dance in our internal dream world. Fortunately, each time I would start to nod off into my mother's and sister's trance consciousness, the energy I had received from Sri Mataji would kick in and jerk me back to full wakefulness. Once restored to this state, I was simply able to watch my family acting out their delusions in the illusion, while observing the parts of myself that would normally have been caught up in it. In other words, *I* was watching *myself* watching them be asleep!

This going in and out of the trance continued all evening. Finally I fell asleep, in the nocturnal sense, awash with joy and ecstasy. When I awoke next morning, I was back in the everyday "perceptual box system," restored to *normalcy* along with my mother and sister. Now they and I were co-participants in a worldview that was just as real and imperatively demanding as it had always been. The only difference was that now I knew, from firsthand experience, the absolute insubstantiality of what we take to be reality. I also knew that the true nature of life is unconditioned bliss and joy and that I was not going to let sleeping people con me out of it anymore.

What Hypnotizes Us? Spirits? Habit? Or Our Own Imagination?

After my awakening experience, I began to puzzle in great depth over what is keeping us in a state of sleep. And I became intensely interested in recapturing that awakened state on a permanent basis. I began studying the lives of saints, seers, and mystics of all ages and climes. I was surprised to learn that some cultures still believe we mortals are surrounded by malignant and benign spirits. Supposedly these entities can impinge themselves upon our consciousness, affecting for good or ill our various states of mind.

Going Downtown with Jesus

Television may be "bubble gum for the eyes," but occasionally we can learn something useful from the tube. I once saw a man being interviewed on television about his NDE—Near-Death Experience. While in a hospital undergoing an operation, his heart had suddenly stopped. As the surgeons tried to jump-start him back to life, his consciousness, now separated from his body, watched them from the ceiling. Then he was drawn into a dark tunnel and hurtled at great speed toward a distant pinpoint of light, which grew larger and brighter as his consciousness advanced upon it. When he reached the end of the tunnel, he saw that the light was radiating from a heavenly personage he took to be Jesus Christ.

This being, whoever or whatever it was, beckoned the man to follow and together they moved rapidly through many otherworldly dimensions. Having previously heard that individuals who "die" on the operating table are sometimes taken by emissaries of light to heavenly realms, the man assumed he was now being led to paradise. But to his surprise, his Jesus took him to a grimy bar in downtown Los Angeles. There, from behind the scenes as it were, they were able to observe the drunken clientele propping up the counter and lolling over the tables.

The man had been in many such places in his life, for he had himself been a longtime alcoholic. Now he was being forced to look at other poor souls caught in the grip of the malady that had been the cause of his own undoing. But this was no ordinary bar. Or at least, his perception of it was most unusual. His angelic guide was providing him with an extrasensory faculty of intuitive perception. He could clearly see that not all the spirits in the bar were being poured from bottles. Behind the scenes of the material world, so seemingly real to the men and women in the bar, there hovered grotesque creatures that looked as if they had escaped from Dante's inferno. Whenever a drinker set a glass down with a feeling of satiation, these dark creatures would quickly impinge upon the consciousness of the drinker and will him to drink again. Some of these disincarnate entities would actually get inside the body of a drinker and experience the vicarious thrill of imbibing once more through a human form.

The extra-dimensional traveling ended when the hospital team successfully restarted the man's heart and his consciousness returned to his body. Eventually he fully recovered and was able to return to everyday life. But it was not the life he had known before the operation and his out-of-body revelations. From the point of his recovery, based on what he had experienced when "Jesus" showed him the "other side" of drinking, he dedicated his life to helping people break free from the apparently multidimensional perils of alcohol.

Reassuringly to skeptics who wish to remain asleep in the great trance, there is no proof that ghostly entities, or even spirits, actually exist. We can, however, agree that we are all creatures of habit. When we get an uncontrollable impulse to do something, we are acting out the biological compulsions of behavioral conditioning. We may not like some of the things we seem compelled to act upon against our will. But at least we can assume that our habits are our own. Or are they? What if some of the impulses our bodies and minds play host to are not always our own, but fragmented aspects of other people's consciousness? Can patterns of thought and habit leap from one mind to another like wind-blown seeds and take root in our consciousness?

Even more bizarre, do we sometimes act out the desires of spirits, living and dead, that troll the psychological atmosphere around us looking for kicks? Can unseen mechanisms of thought and impulse cause *us* to embody archetypal forces? Do even inanimate objects possess a mind of their own and call to us to engage in action with them? Here are two strange tales that should cause us to at least wonder.

Richard Pryor and the Possessed Pipe

When comedian Richard Pryor set himself on fire while freebasing cocaine, he did so in a desperate bid for freedom.

"I set the pipe down," said Pryor. "I didn't want to do it anymore. But the pipe jumped off the table and leapt back into my mouth. Every time I put it down it would jump back into my mouth. I kept on putting it aside and it kept jumping back into my mouth like it was alive and had a will of its own. And I thought I was going mad so I poured lighter fluid over my body and set myself on fire."

Ginger Baker and the Magic Drums

Ginger Baker, drummer of the famed rock band Cream, said in an interview, "Once when we were playing, I got into this state . . . and I thought, Am I playing these drums or are they playing me?"

Did the spirits inherent in drumming or cocaine actually possess Baker and Pryor? Does the latent energy required to engage in any activity actually have a living ethos of its own? Can something external actually rule us? Or was it the creative momentum of their personal energy, imperatively willed desire acting out externally to themselves and then seen as the cause? Are inanimate objects really alive?

Carl Jung recounted in a filmed interview that one day, the pots and pans in the kitchen at his lakeside retreat at Bollingen, Switzerland started to behave willfully.

Nothing was being cooked and the stove was cold, when to Jung's surprise, a kettle suddenly leapt off the stove and hit the floor with a crash. Then a saucepan fell off its hook on the wall and joined the kettle on the floor. Soon the room was alive with falling pots and pans. Jung realized he needed to talk to the unruly implements.

"Look here, this just won't do," he told them. "I'm trying to work and all this noise is distracting me. You are all just going to have to settle down." And they did.

Jung's writings are full of references to the aliveness of the inanimate. He could see a great, unified intelligence manifesting diversely in every physical phenomenon. Throughout his life he remained ever alert to see and hear it talking to him.

Western pragmatists would tend to discount the spirit of a tree or a kettle as a reality. Likewise, our medical approach does not see physical illness as a manifestation of disturbed life energy and certainly not invasion by disembodied beings. But many Eastern cultures have elaborate practices for dealing with unfriendly spirits. Which approach is correct? Perhaps the truth lies somewhere between the pragmatic realism of modern science and the psychological dangers of an unscientific acceptance of any enigmatic phenomenon as evidence of the paranormal.

We might reasonably assume that every action or thought carries a charge of energy. That energy has to go *somewhere*. Our actions are generally based upon desire for a particular outcome. Since so little of our activity reaches the intended or desired conclusion, then we human beings must be carrying around multi-watts of frustrated impulses in our energy fields. Consider a city, filled with thousands of people. The confused energetic accumulations of frustrated intention in a metropolis can be overwhelming and enervating to sensitive souls.

Can You Eat the City Heat?

Cities are like large hives that generate, store, and process the energy of human activity. Teeming with thousands of people and untold trillions of heterogeneous thought patterns, it can be very difficult to maintain one's sense of individual identity amidst the noise and filth, particularly if one is a spiritually sensitive person. The unfulfilled desires, restless thoughts, and actions of its inhabitants frequent the streets as vagrant negative energy and kinetic physical impulses. These are the "spirits" that haunt the sidewalks of the modern world, seeking susceptible bodies and minds through which to run potentiality as actuality. To deflect them, we must learn to be energetically pneumatic. Like the tires on a car, we need to surround ourselves with such a huge force field of energy that everything inharmonious just bounces off us.

Every human being emanates a particular vibratory atmosphere. This force field contains and represents the totality of that person's life experience. It is the atomic weight of *who the person is.* More accurately, it represents what that person has made of himself or herself as part of the process of evolution. If we ourselves are weak, if our pneumatic force is too low, we shall be overwhelmed by the complex, negative energy fields of other people, particularly in dense atmospheres such as we encounter in cities. Fortunately, we can train ourselves to keep our own emanations from leaking out wherever we go. Additionally, we can learn to transform the negative emanations surrounding us and convert them into useful fuel for our drive forward in our own life processes.

To the person who knows how to feed off it, a large gathering of people can become a tremendous source of energy. Think of the electricity in the atmosphere at a football game or a rock concert. The players get highly charged up by the intense power generated by a large group of people who are focusing upon them. When we walk down a city street, hardly anyone notices us. But if we focus upon ourselves by *sensing and feeling* and *self-remembering* as we make our way through the crowds, we can accumulate energy from the surrounding atmosphere. This type of *total body awareness* can then take the energy *behind* the filth, noise, and negativity and convert it back into useful fuel. Here is a metaphor that describes this process very well.

The Spaceship That "Eats" the Universe

A spaceship was traveling through the universe. One of the passengers, curious about how the propulsion system of the vessel worked, asked the captain to explain it to him.

"This is the latest model," replied the skipper. "As it moves forward, it ingests into itself all the space dust, bits of broken meteorites, and other junk lying around in the universe. Since all matter is essentially made up of the same molecular substances, it then breaks what it ingests back down to its original nuclear component—pure energy. This force is then emitted from the rear of the vessel and thrusts it forward."

"Fascinating," said the passenger. "It sounds very economical."

"Oh, it is," assured the captain. "Since there is so much useless stuff all around us, we never lack for something to convert into a force we can use. In fact, the more we are surrounded by, shall we say, the negative fallout from creation, the more we can profit from the experience. We have a little saying to remind ourselves of this. Would you like to hear it?"

"Certainly," answered the passenger. "I am most interested."

"The formula is very simple and easy for us to remember in the face of apparent difficulties. It goes like this: *The denser the fog, the faster the vessel goes.*"

Your Body Is a Device for Transforming Energy

The spaceship described in the above story is the human body. Your physical vehicle is a device for receiving, processing, and transforming the energy contained in the impressions it receives through the five senses. Everything we see, taste, touch, hear, and smell contains an energy of a specific density. Some of the things we perceive repel us because their innate frequency is too gross for us to process. Other impressions, such as from flowers or a sunset, affect us harmoniously. But quantum physics tells us that essentially, there is no such thing as a flower or a sunset. There is only a unified field of energy in which a play of atoms coalesce into the various forms we see. Theoretically, if we ourselves can vibrate energetically in resonance with the *creative power* from which the play of external impressions arises, the *I AM* within ourselves, then we should be able to sense and experience that same underlying resonance in all objects to some degree. As we become more and more accomplished at this, the gross energy generated by the unpleasant aspects of human behavior should be as "eatable" by us as when someone is showering us with compliments and adoration.

By maintaining conscious connection with the underlying substratum of visible creation, we can train ourselves to become experientially rich in almost any circumstance. Let *others* lose energy through reaction, self-justification, and identification with external circumstances. We can eat the energy they cannot tap in any environment. They cannot draw it into themselves because, in regard to consciousness, they are out to lunch. Therefore the instant you become coherent, through *sensing and feeling* and *self-remembering* into *I AM* consciousness, all the transmutable energy in the dynamic of the situation flies to you! Instead of weakening, you become enormous.

Going Beyond Positive and Negative

We convert the forces of tension into usable fuel, by refusing to become identified with our negative emotional reactions to the external triggers of circumstance. Thus we avoid the consequent possession of ourselves by internal or external static energy as a consequence of falling into reactivity.

We do not remain ridiculously positive, smiling passively in the face of inappropriate behavior and boundary crossing. Instead, we stand, psychologically speaking, right in the middle between "yes" and "no," the affirming and denying poles that normally characterize conflict. We ground ourselves in a place of personal reconciliation that is more powerful than either of the other two extremes.

In the words of Carl Jung, we understand that "reality lies at the point of tension between the opposites," and we center there at a moving point of balance and act from it!

The "point of tension between the opposites" is where we find the missing *third force,* the energy of reconciliation. This is the neutralizing element that plays mediator between plus or minus, yes or no, attack or defend, affirm or deny, and all the other dualistic pairs of opposites.

It is only through the action of and awareness within ourselves of this third force that we can feel a connection with our sacred center, the *I Am That I Am.* Awareness of the third force produces the state of self-remembering. When we self-remember, the energy running the play of opposites constantly surging back and forth within and around us pours into our center and vivifies the spine and the brain. The cerebral-spinal structure, our inner *Tree of Life,* is the residing place where *I AM* sleeps within us. In the human embryo, the first elements to form are the medulla oblongata and the spine. Reversing the flow of life energy from the hypnotic external trance transfers habitually outgoing life energy back to the spine and brain. This is the goal of sitting forms of meditation: "Be still and know that I am God." But we are learning to do this while in the midst of activity. Self-remembering through *sensing and feeling* allows us to be within ourselves and engaged in even the most demanding external activity. We are hitting enlightenment on the run!

By self-remembering we become supercharged. In social conflict situations, when other people refuse to join you in the place of reconciliation, they will lose force as a consequence of their folly and misbehavior. The good they refuse will fly to you and add to the atomic weight of *your* being. And if you then have to speak words they may not want to hear, you can be sure they will not forget the experience. Your utterances will be grounded in the laws of the universe, and no fool can argue with the laws of creation.

The Dance of Atoms and Self-Remembering

In the atomic world we find the ongoing play of electron, proton, and neutron. In these three forces, it is the first two that contend as interchanging charges of positive and negative. The neutron is the neutralizing, or *reconciling,* element—the miraculous third force. The human body, and the material world around our bodies, is made up of atoms, charged continually with the dance of electron, proton, and neutron. Instability happens when the neutralizing force becomes weak and the other two agitate each other. The reason heavy water is required to detonate the atomic bomb is that it slows down the vibratory rate of the neutron and, with no reconciling force to keep them in check, electrons and protons collide with world-shattering results. So too in human interactions and relationships: When things get too heavy, the reconciling force becomes weak and people bang their heads together, sometimes explosively.

Self-remembering aligns us with the mighty third, or reconciling, force. This element is referred to in various religions as one aspect of the triune nature of God. In Hinduism it is the "renovating" aspect of Shiva, the other two being "destructive" and "preserving." Biblically, it is characterized as the Holy Ghost, the comforter that "brings all things to remembrance," which of course includes ourselves. The energy of this reconciling element, once it is in motion, can fill us with greatness. It endows us personally with a sense of connection to a destiny greater than the need to be egotistically right.

Without the friction of stressful interpersonal interaction, we might never make the effort to find this third force. We would simply sleep through life, just like everyone else. From this point of view, those who behave with aggression toward us can be seen, in the ultimate sense, as allies. In order to deal with *their self-hypnosis,* we have to become greater than their dualistic perceptions of life. To some degree, we have to step out of the trance that keeps them in the state of sleep. This was what Mataji showed me. So if we want to make a profit around negative people and situations, let us remember the rule that propels the spaceship: *the denser the fog, the faster the vessel goes.*

Remember too that in any large gathering of people, huge amounts of energy are being generated. Just as a dynamo can collect energy from the surrounding atmosphere, so a man or woman who *senses and feels* and *self-remembers* can gather energy from any social environment where people are thronging together. Once you know the right tricks, you can apply them to a trip to a major city like Los Angeles, London, or New York, to the local shopping mall, or even to dinner with the in-laws. Any social situation can be turned into a personally profitable experience by making *sensing and feeling* and *self-remembering* second nature. The more you do this, the greater will be the energetic power of *I AM* flowing into the world through you!

So, practice in a relaxed manner all the time, no matter where you are or whom you are with. Hold fast to this firm conviction, and in any environment and any situation, say to yourself constantly: *I will remember myself. I will always make a profit in terms of energy, expanding consciousness, and spiritual awakening.*

CHAPTER SIX

Workplace Dynamics: Enlightening the Nine-to-Five

Shake Them Up to Wake Them Up

Enlightened personal interaction is not about "making nice" with people, particularly with those who are disrespectful to us. Women know only too well the perils of being a "pleaser"—someone who goes along with bad behavior from others for the sake of harmony. When we stuff our reactions and smile to avoid tension and conflict, we serve no one, least of all ourselves. We can "enlighten" perpetrators of disrespect by letting them know that we are not going to take delivery of any behavioral garbage.

Gandhi used passive resistance and noncooperation to enlighten the British and get them out of India. He gave an empire an awakening shock. You can help those with incompetent social skills who cross your path awaken to a new reality by embodying before them an energy field that puts their dysfunction on hold. This may be done simply with a look or a statement delivered with the authority of personal presence behind it.

People who are asleep may need to be shaken to wake up. If their dreaming harms no one, let them sleep. But if their self-delusion attempts to turn your harmonious life into a temporary emotional nightmare, you are well within your rights to let them have it. But instead of fighting on their terms, being rude and aggressive, you can put them on "Pause" by expanding out of their limited world into the energy of a higher reality—the fourth dimension of higher consciousness and the presence and power that emanates from *I AM*.

Our daily work environments can be a breeding ground for many forms of subtle and not-so-subtle personal abuse. In this chapter we will be looking at the dynamics of rudeness and overfamiliarity amidst the stress and turmoil of the nine-to-five. We will look at some real-world scenarios and explore effective ways to deal with on-the-job intimidation. Let us begin by examining how to overcome the sense of *dehumanization* we can be exposed to while at our place of employment. The following is a true story of subtle workplace harassment from my own life. It was perpetrated against my coworkers and me when I was a teenager in England.

He Turned His Employees into Objects

Upon leaving school I worked for a boss who deliberately acted as if he could not remember anybody's name. If he needed you to execute some task, he would flap his hand vaguely in your general direction and say, "Er, you, there . . . uh . . . *Thing!*" and then send you off on some task of colossal unimportance. Talk about turning people into objects! Thing, indeed. But there was an added danger to being so addressed. This provider of minimal wages sometimes sprayed the atmosphere when he spoke. "Thing" is a word that lends itself to projections of saliva from the mouths of those nature has fashioned to so emit when they speak. The ability to weave and dodge, although not listed as a job requirement, was certainly a helpful survival skill in this situation.

"Thing" was our employer's name for everyone who worked for him! But when we weren't busy ducking, we employees had our own name game, a special way of redressing the balance. Unbeknownst to the boss, behind his back, he *himself* was known to the entire staff as Thing!

If my buddies and I were goofing off and one of us saw him coming, the heads-up would be given that he was advancing upon us. "Look out. Here comes Thing!"

And sure enough, Thing would bear down on us, flapping that vague hand in our direction, while we tried to look as if we actually enjoyed working for the twit. And he would say, "Er, you . . . um . . . Thing! Don't just stand around doing nothing. Go and tidy up the, er, um . . ."

"Thing?" one of us would suggest hopefully.

"Yes, exactly! The uh . . . um . . . Thing!"

I suppose we shouldn't have taken it personally. After all, he even called inanimate objects "Thing." Perhaps he had some brain deficiency and just lumped everything he saw, sentient or not, into a one-definition-fits-all system of collective categorization. But I doubt it. There was a subtle twist to the lips as he said the word.

A disdainful air flickered about his eyes as they looked down his nose at you, before they closed to banish your living image from the visual receptors in his brain. The bottom-line message was always the same: *You* are not important. Only *I* am.

The Antidote

The above true story is an extreme example of mildly dehumanizing behavior. Fortunately, my mates and I were able to laugh it off. I hope you never have to work for someone who refers to as if you were a mere object. However, we have all known moments when someone tried to take away our dignity and turn us, if only in our own minds, into a thing instead of a living soul. The answer, in any situation where someone is attempting to make us feel dehumanized, is to *call the perpetrator to accountability right away.*

Give an abuser a head start and it is very hard to catch up. Once the precedent is set and you have lost the ground of being treated with respect, regaining it will require conscious effort on your part.

Being prepared to respond *immediately* to any unacceptable behavior does not require that we go through life perpetually expecting the worst in human nature. It simply means that we maintain a relaxed state of attitudinal flexibility. Even when we are relaxed and everything is going well in a social interaction, we can still manage to keep an eye open for the odd curve ball. Human beings seem to come with a built-in sixth sense about unacceptable behavior. Keep yours handy and as soon as any manifestation of verbal abuse is sent your way, *nip it in the bud at once!*

If I had known then what I know now, I would have said to my boss,

"Excuse me, sir. Perhaps you are not aware of this, but you never call me by my real name. I would really appreciate it if you would address me in a manner that reinforces our respect for each other in our working situation."

Notice that there is nothing in the above statement to make the other person intrinsically wrong. It actually gives the person an out by implying that he is not doing what he's doing on purpose. Additionally, it offers him a chance to be appreciated by you, while you both cooperate on the work at hand. It opens the door to a more *enlightened personal interaction.*

Handling the Boss

If you are dealing with immediate superiors, it is important not to stare them down face to face with the x-ray vision you are acquiring from this book. If you do, your job could be on the line. As soon as you get a hint of troublesome behavior from your superior, shift into inner neutrality and just look at him or her nonreactively. It is probably better to look into the essence eye—without staring, of course. If you look into the personality eye, he or she might feel threatened when you see egotism on display there.

At the same time, be sure that you drop out of your head and into feet, legs, hands, and arms awareness. Don't respond to any verbal bait or desire to act in a tit-for-tat manner. Even if he or she throws you a perfect opening to be a smart aleck or a put-down artist, don't fall for it. You are within your rights to ignore any loaded remark and respond by bringing the conversation back to matters of import to the company. That's what you are both there for: to work in service for the benefit of the whole.

Sorting Out the Rebellious Subordinate

If you are in a supervisory position and need to give directions to others, you can empower your position by using the eye-to-eye differential. Resentment toward authority figures is an endemic human trait. It often manifests in slyly resistive innuendo, passive-aggressive behavior, and even outright resistance. If you want to make sure an order is carried out, keep your commands short and direct your attention at the *personality eye* of the person to whom you are giving directions.

Veronica came to me for some personal training shortly after starting a new position as head of human resources at a San Diego manufacturing plant. From the outset Jim, one of her colleagues, started making life difficult for her. Apparently, he had been hoping for a job upgrade when Veronica's new position became vacant. But not only was he passed over, an outsider was brought in, and a woman at that.

"I don't like to act in a hard manner," Veronica told me, "but it seems the only way I can get him to do what I need him to do is to act like a cold bitch. Now I've heard that he calls me names behind my back. I can tell he really resents me and I do find myself acting like a man. I don't want to report him, but every day now, I'm just getting too stressed out. What should I do?"

It was hard to imagine Veronica behaving like a man. She was a very elegant woman with a good figure and a lively, intelligent face. I had to hide a smile before answering.

"Well, unless he name-calls you to your face, there's not much you can do about the labeling. But you do need to make him back off of you personally. Let's see if we can give you some strategies that will enhance your authority over him and bring down your stress levels at the same time."

Veronica Learns to Use Her Eyes

I went on to explain to Veronica the difference between the personality eye and the essence eye. Then I suggested we stand facing each other and practice for a while.

"I will be partner A and you will be partner B," I suggested. "Because I am right-handed I am now going to cover up my right eye with my right hand. The left eye, the one that is exposed, is my essence eye. Just look into the center of my uncovered left eye with both your eyes and tell me what you see there. What sort of feelings do you get in relation to me by looking in my essence eye?"

"Well, I feel as if somehow I know you . . . but on an impersonal level. I mean, it is really hard to form an opinion of what your character is like. But there is definitely a familiar feeling."

"You feel comfortable, then?" I inquired.

"Oh, yes. No question."

I then lowered my right hand and covered up my left eye with my left hand, thereby exposing my personality eye. "What do you think of this one?" I asked

"Oh, my. Well . . . um . . . interesting." Veronica was now looking at me rather warily. "It seems colder . . . more distant. Harder, even. It has certainly seen the world and knows people."

"You prefer this one, then?" I inquired, shifting hands yet again to cover the personality eye and reveal the essence eye.

"Oh, yes. Definitely more comfortable."

I led Veronica over to a nearby wall mirror and, facing our own images, had her practice covering and uncovering her eyes to check the differences.

"That's amazing," she said. "It's like I'm two different people in one."

Now that she could clearly see it, I explained in detail how to use this difference to her advantage in her current predicament at work. I also taught her the sensing and feeling exercise with her arms and legs. Finally, I gave her a secret, very effective, technique for defusing someone's anger. Then I had her sit behind my desk as if she were in her own office, and I momentarily left the room. I was going to pretend to be belligerent Jim and together, Veronica and I would improvise some educational psychodrama.

Rehearsing for Action on the Stage of Life

Never having met Jim, I conjured what I imagined to be a suitable image of him in my mind and assumed that persona. Then I swaggered into Veronica's "office" as if I owned the place.

"You wanted to see me?" I inquired, as I flopped into a chair, barely resisting the temptation to put my feet on the corner of her desk. Veronica kept scribbling away on some imaginary papers as if I weren't there. Then she abruptly dropped her pen onto the desk and looked straight into my personality eye.

We were only acting, but as soon as she looked at me that way, the smirk left my face.

"Yes, I do," she said in a direct, no-nonsense manner. "I've been meaning to talk to you for some time."

I abandoned the slouch in my seat and found a somewhat more upright position.

"I hear you have been calling me names behind my back." Veronica's voice was as steady as her gaze. I was the one who looked away.

"Well, I ... it was just in fun. Doesn't mean anything." I looked back at her with a bit of a leer, as if to let her see that I was pleased it bothered her.

"Oh, I think it means plenty. I think it represents your inability to accept a woman in a position of authority!"

Wow, I thought, she's got authority now. There was a strange remote atmosphere surrounding Veronica. She was obviously sensing and feeling her arms and legs and grounding herself through her feet. I felt as if she were filling the room with her presence and I started to bluster angrily as I improvised what Jim might do and say next.

"Look here!" I yelled. "I have been with this company for fifteen years and I'm not going to sit here and ... and ... listen to ... er ... um ... if I want to call you a ... ummm.... then I'll uh...."

And then I dried up.

The Secret Anger Taming Technique

Veronica wasn't looking in either of my eyes anymore. She was staring directly at the point between my eyebrows and suddenly, I just couldn't go on. She had turned me into a babbling idiot and then put the brake on me with a look!

We both burst out laughing and the game was over. She came out from behind the desk and I shook her hand warmly.

"It works," she cried out happily. "Your secret technique works. Or was it *all* an act on your part?"

"No, no, I was really trying," I assured her. "I just couldn't do it, even as playacting. When I was yelling and you looked at the point between my eyebrows, the connection between my brain and my mouth snapped apart."

"Nothing you said made you sound as if you had a brain," laughed Veronica. "From the get-go you seemed like a very small person hiding behind a smoke screen of bluster. Like the Wizard of Oz!"

"That's because I was coming from false personality and you were operating from a preliminary state of *self-remembering*," I said. "As long as you remain connected with your arms and legs, while feeling your feet on the ground and staying out of your head, you will be able to stay nonreactive. The energy you save in that way can then be used to power up the state of presence around you. And you will quickly feel the sense of certainty that always develops as soon as you start to self-remember."

"I definitely felt it," she affirmed. "It just seemed to come out of nowhere the minute you walked in the room with that bad attitude. Instead of feeling small or intimidated by your bluster, I just dropped out of my head, did my arms and legs, and all of a sudden, it's like I was in this huge space and nothing could move me against my will."

"Well, it moved me. It almost pushed me out of the room," I said, laughing.

"And the clincher was when I looked at the point between your eyebrows as you got angry. You looked and sounded like a complete idiot and I wasn't affected by it at all."

"It's a great technique," I concluded. "And you are a natural at this stuff. All you have to do is *remember to do these things* and not let other people's craziness hypnotize you into responding from old patterns of reaction. We all carry a lot of automatic responses to social pressure with roots in forgotten causes. Some even stem from early childhood conditioning. But the joy that comes from having power over our *own* unconscious stuff is very satisfying. The more you learn not to submit to your own nonsense, the less you will buy into other people's rubbish."

"Sounds great to me," smiled Veronica. "I want to sign you on as my personal coach."

And so she did, becoming one of the finest practitioners of this system.

Removing the "Beam" of Reactivity from Our Eyes

Most of us are afraid to speak out in the face of any kind of verbal insult. Part of the dance is that we don't want to show others that we are affected by their lack of respect for us. It is not considered cool to let people see that they are getting to us, so we smile wanly and shrug off an insult as if it doesn't matter. But deep down we know it does. Veronica learned to center herself in a place on nonreaction. She learned to deal with Jim impersonally as a surgeon would when removing an offending object from someone else's eye. She had followed Christ's injunction to first remove the beam from her own eye. Then she could see clearly to remove the impediment in the eye of the person who was seeking to offend her.

The "beam" is composed of sensitivity, reactivity, our own irritation and sense of annoyance, plus the desire to hit back and make the perpetrator suffer. We are within our rights to remove the external source of disrespect toward us from the consciousness of offenders, but we must try not to leave them damaged in the process.

There is no greater arena in which to acquire these skills than the one where we make our living. Many people are allergic to their jobs. Bored to the point of distraction, they function largely on automatic pilot for eight hours per day. Feeling that they have sold out their freedom and potential for money, some individuals will seek diversion in game playing and baiting coworkers. The average work environment thus becomes a breeding ground for subtle disrespect and game playing.

The Mechanics of Annoyance

The more time we spend with anyone, particularly those with whom we have little in common, the more they tend to get on our nerves. What we fail to see is that what annoys us most about other people is *their mechanical behavior.* And that is exactly what is behind those things about *us* that get on the nerves of others—our ingrained, automatic, habit-driven behaviors. Entrenched mannerisms subliminally remind us that we too are creatures of habit. Often we ourselves act mechanically, going from one thing to another in a daze, present neither to ourselves nor to the moment unfolding before us. No one wants to feel like an automaton, so we tend to avoid or despise anything or anyone who reminds us that we sometimes pass through life like a sleepwalker. Someone else's automatic way of talking, eating, or walking, even the sound of their breathing, can become a source of irritation. If that person is someone we would not normally choose to spend time with, they can drive us nuts.

Our tolerance capacity can be so consumed at work that, by the time we get home, those with whom we live can easily annoy us still further. I saw this clearly when I visited two professional women who share a home out of financial necessity rather than friendship.

Patty and Vicki and the Irritation Shuffle

When I stopped by for a visit one evening, Patty was sitting at the table eating her salad, devouring sticks of celery and nuts and chips with loud crunching noises. Vicki was sprawled out on the couch with her fingers in her ears trying to read. Occasionally she would roll her eyes heavenward, as if petitioning God to give her strength. All the while, Patty chewed on in blissful oblivion. What Vicki didn't realize was that her reactions to her housemate's eating habits were just as mechanical as Patty's chewing. Patty was of a disposition that detested confrontation. For two years she had never bothered to tell Vicki how much the black scrape marks her high-heeled shoes left on the tiled kitchen floor annoyed her.

Finally, the lid blew off the pressure cooker. Patty and Vicki had a flaming row that cleared the air for a while. But when I came by to see them again a few months later, they were back in their annoyance boxes again, although they had upgraded to a fresh set of irritations. Old habits never die, it seems. They simply metamorphose into different themes on the variegated distractions of human incompatibility.

Using the Irritation Factor to Good Advantage

It is easy to be irritated by others. Being able to see that we may be equally annoying to someone else requires a special kind of honesty. Most of us would probably be offended if we thought that a person who annoys us could dare to think that we ourselves are annoying!

Learning to tolerate others can be used to cultivate compassion. But we must be able to clearly discriminate between the automatism of annoying habits and *intentional rudeness*. Patty's celery crunching and other annoyance factors were unintentional habit mechanisms. No conscious intent to harm another person motivates such actions. On the other hand, the person who makes cruel, cutting remarks has every intention to violate your space. In the first case, forgiveness is called for; in the second, action is required to prevent further manifestations of wrong behavior coming our way. One of the problems today is that through television and the movies, people are getting en masse instruction on how to ridicule other people. Our media thrives on and even celebrates the art of the put-down as if it were a virtue.

The Age of Rudeness

Most television sitcoms are based around how people annoy one another. The humor generally consists in the expression of clever wisecracks that put someone down by pointing out how innately stupid and annoying they are. Since television reflects popular life and vice versa, we have in this type of "entertainment" a mirror of how people misbehave toward each other. Whether done in the home or on the job, overfamiliarity is the breeding ground of contempt. Rudeness has become an escalating social disease, symptomatic of an age that is rife with discourtesy and outright bad manners. Turning around the collective juggernaut of massive social disrespect is a Herculean task, one not likely to be accomplished anytime in the near future. But that does not mean that you and I need to submit to the prevailing vulgar populist winds and be blown off course. Acquiring the will and consciousness to go against delusional mass trends can turn ordinary men and women into spiritual giants.

Continued application of the methods you are reading in this book will place you head and shoulders above the common meanness of our times. As you absorb and implement these ideas and techniques, you will automatically command respect, even in the workplace. Bosses and coworkers will forsake abusive attitudes they may be in the habit of directing your way. Through the example of your quietly powerful, unruffled yet determined response, you will be training them to be respectful of you and others. Through the example of your right behavior, you will also be demonstrating for everyone in your work environment that change is possible. You will be embodying the energy of enlightened interaction through your very presence and actions.

Wrong Familiarity Breeds Disrespect

Please memorize this phrase: *Wrong familiarity.* Offering courtesy and respect to others should implicitly mean that we are not willing to accept anything less than absolute courtesy from them. To be wrongly familiar is to violate the human rights of someone else. Bringing another person down, insinuating by words or a look that he or she is somehow less than you, is despicable. *Letting* someone do that to you is almost as bad. By allowing it you are encouraging and perpetuating the abuse.

Awakening Exercise: Make a List—Name Some Names

Because we tend to push bad memories out of our conscious minds, it is a good idea to actually make a list of people who are sometimes verbally abusive to you. Be sure and take into account those who deal in subtle forms of put-down and "rough kidding." Choose one instance where one of the people on your list said something offensive to you, but you failed to speak your feelings at the time. Write down what the other person said. Study it for a few moments, then close your eyes and recreate that scene in your mind.

Next, give your highest wit and intelligence permission to come up with the perfect response, the marvelous thing you should have said, but didn't. Then write that statement down. Look at it carefully and see if it contains any "getting even" or "you" messages, subtle put-downs that make the other person wrong.

Avoid "You" Message Statements

A "you" message is a loaded statement, a stress-accented word in a sentence that tells someone they are a *this* or a *that*. An exaggerated example would be something like "*You* are such a loser. I lend *you* my car and *you* always bring it back low on gas. *You* drive me mad."

In that statement the four heavily accented uses of the word *you* will probably drive the recipient right up in the air as soon as they are uttered. Then the recipient will retaliate in kind. More subtle forms of this type of shaming and blaming are of a stripe that doesn't actually use the "you" word. A look of contempt or a tone of voice may imply that someone is a loser. When we are on the receiving end of this type of loaded statement, we don't want to behave like the perpetrator. Ideally, we want to go one better and bring that person to a higher level of expression and mutual respect.

Look carefully at the statement you have written down. You may have to fine-tune it a bit but you will know when you have got it right. You will feel an inner click, as if you just hit a golf ball right down the fairway onto the green.

When you have got your statement just right, try reading it out loud. If your voice sounds thin and reedy, shaky and uncertain at the thought of speaking out, go and stand in the bathroom where the echo will make you sound better. Look in the mirror and say it to yourself. Try saying it to your essence eye. Then switch and say it to your personality eye.

Next, put your statement to one side, close both eyes, and get really centered. Drop your attention down to your feet. Feel them rooted on the ground. Then *sense and feel* your hands, arms, and your legs. See if you can get them to fill with energy just by putting your mind in them. Finally, drop down into your stomach mentally and feel the power gathering behind your navel.

After a second or two, open your eyes and say *an approximation of your statement* to yourself in the mirror. You don't want to get hung up on trying to remember the exact words you have written. Trust your mind and intuition to improvise the perfect utterance, based upon what you have written, but expressed in a fresh way.

Then take a good deep breath and *as you breathe out,* open your eyes and say your statement to your own face in the mirror as if you were speaking to your nemesis, the one who insulted you. Make sure there is no passion in your voice, no anger or trace of personal retaliation. If you inject venom or express a personal desire to wound the other person, you have lost. But this does not mean you have to be passive or act in a fawning manner. Just stay body-conscious and speak from there rather than from your head.

It is fun to try different acting styles and experiment with various degrees of assertiveness as you speak. With a few minutes of practice and modification of your statement, you will be surprised by how you are expressing yourself. It will be in a manner that clearly states you are a force to be reckoned with. Looking in the mirror, you will sense about yourself an air that affirms you will brook no wrong familiarity of expression toward the sanctity of your soul. Practice holding this positive state on a continuing basis and you will naturally and easily deflect negativity thrown your way.

Breathing and Speaking with Forceful Expression

Whenever you speak to anyone, get in the habit of taking in breath and then speaking out as you *exhale* through your mouth. I once asked a public speaking student of mine to take a good long breath and start speaking. He inhaled deeply, and then exhaled completely and started speaking with no air in his body! This is a common phenomenon. Observe people around you as they speak and notice how often they exhale before they talk. No wonder their words have no effect on people. They are running out of breath the minute they open their mouth. You can use their fault to remind you not to duplicate it in your own life.

Recall the story of the snake that wouldn't hiss. Don't be afraid to express yourself forcefully when necessary. And remember Kimberly? She told the waiter that if he continued to behave rudely, he would awaken something in her that he would find very unpleasant. She issued an almost perfect statement. Even though it carries implied consequences, it places responsibility for activating them in the other person's hands.

It is a personal demand for respect and an invitation to the other person to embrace maturity, responsible behavior, and a more enlightened personal interaction with you.

Finding the right expression of self-autonomy and assertiveness may seem like a scary thing to do in a work situation. After all, your job could be at risk if you give offense to a superior. But without pushing things to the extreme, there should be something about you that clearly signals you expect to be treated with respect by others. Speak clearly, but don't raise your voice. Say the truth, *as it appears to you*—but *not* as if it were a universal assumption that only an idiot could fail to see. Maintain an aura of quietly powerful inviolability at all times, not just when facing difficulties. Gradually we can train ourselves to be relaxed and dignified, ready to say and do what *I AM* requires of us for our highest good as we move through our day.

The more you practice these qualities, the more you will build around yourself a force field of energy that will speak louder than your words. Your invisible message should be similar to the following:

> I am a person of great integrity. My genuine desire is to treat you with respect and have you honor me with the same. If you try to treat me badly, I will look briefly into your personality eye in such a way that you will subconsciously know that I can see you are out of integrity.

I will then look into your essence eye and invite you to come into rapport with me and our highest shared good. If you fail to join me at that level, then it is you and not I who will suffer, through no direct cause of mine. You will simply remove yourself from the beneficial influence that you could derive from having someone like me and my spiritual gifts as a positive force in your life.

I like to think of myself as a socially generous person. When I first started to implement these techniques socially, I still tended to give other people the benefit of the doubt. If I were unsure that someone was attempting to put me down, I would let it go, thinking that perhaps I didn't hear correctly or I was being slightly paranoid. But gradually, as my skills increased, I became an infallible detector of subtle forms of rude behavior. My inner radar has now become very acute. I can sense, even without looking directly at the person, when someone is about to cross the boundaries of courtesy and right behavior into overfamiliarity and disrespect. My practice is so developed that once I have sensed that people are about to try something, if I turn and look into their personality eye, they will usually clam up and back off at once.

Knowledge is power! When people are about to behave unconsciously and you *know it,* look at them in such a way that you let *them* know that *you* know what they are about to do or say. In this manner you have the drop on them. I have even actually said out loud in some tough situations, *"Don't try it. I know what you're thinking before you do and you won't like the outcome."*

Most of us tend to avert our gaze when someone is acting out of integrity with that which we might call their higher self. It is almost as if our souls abhor looking at offensive behavior. But our looking away signals to egotists that *they* have the power. They will think they have backed you down and that they now have the upper hand. When you look at someone, really look. See them! Don't be afraid to look directly into the eyes of a troublemaker, even at work. But if it's the boss, be sure to smile when you do it.

CHAPTER SEVEN

Dealing with Energy Vampires

On the Stage of Life with Carl Gustav Jung

Psyche means soul and the psychological aspect of spiritual development is essential to our *sociological understanding and ability to function from a place of wholeness.* To be whole means that we are able to accept and handle the manifold contradictions in our nature. And do this in such a manner that the more potentially disruptive ones do not interfere with our lives against our will.

While I cannot claim to be anything other than a lay psychologist, I have had an unusual personal connection with one of the founding fathers of visionary modern psychology. From 1995 to 2002 I played Carl Gustav Jung and twenty other characters in *Forever Jung,* a self-penned one-man show based on the life of the pioneering Swiss psychologist. I gave more than two hundred and fifty performances in theaters, universities, and churches in the USA, Canada, and Great Britain. These presentations were often hosted by societies dedicated to bringing Jungian thought to the general public. Playing Jung is like doing Lincoln or Jesus. Everyone has an idea of what he should be like. I played Jung as he was to me and even collected a prestigious "best actor" award in New York for my interpretation. One thing I can say with certainty: You can't walk in the shoes of someone like that for seven years and not have him rub off on you. I learned about Carl Gustav Jung *by becoming him!*

The Light of the Shadow

One of Jung's great contributions was the recognition of the *shadow*—the dark, repressed, unconscious side of human nature. While undergoing a major mental crisis himself, Jung was able to identify with and even draw a picture of his own shadow—a little dark man crouching in the corner of a checkered room. By accepting responsibility for what he could see and recognize as his own dark side, he was able to reconcile with it and integrate it into his consciousness. Thus he was released from the night of his own fearful projections. From this came his famous statement, "One does not become conscious by imagining figures of light, but by making the darkness conscious."

But how do *we* deal with the shadow when we encounter it in the people with whom we must interact every day? It is one thing to integrate one's own shadow. In the world at large, however, the *collective shadow* of the human race has not been integrated and is therefore on the loose. In fact, it has become so powerful, it now has the potential to destroy the very planet we live on. Individuals who are filled with negativity, whose conversation constantly gravitates toward morbid things and drains us, may be people who are unconsciously aligned with, and thereby possessed by, the collective shadow. They might even be the most difficult type of all to deal with: They could be *energy vampires!*

Most of us have had the experience of encountering someone who feels like a black hole in space. This type of individual puts out little or no light. Standing before such a person, you feel as if your life energy is being drawn into a psychological and emotional vacuum. While you are talking to this person, an uneasy feeling spreads through your being. You are possessed by the urge to get away before he or she possesses you!

These are the signs and symptoms that you are dealing with a major energy vampire—someone who specializes in stealing life energy from other people. In such a case, follow your instincts and get away from such a person as quickly as possible. I have turned on my heel and just walked right out of the room, leaving an energy vampire spouting words into thin air. And I will do it again. We are under no obligation to let *anyone* siphon off our life energy, especially those who are addicted to deliberately creating negative situations from which to feed.

Not all energy vampires are as easily recognizable as the type I have just described. There are lesser and greater degrees of addiction and different types use different ways to seduce you into compliantly giving your power away. There are many forms of energy vampire attack, ranging from the mild to the severe. Perhaps you work with someone who is conversationally negative and tries to constantly engage you in debilitating conversations? How about the "hostage taker"—the one who backs you into a verbal corner where you can't get a word in edgewise and then forces you to listen to all his or her stuff?

There may be someone in your own family—a parent, an in-law, a relative, who seems to take pleasure in being a source of irritation and annoyance. These people all share one thing in common. They want to put *you* on hold and force you to pay attention to them while they suck the life out of you. So whether the degree of drain is subtle or gross, when you are dealing with an energy vampire, remember that this is someone who gets life energy by stealing it from other people. In this chapter we are going to explore garlic- and stake-free ways to dissuade such types from messing around with us!

A Southern Gothic Experience

In 1998, while traveling the USA with *Forever Jung,* I was set to give a performance at a New Thought Church in the South. As was my custom when presenting the show at a church, as opposed to a theater or university, I gave a three-minute "preview" at the Sunday service before the event. The church had a warm, friendly feeling and the little scene where Jung proposes marriage to Emma, the woman who was to become his wife, went over very well.

After the service, as people surged into the lobby to buy tickets, Rev. Lisa, the minister, invited me to have lunch with her. I readily accepted, but she asked if I would be willing to wait for half an hour, as she had to have a meeting with a church member. I happily agreed and Lisa disappeared into her office with one of her parishioners, a smartly dressed woman in her late fifties. No one would have suspected from this person's outward appearance that Rev. Lisa was going to be dealing with an energy vampire disguised as a "church lady."

When the pair emerged from their meeting almost an hour later, Lisa's face was ash white. And I noticed that she was trembling slightly. We left the church together and got into her car. But instead of starting the engine, Lisa just sat staring out the window at the trees that fringed the parking lot.

"Anything wrong?" I ventured, not wanting to pry, but sensing she needed to talk.

"I'm sorry," she replied, smiling wanly and shaking her head, as if trying to divest it of some unpleasant impingement. "It's that woman. I know I shouldn't let it get to me, but she just drains the life out of me. She is power mad and constantly negative. There's always some drama going on in the church that she has cooked up. She deliberately stirs things up and when everyone is up in the air. . . ." Lisa paused, fighting back tears. "Well . . . it's like she loves it. I see this gloating look on her face, as if she gets power from being the instigator of friction between people."

"Have you called her on it?" I asked gently.

"I don't know how to handle her," Lisa replied. "She is very smart. She has a way of denying her personal responsibility that makes the problem appear to be in *your* head and nothing to do with her at all. And worst of all, she is always going on about *love* being the answer and how she is a *heart-centered* person."

I told Lisa that I had some special tools and techniques that might help her to get the better of the situation. Over lunch I shared with her some of the techniques I work with. Soon I was going to need them myself. I was about to have my own encounter with Rev. Lisa's source of frustration.

The Vampire Goes for Me

Forever Jung was performed on Friday night and was a smash hit. The next morning I gave a class I call Sociological Aikido in the sanctuary. About seventy people were in attendance and all was going well until ten minutes before the end. By this time, I had explained all the principles involved, drawn diagrams illustrating the eye-to-eye differential, and paired people off for experiential exercises. Then I noticed a hand waving in the air toward the back of the room. It was time for questions and answers, so I acknowledged the gesture and who should stand up but Rev. Lisa's nemesis. As soon as I saw who it was, I immediately started putting awareness into my feet, arms, and legs.

"This is all very well," she began with a tired, supercilious air. "But here at our church we believe in *love*. We don't see anything but the best in people. So we don't need your spiritual defensiveness."

Notice the structure of this verbal attack: "This is all very well," delivered with a dismissive tone of voice, implies that the content of the workshop is really *not* well at all. She was saying that what is being presented is in fact inconsequential, *if* one knows what she knows. "We believe in love" sets up her and her alter ego—the church and its members—as upholders of an unarguable standard of spirituality. How can one argue with love, the acme of goodness. The *we* in "We don't see anything but the best in people" effectively excludes me, while implying that I lack love. So my "defensiveness" and I are not needed, thank you very much.

I surveyed the faces in the room that had been lit up with appreciation and interest in everything they had been learning so far. Now they looked at me with a combination of apprehension and curiosity. How would I deal with this confrontational situation? Could I put into practice what I had been teaching them all morning? They needed to know whether I could walk my talk in relation to her. While sensing and feeling my arms and legs, I deliberately let an atmosphere of protracted expectation build up in the room. When the silence was practically screaming, I said:

Love is without doubt the most potent force in the world. Yet many crimes have been committed in its name. One of the biggest challenges we face as human beings is lying to ourselves about our motivations. We may delight in creating pictures of ourselves as good, kind, loving people. But we must also be able to see that *we ourselves,* like everything in creation, possess or are possessed by a dark side. Until we accept and take responsibility for this shadow within us, we may become its unwitting instruments. Without realizing what we are doing, we may make other people suffer, while forcing upon them imaginary pictures of our own *goodness.*

"What's wrong with goodness?" she snapped back nastily. "I'm a good person. Jesus told us to be perfect like our heavenly father and that's what interests me."

As she said this, the entire room cringed. A few people looked at her and each other as if they would like to form a lynch mob. They had obviously heard all this before. I responded:

As I recall, when the disciples praised Jesus for being good and virtuous, he said "Why do you call me good? There is no one good but the Father." Of course you are a good person. We are all basically good people. But if you are like me, you also have human inconsistencies, lapses of judgment, and don't always treat others as well as we might wish. For myself, I know that under certain forms of provocation, I could resent being pushed and behave badly. So I use these tools and techniques to manage my reactions, so that I don't wound other people or myself. Rather than be seduced by my self-created pictures of what a good and loving person I think I am, I take responsibility for the light and the dark aspects of my human nature. Then I try to offer myself as a reasonably balanced instrument to the Supreme Intelligence that *It* might flow an all-encompassing goodness through me should *It* so choose.

"That's all very poetic," she said, twisting her mouth, her eyes glaring at me from the back of the room with an arc welder's cold heat of intense dislike.

"Yes, I suppose it is," I replied. "The truth has a certain poetic ring to it."

The people in the room burst into appreciative applause. Apparently, my words had rung with truth for this statement took the wind right out of her sails. She sat down to chew on it, disgruntled. The feeling of apprehension others had been feeling during the initial phases of the confrontation had now melted away and everyone in the room was relaxed and smiling up at me. I had not forgotten them while I had been dealing with my antagonist. I had in fact been addressing *them,* even though I had been focusing my attention on the aggressive words coming from the verbal attacker at the back of the room.

Teaching Indirectly

This technique might be categorized as *teaching indirectly*—making a point that might benefit others, while directing your words to someone who may, in fact, be a lost cause. In such a situation those who are receptive may pick up something useful from observing the interchange. As soon as my "loving" challenger spoke, I knew from her body language and tone of voice that I was not going to be able to change her rigid outlook. But I was able to use the time and energy required to respond to her, to plant thought seeds in more receptive minds. Also, by enlightening myself with arms-legs-body awareness throughout the situation, I was able to build up energy in my body and radiate the overflow from that energy to others in the room.

A Warm Ending

After everyone had left, Rev. Lisa and I were closing up the church when she turned to me and said, "You know, this has been really helpful to me, especially seeing the way you handled *her.* She is obviously too stuck in her head to see anything beyond her own ego. But I think I can deal with her from now on by using the tools you have given us today."

"Lisa," I replied, looking deeply into her essence eye, "I know you not only *can* do this but you *will.* One of the highest forms of love is knowing enough to be able to do what is necessary to help other people, even if they don't know they need our help and are actively resisting us. She is not your enemy or mine. In a strange way she is an ally. Without her creating trouble and friction, we would not have had to go out of our way to find the hidden wellspring of strength within us."

"Perhaps that is why Jesus told us to bless those that curse us and do good to those that spitefully use us," said Lisa thoughtfully. "Maybe when we do that, we are actually blessing ourselves."

"You're terrific, Lisa," I said, as we gave each other a good-bye hug. "Now you've really got it."

We had both benefited from knowing each other and profiting from our garlic-free neutralization of an energy vampire's disruptive influence.

The Energy Vampire Checklist

I don't think anyone wakes up one morning and decides "today I am going to be an energy vampire and drain everyone I encounter." Nevertheless, by body language, tone of voice, look of the eyes, even their walk, some people *can* drain everyone they encounter who is susceptible to their negative influence. Let us now take a closer look at various types of energy vampire. With a little foreknowledge, we can more easily spot those who are looking for a free lunch and make sure we are not on the menu.

There are two main types of energy vampire: the *passive* and the *active*. Passive energy vampires do not usually enjoy or resort to actual confrontation. They come at you sideways in a manner that you can't quite pin down. This suits them fine, because if you were to accuse them of deliberately trying to drain you, they would deny it and probably accuse you of being paranoid. This type has no *obvious* ego. They are more likely to suffer from low self-esteem, which is still egotism and self-love, but in a reverse, negative mode. Since they fear direct confrontation, these individuals generally rely on a *passive-aggressive* approach.

Signs of a Passive Energy Vampire

Dull eyes that won't connect

Voice often has a whining tone

Likes to gossip about others
Finds fault with everyone and everything
Most utterances contain a negative
Thinks life is unfair
Has victim consciousness
Dwells on past traumas
Feels abused by others
Sighs heavily for others to hear
Complains all the time
Sits slumped over
Walks in a lifeless manner
Is addicted to feeling sad

Signs of an Active Energy Vampire

The second type is more easily seen because they *like and enjoy* the sense of power that comes from dominating social situations. Active energy vampires can be loud, obnoxious, and obvious. At the same time they can manage to be just as sly and manipulative as the passive-aggressive type. In either case, the intention is to control others, one way or another. You can recognize them when they:

Take an aggressive attitude on meeting you
Need to have the last word
Want to be right all the time
Constantly tell you how to do things
Look for moments when you feel uncertain and play power games
    on that uncertainty
Try to trip you up conversationally and make you look stupid
Make jokes about you with a personal edge
Make sarcastic, cutting remarks
Tell dirty stories
Enjoy making you feel uncomfortable

Like to see people squirm

Smirk as if you are an inferior

Talk to others in a room as if you are not there

Use any authority over you at work to bully you

Talk about themselves all the time

Will not respond to essence-eye contact

Regard gentleness as a sign of weakness

Energy vampires specialize in disconnecting people from their sense of self. When this happens to us, it is a psychological catastrophe, because the temporary identity loss drains us mentally, physically, and emotionally. Given the pace of modern life, who can afford to be out of the driver's seat for more than a few seconds? When we are dispossessed from ourselves, there is no one home to take delivery of the good that life can offer us. To be internally short-circuited is to be in a state of chaos. When we have chaos within, the world around us quickly begins to reflect this as a series of external chaotic events. Most of us have had the experience of life seeming to conspire against us, or times when nothing appears to be going right. And the more we react and become internally disturbed, the more ridiculous we appear to ourselves and to others. Energy vampires know this and delight in putting us in a state where our inner upsetness, triggered by them, makes us look outwardly foolish and them feel temporarily powerful. The fact that they are able to manipulate our reactions and make us behave from dysfunction is very empowering to energy vampires.

An ego in the delusional state of disconnection from the soul delights in putting other people into the same state of delusion. The energy vampire *wants* to disconnect you for the quick thrill of power, the rush that comes from making you reveal your human weakness. It is as if he or she is saying on a very subtle level, "See . . . you are not a soul after all. You are just a piece of live meat. Since I have power over you I must be better, or more important than you."

Eventually, however, the karma that accrues from perpetrating any form of abusive behavior on others is going to require payoff.

Power Abuse Eats Up the Future

In Orson Welles's classic movie *A Touch of Evil*, Captain Quinlan, a cruel, shady police detective (played by Welles) goes to see a psychic, played by Marlene Dietrich.

"Tell me my fortune," asks Quinlan, as he sits slumped and worn out before her.

The gypsy flips a few cards and says, "You haven't any. Your future is all used up."

Energy vampires may appear powerful in the moment, when they seem to be in control of a situation and are playing their games. But the power they are using is all on loan. More accurately, they are stealing from themselves. Every time they act in an unconscionable manner, they are in fact *using up their future.* Try to remember this when you feel that you are becoming weak in the face of their negativity. It actually helps to say to oneself mentally, *"This person is an energy vampire, and energy vampires use up their future."*

When you truly see the weakness behind their self-aggrandizing facade, their lack of self-love, and sense of personal emptiness, this type of individual will have no power over you. If your life force can stay powerful before them and you manage to remain centered, *their souls will become embarrassed for them* and they will leave you alone.

Don't Bring Me Down

To get energy from you, people who are down must bring *you* down to their level of negativity and confusion. That is because in order for energy transference to occur, the parties involved *must* be on the same frequency. When your personal equilibrium feels the fluctuations of uncertainty in relation to another human being, you are vulnerable to leakage. Energy vampires know this, albeit unconsciously. By initiating a negative conversation, they cause the molecules of *your* emotions to vibrate in resonance with fear and uncertainty. Your consciousness will drop down to their negative level of being. Once you are vibrating in dysfunctional sync with an energy vampire, what remains of your positive life force will fly to him or her. This sudden deprivation will cause many subtle energy circuits in your body to malfunction.

In behavioral kinesiology, pioneered by Dr. John Diamond, author of *Your Body Doesn't Lie* and *Life Energy,* this state is referred to as being "switched." When our circuits are switched, the life force that would normally be flowing through the acupuncture meridians of the body in sync with nature suddenly goes haywire. Instead of coming up the back of the body, over the head, and down the front, it may be reversed, traveling up the front of the body and down the back. Additionally, the activity of the thymus gland is reduced to practically nothing. Loss of connection to the thymus is instantly debilitating. It was believed by the ancients that the function of the thymus gland was to connect the soul to the body. When life delivers a shock to us, we often feel as if we have been knocked out of our bodies and lost touch with who we really are. Our souls and our personal selves have become separated.

Your Original Chi, or Life Force

Dr. Diamond's work has strong connections with the theories of acupuncture, which meticulously chart the natural flow of energy through the human body. This ties in very closely with Taoism, a philosophy that has its roots in the reconciliation of opposites. Taoism sees reconciliation possibilities between the Yin and Yang in man and woman, and between heaven and earth through man and woman. Extensive knowledge regarding the flow of energy in all forms of creation throughout the universe has been cultivated over millennia, even to the study of life force in the act of conception and in the developing embryo.

The Taoists claim that all people have within them a special storehouse of life energy known as the *Original Chi.* They believe that this legacy, gifted to us by our mother and father during the sex act, combines universal, higher-self, and earth forces with the Yin and Yang of orgasmic energy. These forces merge with the sperm and ovum of our parents as they unite and ignite. While serving as instruments for a cosmologically rooted creative process, our mothers and fathers also give a portion of their life energy, that we might have life.

I have seen people roll their eyes and look allergic when told this because they had a bad relationship with their parents. Things may have been so difficult outwardly during childhood that they don't even wish to feel any inner connection with those who helped give them life. But the creation of a child is a divine act. No matter how dysfunctional human beings may be on the personal level, the intelligence in the sexual seed exists on a level of consciousness far above the human plane.

This Original Chi is powerfully stored in the body of the developing child in the area behind the navel. As we mature we can lose connection with this vital energy source and our evolution may start to deviate from its highest potential. When we become disconnected from our prenatal Chi, we don't know who we are. We feel out of touch with ourselves. Our behavioral choices, habitual mental and emotional attitudes, the ebb and flow of positive and negative events in our lives, even the food we eat, drain or enhance our original life energy legacy. However, much like a car battery, the Original Chi can be recharged through techniques like the ones you are learning in this book.

Conversely, it can be siphoned off from us by those looking to recharge their own depleted battery from the nearest handy external source—*you and me!* When people have a low-level sense of connection with their own Original Chi, they will be active to deprive others of theirs. Developing *I AM* consciousness automatically leads to recharging the battery of this prebirth source of energy within us.

Cruelty Stems from Loss of Original Chi Connection

There is usually a sense of innocence and childlike joy about people who manage to stay well connected with their Original Chi. Those who have lost connection with this precious part of themselves, through poor behavioral choices, will often ridicule people who still have their connection intact.

When we encounter those who habitually make cruel remarks, or put down and belittle others, we can be sure that such individuals have lost their innocence and possess little or no connection with their Original Chi. What motivates them? The motive behind the abuse of innocence is jealousy. It is rage that someone else still has what the abuser has carelessly thrown away.

My mother suffered terribly from attacks by this type when she went to work at the Air Ministry in Britain during World War II. Not only was she very beautiful, as pictures taken of her at the time attest, she was like an innocent lamb sent to the slaughter. During a war, necessity flings together many people from disparate backgrounds. While serving her country, my mother was daily surrounded by coarse, cruel individuals who delighted in recounting crude jokes and telling lurid sexual stories just to shock her. She never descended to reply in kind and kept her composure. But in private she wept bitter tears to be so hurt and disillusioned. She still says, years later, "I never knew people could be so cruel."

When you are confronted by people who seem to go out of their way to disrupt your sense of connection with yourself, it can be very helpful to remember that such individuals may have lost connection with their prenatal energy (innocence) a long time ago. You may feel compassion toward them as you become aware of this. Nevertheless, your compassion is unlikely to change their habitual modes of negative expression, since they may have become too ingrained. Practical compassion means that you do not feel compelled to strike the other person with intent to hurt or wound. But you will still be called upon to act and to exhibit an appropriate response to prevent yourself being drained.

Most energy vampires will see love and compassion as weakness and will want to eat you alive, thereby trying to get rid of, *in you,* that which they despise in themselves, namely, *the need to connect with others in a loving way.*

If you get angry, hurt, or resentful, they have won. They have divided you against yourself and separated you from your ability to feel positive emotions. Your personal discomfort under their provocation appears to them as evidence that you are just as messed up as they are. Again, they feel powerful because they were able to make you feel weak.

Why We Lose Energy to Negative People

When we are verbally attacked and our life force becomes unnaturally switched within us, the positive charge we were using up until the point of disconnection suddenly has no point of reference. There is no *I AM*. Energy in the molecular world of subatomic particles always seeks to line up around the nearest coherent source. So too will the energy in an unfocused human body gravitate toward the nearest external source of strength, *even if that strength is negative*. For electrons and protons, a negative can suddenly become a positive and a positive a negative. They don't know the difference and they don't make judgments. They simply do what nature programs them to do. But they are not conscious that they are doing it and therefore have no choice. Human beings have choice in one major sphere of activity. We have the possibility of attaining sovereignty over our reactions and can *choose* to be positive or negative.

The negative person who is trying to get energy from you knows intuitively that to draw on your energy he or she must make you upset. In order not to react, we must know how to make ourselves nonreactive under pressure. We do this by throwing all our attention on every part of our physical being simultaneously (hands, feet, arms, legs, torso, and so on) the second we smell trouble. This is an art that takes some practice, but is well within the reach of anyone because full-body awareness is the natural state of a *normal* human being.

A baby inhabits every cell of its body. It feels its consciousness in all parts of itself simultaneously. If our children today grew normally and naturally, they would preserve this *sensed and felt* connection with themselves. Unfortunately, the constant overload from informational bombardment quickly seduces our young people out of their bodies and puts them into their heads. Most adults possess no ability to be aware of their feet, legs, hands, arms, head, body, and torso simultaneously. But we were not designed to have heads that feel separated from our bodies. Or to have front-to-back body splits. Nor were we meant to have upper torsos that lack connection with our sexual power and the lower half of our physical selves.

These states are unnatural. When we make conscious efforts to reverse the sense of disconnection, we can actually feel, sometimes instantly, that we are attracting the attention of nature. As soon as we take steps to normalize ourselves, she stirs to align our natural resources in such a way that her original intention—wholeness for men and women—starts to manifest in our body cells. Far from being our adversary, nature wants us to win. To be "normal" is to be in tune with nature by being fully connected with oneself. This strongly establishes us in a powerful psychological energy. It is the dimension where opposites can become reconciled and manifested through us personally as the quality of *wholeness.*

Man and woman are biologically and psychologically conditioned beings. If we want to change our lives, first we have to change our psychology, for what we see externally is directly related to the health of the psyche. Fortunately, reordering our psychological world can restructure us biologically, and vice versa.

In the next chapter, we shall take a look at some powerful tools for reordering our psychological-biological interface. If the brakes on our cars are faulty, the wheels need to be aligned, or the transmission is failing, we run the risk of ruining our means of transportation, unless we get everything in right working order. But to fix our cars, we must first be made aware that they are *not* working properly and are in need of repair. So I am going to show you how to upgrade the bodily vehicle you are driving through life to obtain optimal working capacity.

The driver should be the *I* of the *I AM.* Unfortunately, our sleeping selves are behind the wheel most of the time and we never seem to arrive where we want to go in life. In addition, our machine is not working properly due to bad habits and mistaken conceptions of what it means to be a man or a woman.

When you came into this world, no one gave you an owner's manual that showed you how to operate body, mind, and emotions and get them to work as a team. You are about to learn what we should have known all along. As you absorb these ideas, you can have a life-changing perceptual shift. Suddenly you will find yourself behind the wheel of not a beat-up old Ford, but a solid-gold vehicle of the future. Only the man and woman of tomorrow, those who know themselves by direct experience as *I AM,* can drive such a car in the here and now of today. So if you are ready to make such a shift, let's change mental gears and travel together to an amazing world of optimal operating possibility.

CHAPTER EIGHT

Changing the Brain-Body Dynamic

The New Model of Man and Woman

Amidst the chaotic crash of falling worlds as outmoded models of human behavior disintegrate, a new type of human being is starting to emerge. The body-mind-emotional vehicles that our souls inhabit are being rewired to withstand the greater voltage of a higher type of consciousness. It may take centuries for all the dysfunctional models to be gradually replaced. However, you can drive the latest version of the human machine right now. Not only can you drive it, you can *be* it, if you are willing to fully participate in the rewiring process that will enable you to live in the energy of a positive future world right now!

What I am going to share with you next is so profound in its simplicity that it is amazing hardly anyone sees it.

The old model of a human being functions on what I call a *two-stroke system.* Bodily sensations, actions, and movements are triggered by a continuous process of interaction between thought and feeling, or feeling and thought. This process goes on inside us all day long, unchecked and unnoticed. Too often we simply become this pattern of dualistic action and reaction, continually engaged in processing our thoughts and our feelings. Reacting to these patterns moment by moment, we speak *from* them as if we actually *were* them, as if this "thing" of the moment, this micro temporary aspect of ourselves *is who we really are!* And this frightening reactive process always happens so incredibly fast that we don't even notice.

The Two-Stroke System Person, Defined

Let us designate numerical identities in the two-stroke system.

First, we shall call the activity of the brain thinking *function #1*. When a person has a thought, function #1 is active.

This thought produces a feeling somewhere in the body—a sense of fear, excitement, anger, or annoyance, perhaps. We shall call this second, *reactive*, process *function #2*.

In the average person, as indicated above, only these two functions are operational most of the time. A thought, function #1, arises. This activates a feeling, function #2. Sometimes the process operates in reverse. A feeling, function #2, produces a thought, function #1. This usually happens when something emotional has occurred and the mind then tries to figure out what is going on.

To repeat, the old model of man and woman works on a two-stroke system of alternating currents between function #1 and function #2. Mind triggers emotion—or emotion triggers mind. In either case, *duality* is in operation and where there are only two possibilities, tension arises. To find resolution we need a third, *neutralizing* element to make the tension of duality work for us by turning it into a positive, usable energy resource.

The Trouble with Duality and How to Transcend It

Philosophers in every culture figured out long ago that *duality equals trouble*. As night follows day, so pain often attends pleasure. The old world of sleep is run by opposites continually contending. Even-mindedness has been prized by stoics, like the Roman emperor Marcus Aurelius and Eastern sages like Lao Tzu. Deeply meditating yogis try to rise beyond the alternating dual currents of electricity in the body and mind. Through meditation, they seek to neutralize or cancel out the positive and negative polarities of ordinary consciousness. *Dualistic consciousness = delusion!* An ancient chant from India serves as a call from the spiritual neophyte to God as being *beyond all duality*. It carries an appeal to "deliver us from delusion." Again, "delusion" is the world of collective automatism, the mass trance of reactive consciousness around us, *the direct result of centuries of dualistic thought and activity.*

The development of Western consciousness has been based on the perception of people operating in the two-stroke system of function #1 and function #2. *Dualistic self-perception* has shaped the world we live in and has become, by default, the collective condition of human intelligence. At our current critical juncture in human evolution, many people all over the world are inclining toward a spiritual understanding of themselves and the world. The evolutionary thrust of human development, along with the energy field of the planet we live on, has shifted. The will to real consciousness is strong, as is the sense that we have been asleep and now want to wake up. Because of this, a new type of human being can emerge. Instead of the old two-stroke system of function #1 (thought) and function #2 (emotional reactivity), any sincere person can embody the powerful results that naturally flow from transforming oneself into a model of the new man and woman. What is required for this to happen is that one becomes a person who can embody not just two, but *three functions at the same time.* Functions #1 and #2 become balanced by the application of a third, reconciling, force—*function #3.*

How a Three-Stroke System Works

In this new paradigm, the mind is still designated as function #1. But instead of being preoccupied with automatic thinking, our power of thought is being focused and consciously directed to global body awareness by sensing and feeling arms, legs, and so on. The second response, function #2, ceases to be random feeling responses to the mind. No longer is automatic thought and feeling being transformed into psycho-emotional physical reaction. Function #2 now becomes a self-willed sensing and feeling of whole body as sensation.

This gives rise to a feeling of ourselves in the stomach and chest of balanced emotions as the sensing and feeling naturally transforms the energy of mechanical, dualistic operation into function #3—the third force, or reconciling, activity. Just as the neutron balances the activity of electron and proton, the almost constant duality of the usual function #1-#2 interaction is transformed into a triad, a state of balance between opposites, by the introduction into consciousness of function #3.

The active effect we feel as a result of activating function #3 is the experience of naturally arising positive emotions, personal peace, well-being, and a *felt sense* of *I AM*. There is a knowing of exactly who, or more accurately *what*, one is, completely independent of external situations. Mind and body are thus placed in the service of emotional health and happiness. These are natural, desirable goals for any reasonable person.

The Flow of Attention, Again

So in this new model, instead of mind going directly to emotional reactivity, the order of the flow of conscious self-awareness now becomes as follows:

Function #1 = the mind is scanning every part of the body simultaneously

Function #2, which used to be direct emotional response to mind, now becomes a simultaneously sensed and felt awareness (arms, legs, hands, feet, head, torso, and so on)

Function #3, the *result,* is consciousness of energy as presence, emanating from, through, in, and around the *whole body as awareness.* This produces a massive increase in one's level of being. *One becomes conscious of consciousness itself!*

The reason we do not normally feel the power of presence and being is because our emotional energy is continually being used up in useless automatic feeling reactions. Imaginary fears, self-doubts, worry, and anxiety are examples of wasteful internal states that run on energy stolen from our feeling function. Since the energies normally used to generate positive emotions are very subtle substances, negative emotional states convert or downgrade that fine energy as they use it up. The result is that we feel emotionally sick when in the grip of such states. We are poisoning ourselves with our own disturbed energy. This process can be largely eliminated from our lives by using the mind to continually entertain a state of whole-body awareness, thereby freeing our feeling function from mechanical, mind-driven, negative emotional reactivity.

When we direct the mind to sense and feel the body, the fast-moving energy of our feelings is buffered for a few seconds. Before reaction can kick in, causing the body to have negative emotional reactions that it then acts out against our wills, we have taken custody of the body by *sensing its totality and feeling the presence.* This anchoring process allows our feeling function to find its right place as an expression *within* the body, not as something that takes it over and runs away with our personal identity.

Sensing and Feeling: Generating Self-Reconnection

Turning oneself into a three-stroke system is a prerequisite to establishing and maintaining connection with *I AM* awareness and the attendant presence and energy of that state. This begins with sensing and feeling—intentionally directing our attention to awareness of feet, legs, hands, arms, head, neck and throat, chest, abdomen, and pelvic area—in short, the entire body all at the same time. We can train ourselves to do this at will, on demand, in any social situation, quickly creating a sense of our totality at a moment's notice.

To repeat, this simple practice will, by itself, effectively confound negative intentions toward us *because the perpetrators are usually coming from their heads!* Once we make up our minds to continually practice the reconnecting techniques, the results appear automatically and quickly. Our bodies get the subliminal message that we are actively reclaiming our right to be in them. Our bodies' cells welcome our support and respond by generating high-voltage, coherent intelligence, enabling us to become who we were born to be, instead of a counterfeit caricature we have cobbled together to mask our insecurities. Our bodies will do this because they have been created to house and express *I AM* consciousness. They respond and live most fully when touched by authenticity, not our idiotic ideas of who we think we are when hypnotized by our reactions to the great illusion out there. Our bodies know when *I AM* is present.

Staying coherent in our own field of energy at all times depends on our willingness to develop *a continuously sensed and felt connection with every part of the body simultaneously.* Not only do most people have no awareness of their feet, legs, hands, arms, head, torso, and so on, separately or simultaneously; it would never occur to them that this is an unnatural state to be in. The advantage of this for you and me is that if we live *body sensed,* as we were intended to live, we can move through the world like giants instead of disembodied heads.

Sensing and feeling is a lost art that can quickly be recovered with a little daily awareness practice. In the beginning you may only be able to sense your feet while you converse with others. While someone is talking to you, just drop your attention down to one or the other or both your feet and they will respond by feeling warm, tingling, or getting heavier. Just keep your mind in your feet and see how well you can maintain connection with them while your head is talking to someone. Gradually you can progress to feeling feet and legs, then hands and arms. Eventually you will be able to sense your feet and legs, hands and arms, head and torso— all at the same time. Try getting centered this way before you walk into a room, and enter *in presence.* You will see how people gravitate toward you and respond positively.

Master this simple art and you can live in our mad world in a state of profound security. No one will be able to mess with you, including energy vampires. As a result of your sensed and felt whole-body awareness, others will be confounded by the power and presence emanating from you. This presence, the energy of your own being, comes from *I AM,* the core of your being. When active, it is as if a tuning fork has been struck inside and harmonic vibrations radiate out in all directions simultaneously. From the bones of the spine and rib cage, these emanations pass through the skin like a force field, extending the radius of magnetic influence to all who cross your path.

Practicing *Being* and *Presence*

Here is an example of how I might induce in myself a sense of presence and increase the sense of my own aliveness, while executing a mundane task. Even though it is something that actually happened in the past, when I was writing this book, I include it here in present tense, so you can feel the immediacy and see how it might work for you.

As I am sitting here before my computer, writing these words, I have let my mind become completely aware of the position of my body, the temperature of my skin, the background noises in the room and those coming in from outside. I am also cognizant of my body breathing and my hands flying over the keyboard. This relaxed directing of my attention away from the head-state into which one easily migrates when working has given me a global, rather than a localized, *self-awareness.* There is no sensation of being *out* of my body, as if I am up on the ceiling looking down at myself. Rather, I am aware of focused energy permeating my hands, my arms, my legs, my head, my torso, my feet, and so on. Something has started to emanate in, from, around, and through me. It is a subtle atmosphere and produces a specific energy that I recognize as *presence.* It manifests as a thick sensation of all-pervading warmth that permeates my flesh and makes me feel very secure spiritually and personally. Now that I am writing about it, this presence is increasing even more. It seems to thrive and multiply from receiving attention. My sense of connection with my personal self *and* as a soul in human form seems to be merging. I feel solid and connected in many ways. I am becoming a *three-stroke system.*

Additionally, my *level of being* seems to be increasing. *I* am here, in this place in this room, fully aware simultaneously of myself and of the task I am executing. In this state I know what I know. No one is going to be able to take that awareness away from me. There would be no need to argue with anyone about anything. No need to justify myself in any way. Yet at the same time, if I were called upon to speak or act, to bring about a specific result in a social situation, I could do so with dignity and power. There can be no hiding out from life in this condition. One *becomes* life and what else is life but the movement of creative forces in action. So, from this state, one could act out any role required by the moment and enjoy it as a part one is suddenly required to play in the improvisational theater of social interaction. *One is creating a new world of enlightened personal interaction with oneself!*

When I stop writing and sit still, there is a sensation that this presence not only now fills the room—it *contains* the room. The room is now outside of me. I have become presence and the room is contained within the presence that is *I AM*. As I look up and out the window at the trees, the landscape, and the sky, they too seem to be made up of this substance. Whether my perception is expanded out to the horizon, or focusing upon the task of writing these words, it is the same. An atmosphere of presence is emanating through me and it is coming from *I AM*.

Reaction + Identification = Loss of Presence

Now let us suppose the phone rings just as I am writing something particularly pertinent. Irritation arises within me and the presence vanishes. I forget to sense and feel and, as I cross the room to pick up the phone, my foot hits the leg of the table. An expletive slips out of my mouth. By the time I get to the phone, I am certainly not the same person who was sitting and writing a moment before, enveloped in self-remembering and in the extra-dimensional awareness permeating my three-dimensional form. Becoming *identified with my irritation* and lost in self-forgetfulness, I have turned into a reactive idiot—there is no longer a sense of *I AM*, just a confused, malfunctioning machine that I now think is me. And an upset me at that!

This is the opposite of self-remembering. I have turned into a mechanical reaction instead of a self-directed soul. I pick up the phone and hear only a dial tone. No one is there. Now I realize I have behaved like an idiot. My negative reaction turned a part of myself into an energy vampire. It ate the subtle energetic substances consciousness requires for me to be immersed in the subtle emanations of my own being—and *I* disappeared. So too did the presence and connection with *I AM*. If my old boss suddenly materialized he could justifiably flap his hand vaguely in my direction and say, "You, there … um … Thing!" and I would deserve it.

The moment we react negatively to anything, our own inner vampires can spring into life and quickly feed upon our positive life energy. The more we supply these forces with the negative responses of grumbling and self-justification, the bigger they will grow. Such is the power of reactive identification with any event, internal or external. In seconds, we can lose all sense of balance and normal identity. Becoming identified with our reactions, we actually *become* anger, impatience, irritation, cruelty, despair, or depression. How can the subtle sensations of presence that attend spiritual consciousness remain in an internal environment that is in a state of such upheaval? The gross and the subtle cannot exist for long together, either within or outside of us. It is impossible, for the denser vibration of the one obscures the finer quality of the other.

Constant practice of intentionally staying in full-body awareness through sensing and feeling is essential if we wish to stay conscious. Since I AM can only be felt, we have to be home in our body—our "sensing mechanism"—to feel it.

The powerful sense of our own being, of *I AM,* that is generated through the sensing-and-feeling practice is our greatest asset, and it is a warning system. When personal reactivity kicks in, our level of being will instantly drop away. Quickly perceiving this sense of energy loss can serve as a trigger to help us get off our reactions and come back to personal autonomy at once. This is essential if we are to avoid being seduced by energy drains from without and within. With practice, we can learn to stay present *in* presence and keep our level of being high on a nearly permanent basis.

Embodying the Future to Achieve Success Now

On the most practical level, the results of the three-stroke system translate into a great sense of personal security and self-confidence when dealing with the unpleasant behavioral manifestations of other people toward us. These benefits happen naturally as function #3, body sensed and felt living, becomes a more or less permanent state as a direct result of putting functions #1 and #2 in correct order.

Since average energy vampires or negative people are nothing more than an outmoded two-stroke system gone bonkers, they are nothing to be afraid of. When you can switch, at the moment of peril, from reactive weakness to a powerful embodiment of the emerging man or woman, you become a troublemaker's worst nightmare. They thought they could turn you into a mouse, but instead you become the future person in the here and now!

However, those who are trapped in negative past patterns, and yet possess the potential to break out of them and transform, can experience a major shift in consciousness as a result of interacting with you. *Potential* three-stroke systems will resonate with and be affected by your three-stroke energy field. Your self-remembering will cause them to self-remember. They would not be able to put into words what is happening to them. But they will drop out of their heads and experience a degree of enlightening energy as they become more present to themselves.

I have lost count of the number of times this has happened before my eyes. But I pick up on the atmospheric shift in people at once. Their essence eye will glow and radiate at me with recognition and gratitude and their breathing will cease to be upper-chest respiration and become expansive body breath. Sometimes someone will say to me, "I am tingling all over . . . what is this?" And I will reply simply, "It is you."

Serving the World by Transforming Yourself

Through your conscientious practice and ability to generate presence and bring forth the same in others, you can become someone who is paying for your future in advance. But you are restructuring not only yourself. You are recreating life on a new level and rebuilding the world. And life will reward you right now, in the present moment, by creating beneficial circumstances that will further your ability to generate more and more a presence and sense of *I AM*. Why will life back you up this way? Because you have shown that you are willing to serve something greater than your own primary natural inclination toward self-interest. You demonstrate a willingness to function in this world the way a real man and a real woman are designed operate. Life then can make major investments in your well-being and automatically create circumstances that will enrich you as a means to expand your field of influence.

Perhaps you have wondered why some people prosper in the human dream while others seem to suffer? I am going to show you that it is possible to put ourselves in alignment with a constant flow of beneficial events rather than a random flow of unpredictable outcomes. There is the great hidden law of material success. It may be formulated as follows: *Your level of being attracts your life.*

Increase Your Level of Being to Succeed in Life

When you can charge up your level of being, you will naturally draw to yourself a flow of life-empowering circumstances. Change your level of being and your dream of life changes—sometimes instantly! You become a success magnet that attracts favorable outcomes in social situations because you suddenly became highly energized. People's attitudes change the moment yours does. They become cooperative, willing to listen, eager to help. Why? Because you are holding for them a field of supranormalcy and the power emanating from you is *causing them to replicate your state!* They are temporarily feeling *normalized* because you have seduced them from the limitations of the old, dysfunctional two-stroke operation into the experience of being a three-stroke system. To some degree, they can sense and feel their own presence and being. It may not be a full-blown perception of *I AM* but is manifesting in, around, and through them to a degree. And without knowing why, they love you for the gift you are bestowing upon them.

This is the real meaning of win-win. *I AM* in you meets *I AM* in someone else, and opposites are canceled out by reconciliation through the recognition of something in another human being that is greater than the trance of the great illusion. You are giving those who would act inimically toward you a chance to redeem themselves by going beyond who, what, and how they normally are. You and they make a winning circumstance out of a situation that could have caused both of you to lose. Because you changed yourself at will, you changed them by proxy. *Now you and your antagonist are both making a profit!*

Can you see how powerful this makes *you a*nd how truly loving, even and especially if, you had to stand up to people, hiss, or even playact to get them there? The power of redemption is the greatest force in creation and it can flow through you when you are connected with that which underlies everything—the great *I AM!* It can express through you a pragmatic, nonsentimental love that cancels out opposites and draws separation and fragmentation back into a state of unity. To work with that force in creation puts you on the fast track of evolution, so fasten your seatbelt.

We are surrounded by a delusional dream state where atoms and molecules masquerade as material substance. Maya, the cosmic illusion, the supreme creator's sleight of hand, is a conjuring trick behind which are hidden the riches of the primal joy, bliss, and lasting happiness. Our task, as evolving souls, is to see through the trick and steal the treasure for ourselves. And we must learn to do this right in the marketplace of life, surrounded by the clamorous din of people buying and selling their souls to the illusion. Through the techniques and principles you are learning here, soon you too will be able to affirm with me:

> Wherever I go, whatever I do, the *I AM* in me is awake in the dream that keeps others in bondage by their own consent. I, however, refuse to accept the self-imposed limitations of my own sleep or anyone else's. Right here, in the midst of life, in the face of any circumstance, my soul and I generate the power of being and presence. We live in *I AM* consciousness and, from this state, can say to the world with absolute authority: We always make a profit!

The Miraculous Law of Divided Attention

The profit we make is generated by creating *I AM* consciousness from the energy of social turbulence that constantly swirls around us. To do this successfully, we must develop, focus, and maintain about ourselves at all times a presence and an energy that has a twofold quality. We must learn to keep as much awareness upon ourselves (50 percent) as we place upon the people, places, or objects around us we can see, hear, smell, observe, and touch—50 percent of our attention upon sensing and feeling our own self and 50 percent upon external observed phenomenon. It is through successful application of this simple principle of divided attention that we learn how to *always make a profit.* The formula can be encapsulated as follows: *Ensure that in any situation that the amount of energy going outward toward an object or circumstance be equaled by the amount of energy we maintain focused upon ourselves.*

This is the law of divided attention. When we look at something external in a fixated manner and abandon all awareness of our self as the source of the experience, we become hypnotized by that which we are looking at. We ourselves no longer exist. We lose all sense of ourselves in the thing observed. When I look at a tree and misplace awareness of that which is doing the looking—*I* myself—there is nothing for the impression of the tree to fall upon. There is nobody home to take delivery. I have gone to sleep.

If I look at the tree and become *fully aware of myself,* sensing and feeling every part of my body and all its energy, while looking at it, then an active power—*I* myself, again—is participating in the process of looking. Thus, the sensation changes from hypnotic self-forgetfulness to a state of self-recollection. The experience of seeing becomes one of "I . . . in this place . . . looking at the tree."

Imagine someone looking at a tree; the arrow tip of attention points away from the looker, toward the tree. This is a *one-way* process. There is no attention upon the looker so there is no *I* to have the experience of looking. The act of seeing has swallowed up the individual, who has become dispossessed of self.

Now visualize an arrow of attention with two tips, one pointing toward the looker and one toward the observed object *at the same time.* Half of the person's attention is focused upon a sensed awareness of his or her own totality—feet, arms, legs, head, torso, and so on, through sensing and feeling; the other half of the person's attention is going out to the tree. As a result, the looker becomes surrounded by a presence that builds up, in, around, and through that person as a direct result of this act of divided attention. Not only is there somebody home to do the looking, but the looker is also *making a profit.* Energy is flowing into the looker from the tree.

People who apply this two-way looking are building up their life force and increasing their personal power by being fully present. Not only to the situation, but also by being *present to themselves!* As a result of this, they are receiving the impression of the tree as a conscious act. The spell of duality and separation is being canceled out. They have made a connection with the underlying unity of all things.

Plato spoke of seeing "the thing in itself." What, for example, is the "cup-ness" of a cup, the "tree-ness" of a tree? What are things, in and for themselves, before our socially conditioned perceptions fall upon them? If we gaze at anything in the external world in an unconscious manner, we automatically become hypnotized by the objects of our one-way attention. The arrow of attention has only one tip and it takes us away from ourselves into the world of sleep to be hypnotized by objects or people. And we certainly don't want to be put into a compliant trance by someone who is trying to force a personal agenda on us.

Divided Attention in Tense Social Situations

No matter what happens during a conversation, our task is to make sure that we stay grounded and self-connected throughout the interchange. By feeling the presence of our own being, no matter which way the conversation goes or flows, and regardless of outcome, we try to stay focused on maintaining a palpable connection with ourselves. Even if we initially expend 75 percent of our energy dealing with the other party, if we can maintain 25 percent with ourselves, even during the difficult moments, soon the energy dynamic will shift our way and our 25 percent will start to increase dramatically. Remember that it takes more energy to be negative than to stay positively self-connected. The long-term goal, one that can be reached with daily practice, is to eventually have 50-50 divided attention at all times.

In tense situations, practice the above while giving other people some rope to tie themselves up with words and thoughts, while you ground in the earth through your body. Connect with your arms, legs, and torso and feel the presence build. Don't try to leap into verbal responses or override what others are saying, even if and *especially* when they are trying to make you wrong. Wait and just listen. Watch the eyes and practice sensing and feeling. Your energy will increase, and they will run out of steam. When they do, you will have the position of power and authority. Then you can use it with dignity and wisdom to command the respect you deserve.

After the moment of tension has passed, you will notice how empowered you feel. Your arms and legs, even your entire body, may be tingling and vibrating with energy. *You will have made a profit!* If in the making, you have been able to assist the other person to come to a higher perspective, then your presence-energy profit will be doubled. Why? Because the other people will also have benefited from interacting with your self-mastery of reactions through divided attention. They might possibly have been transported from isolation into flow with you, as in our tree metaphor. It is like releasing God from the prison cells of self-limitation so many people erect around themselves.

Self-Remembering and the Essential You

If you have the willingness to practice these techniques on an ongoing basis, you will reawaken the dormant, primal, direct perceptual capacity you were born with. You can reclaim the lost sense of knowing yourself as *I AM* that you sometimes experienced as a child and express it *now,* through the mature adult that you are, in a responsible fashion. Our all-knowing child power gets taken away, between the ages of five and seven. This is so that we will be compelled to adjust to the world of sleep around us and learn to participate in the dream as most people dream it. Through these techniques, you can consciously reestablish a powerful connection with the essential being you were in early childhood. By cultivating this connection as a now mature force and drawing it into your social interactions, you will access a power that is greater than the confusion of the madness that surrounds us. You will start to be awake in a world of sleeping machines! You will be stronger than those sleeping people who would unconsciously drain from you the radiant energy that is the depth and substance of your soul.

The opposite of being drained is to be nourished. Life energy may well be our "daily bread." Without sufficient amounts of it, we hardly feel to be living. All of the practices in this book naturally and easily increase our life energy. Paradoxically, when we implement the key strategies that prevent our leaking life force, we actually increase it within ourselves because *we are remembering who and what we really are.* To lose our own connection with ourselves when confronted by difficult people and situations is to enter a state of *self-forgetfulness.* Reversing that process, so that we connect with our own essentiality when pressured, requires self-remembering.

We answer the age-old question "who am I?" by remembering ourselves into the I AM experience. It is only through practices that lead to self-remembering that we can ever know who we truly are and make for ourselves the successful lives we long to live. Later on we shall explore key techniques in depth to call forth the unshakable power and presence of the *I AM* that lies beneath the limitations of who and what we normally think we are. Since interpersonal friction can provide us with the catalytic material to convert into consciousness, let us turn our attention now to an area of life where the possibility for explosive confrontations continually lurks just beneath the surface of our dreams of happiness. It has been called "the battle of the sexes" and yet it is more accurately the play of opposites seeking reconciliation through harmonizing energy. Until we understand the dance of Yin and Yang and primal forces that are set loose when we fall in love with someone, our hearts will never know peace and happiness in our intimate relationships.

Carl Jung had great insight regarding the dual nature of human beings. Inside every man is a woman. Inside every woman is a man. In every relationship there are really four people: the external man and his inner woman and the external woman and her internal man. So if you want to stop wrestling with the dual aspects of your lover, wife, husband, partner, or anyone you may encounter in social situations, join me now for the next dance, the enlightened man-woman, woman-man quadrangle!

CHAPTER NINE

Enlightening Relationship Dynamics

The Battling Couple and Their Inner Antagonists

Most of us have experienced the sense of power and ease in relation to life that flows through us when things are going well with our significant other. We also know the pain and personal constriction that can possess us when we get swept into the maelstrom of battling egos. The emotional disruption that attends falling out of harmony with someone who normally brings love and companionship to us can be devastating. Not only does our emotional and physical health suffer. By not being fully present to ourselves because we feel emotionally dispossessed, we may be unavailable to take advantage of the goodness life offers to us.

Ellie and Steve were very much in love but could not get along with one another. They were both bright, attractive, and intelligent. Steve was tall and strongly built; Ellie was petite and had a mind that moved much faster than her partner's. As they began to tell me about their difficulties, Ellie's eyes filled with tears that softened the tension on her face as they fell. She told me she could not understand why they were constantly arguing when they loved each other so much. They were both sick and tired of hurting each other, but could not seem to get off a cycle of verbal attacks upon each other. As Ellie finished talking, I looked over at Steve and saw that he now seemed very small, shrunk down into himself. Her tears pained him and he reached out his hand and took hers.

"I don't want to hurt her," he said softly, in an almost feminine voice.

"But you do, all the time," snapped Ellie, her features straining once more with tension as the pain came back.

Steve shook visibly, struggling to handle his feelings as her attitude grew hard. "I just don't know what to do to please her," he said to me in a whiney voice. "It seems everything I do is wrong and irritates her."

"There you go again, playing the victim," Ellie snapped. "He always does this to get other people's sympathy."

"Do you realize that in those last two sentences you both verbally attacked each other?" I suggested gingerly. "Steve's statement contained a blame message to you, Ellie, and was passive-aggressive. Your response took the form of a direct attack."

"Well, *you* should try living with the guy!" snapped Ellie, turning to face me with a tough energy that hit me like a blow in the chest. "He's totally irresponsible! We're always in debt and it's always left to me to dig us out of it."

I stared at Ellie in amazement. Her female self had completely vanished and been replaced by an aggressive, accusing, challenging *man.* Her male side was on the loose. I glanced again at Steve, expecting to see him still shrunk down into his female side. But instead he was now all swollen up with wounded male pride. He actually stood up and glowered down at Ellie in an intimidating manner.

"We're always in debt because you lead us from one crackpot business scheme to another," yelled Steve, his face flushed red and his eyes bulging. Then he turned to me, livid with rage. "She's the failed multilevel marketing queen of all time. She drags me to these meetings where we get pitched to sell water purifiers, clean air machines, green algae, and God knows what. She gets all enthused and we run up our charge cards to get started. And it always ends up the same way—not enough sales to get back our outlay. I'm sick of it."

As Steve flung himself back into his seat with the crazed air of a man who thought he had just reclaimed himself through this wild, emotional outburst, I looked over at Ellie and saw that she was staring at him in wide-eyed passivity. She looked like a seventeen-year-old girl. There was no sign of her male side *anywhere.* As she reached out and took Steve's hand tenderly, I could barely contain my amazement.

What was going on here? First, Ellie cries and Steve softens. His female side takes over and expresses compassion toward her. As soon as Ellie sees this, her male side comes out swinging and berates him for being a weakling. This inflames Steve and he leaps to his feet and yells at her, acting like a caricature of a tough guy! Then Ellie goes passive again.

Loosening the Grip of Anima and Animus

When a man starts to bluster, yell, and make wildly emotional, irrational statements, you can be sure he is in the grip of demented aspects of his unintegrated female self—what Jung called the *anima*. At such a moment the woman in his life can feel very afraid. Not of him and his bluster, but for the consequences of having melded her fate to such a nincompoop. What has become of the wonderful man she fell in love with when he first courted her? Where is the promise of strength and reliability upon which she thought she could depend? When her man is possessed by anima's peevish, self-righteous behavior, the woman knows intuitively that she cannot love him at that moment and her empathetic side shuts down. Her male side (called *animus* by Jung) comes out to handle a situation that has proved too much for the man in her life to deal with. It is as if her animus is saying "if he can't handle it, I can and *will*." And will often do so in quite a brutal manner.

In order for a woman to feel love for a man, she must know that it is safe for *her* inner male side to relax around her external man. Only through this can she ever truly feel all her feelings. Sensing that women have the power to unman them whenever they choose, men have traditionally used bullying and oppression to keep women in line. But women want men in their lives who are masters of themselves, not of them. And a man can learn to master his anima's tendency to feel hurt by a woman. When he does this, he will not flare up emotionally and behave in a hysterical manner when confronted by animus. If woman's animus cannot draw the man's anima into archetypal dramas, he will quickly gain the woman's respect *and* her love.

When the Parental Influence of the Past Runs the Present

Following the threads of my amazement over how Ellie could become so passive when Steve blustered, I could only assume that perhaps her father had behaved in much the same way. For now that he had yelled at her, she seemed like a little girl, soft and compliant. When Steve saw this, he melted. Tears appeared in his eyes again and for a moment something resembling love passed between them.

"I'm sorry, honey, I didn't mean to yell like that," he said gently

Much as the wind blows clouds from the face of the sun, the brightness suddenly vanished again from Ellie's face. The little girl she had momentarily become disappeared as she pursed her lips into a tart, disgusted expression. There before my eyes, the cold, hard face of animus returned to glare contemptuously at Steve. I glanced over at him and saw that *he* now looked like a little girl. And Ellie's animus proceeded to flay him and his anima alive. All the bottled-up rage of her inner male frustration at having to deal with men through a female form came boiling out like molten lava. As she poured it on, Steve shrank down in his chair again, to almost a point of invisibility. Ellie was his mother all over again, saying, "You are a bad boy. You have failed me and disappointed me and I am withdrawing my love from you. Now you are going to see what it feels like to be hurt and disappointed by men!"

Ellie's animus quickly spent its fury and it was not long before Steve was on the attack, blustering away while Ellie shrank back and wept again. This was the pattern of their lives. It's a wonder they hadn't killed each other long ago. In the back of my mind, some shadow aspect of myself wanted to reach for a rubber stamp with which to emboss on their case the word "hopeless!"

But on a higher level, I knew that I had to find a way to get them out of their heads and help them to recognize anima and animus in action. At the same time, they would have to learn to sense and feel in order to go beyond mechanical personality patterns to connect with each other on an essence level. Somehow I had to turn these two-stroke system, romantically entwined, psychological antiques into three-stroke system embodiments of the emerging man and woman.

An Obsessive-Compulsive Disorder Made for Two

"You are both caught up in a negative feedback loop of joint obsessive-compulsive disorder," I told them, as they both looked at me puppylike through tear-wet eyes. "Certain mechanisms in your brain are being constantly triggered automatically by each other, and your thoughts, emotions, and physical responses keep running way with you. When you first fell in love you were happy . . . right?"

They both nodded in unison and then slipped shy glances at each other. Somewhere, buried beneath the frustration and personal disappointment in each other, I sensed that the love that had begun their journey was still alive.

"And you probably had lots of moments when you thought and felt an incredible sense of oneness." Again, they both softened as the memory of their idealism toward each other stirred. "In those early days, when you did think and feel as one, you most likely experienced only a positive rush of life-affirming energy and love. Now, you still think and act as one, but it is mostly shared negativity. Your brains are still in sync. But they are out of sync with your highest welfare because in reality, there are not just two people, Steve and Ellie, in this relationship. There are four people: Steve and his anima and Ellie and her animus."

"I understand how we are all creatures of habit and our childhood plays out in the present," said Steve suspiciously, "but what's this about four people? Do you mean we have split personalities or something?"

"Yes, in a way, I do." I then hastened to add reassuringly, "Don't be alarmed, we all do. Inside every man there is a woman and inside every woman a man. These are natural components of our psychological inner world and we can learn a great deal from them. But sometimes they get in the driver's seat and act out through us. And they can cause a great deal of upheaval in a relationship. I have been watching them act out through you two on and off for the last half hour."

"Hey, wait a minute," interjected Steve uneasily, as his idea of himself as a man wrestled with the thought that he could also be female. "Are you saying I've been acting like a woman? I'm not sure I like where this is going."

"And what about me?" snapped Ellie, her animus now giving me the male testing look she usually reserved for Steve. "I'm all woman, so don't go trying to tell me I act like a man."

"Makes me sound like I'm queer or something," added Steve, shifting in his seat uncomfortably.

"Not in the least. This has nothing to do with sexual preference but everything to do with whether this relationship will survive. I assume this is something you both want or you would not have come to see me?"

They both nodded, again in sync. As was my custom, I had videotaped this session. Stumbling blocks we cannot hear in someone's voice may be more easily noticed through the visual clues of body language, which can be easily seen on the video playback.

"We're going to watch the video of our session together. We'll see if we can track the dynamic movement of your *invisible partners,* through the body language and conversational tenor of your session so far."

"What do you mean by 'invisible partners'? Are we possessed or something?" asked Ellie, as I positioned the video monitor so we could all see it.

"It's a term coined by John Sanford, an Episcopalian priest and Jungian analyst. He wrote a best-selling book called *The Invisible Partners: How the Male and Female in Each of Us Affects Our Relationships.* I highly recommend it as a most lucid and practical overview of the dual psychological nature of man and woman."

I went on to give a quick overview of anima and animus. Then we watched the video, the three of us paying special attention to when Steve fell under the influence of his anima and Ellie under that of her animus.

The Awakening Shock of Self-Recognition

It is said that a picture is worth a thousand words. What price can we put on a stream of images that reveal to two basically nice people that their relationship is being ruined by unconscious aspects of themselves that they never knew existed? Steve clearly saw how he first shrank down into a passive state like a scolded little boy when Ellie's animus attacked him. Then he observed how, in an attempt to reassert his male authority, he blustered in a wild emotional manner, all under the influence of anima. And Ellie was able to see how her beauty and natural feminine power was usurped when her animus got into the driver's seat.

She was horrified by the mean, bitter look on her face as her eyes bugged out. "I look like a lunatic!" she cried, clapping her hands to her cheeks in shock.

"Me, too," chimed in Steve. "I don't believe it."

The tension was broken and we all laughed as I turned off the video.

"What worries me is that these aspects of ourselves may be coming out with other people, too. Do you think I act like that at work sometimes?" added Steve.

"Oh, certainly," I said. "We are all largely unconscious. So we shift back and forth between the need to assert ourselves and be more open, relational, and receptive to the needs of others."

"So what do we do about it?" asked Ellie. "I can see that these unconscious aspects of ourselves are ruining our relationship."

Saved by Sensing and Feeling

What I told Steve and Ellie was that in order not to be swept away by unconscious impulses, such as anima-animus manifestations, we have to be able to separate ourselves from our reactions.

"The first trick is to stop the mind connecting directly with the emotions by using the mind to focus on the feet, arms, and legs, the neutral zone of the body."

They both seemed willing to try so we did the sensing-and-feeling exercise together. Within minutes, they reported that they could feel a tingling sensation pulsating in their limbs. I noticed that as soon as they had established the connection with feet, hands, arms, and legs, their faces relaxed considerably.

As the three of us continued to practice, I pointed out that mental energy should be used to support our positive feelings about ourselves. Instead, it gets burned up needlessly by our overly active brains and overly reactive bodies. Stressful interactions with other people put us into states of fight or flight and this consumes our natural physical and emotional resources. Arguments set our body house on fire. When our mind and our speech mechanisms get linked up in a destructive way, they will automatically make us fling ridiculous, negatively charged, highly emotional statements at our partner. I asked Steve and Ellie if they ever experience wanting to stop saying hurtful things to each other, while feeling powerless to prevent the caustic outpouring from their mouths?"

Ellie nodded and Steve looked sheepishly at her.

"What I do," I continued, "is whenever the first hint of interpersonal conflict shows up, I connect with my arms and legs and drop down mentally into my body. You'd be amazed how easy it is to do this under pressure. Tremendous forces of energy get generated in the human body whenever stress occurs. It is a natural compensation mechanism to help us get through the trauma. But if we start to vent our emotions on other people and start saying nasty, hurtful things, then we become like nuclear reactors on overload; all our life force flies away uselessly into the surrounding atmosphere. But the split second we begin to focus on sensing and feeling, and switch from reactivity to productivity, we are able to 'eat' the extra charge of energy the body is generating."

"That's a weird concept," interjected Steve. "Eating your own energy."

"Have you never seen that ancient symbol of a snake eating its own tail?" I asked. "Or statues of Lord Buddha with a snake coiled around his head?"

"And the Egyptian statues with the snake head coming out of the point between the eyebrows," suggested Ellie.

"I always thought that the snake had something to do with sex," said Steve with a grin. "You know, Adam and Eve, the fall, and all that good stuff."

It was amazing how quickly they had become creative and involved in the self-renewing process. Now that they were out of their heads and connected with their bodies they were actually thinking more clearly.

"You are both right," I affirmed. "The snake represents the creative energy in the lower half of the human body. The spine is the Tree of Life and the brain represents the branches that are connected to the starry world above our heads and great universal creative forces. When we are relaxed and in touch with ourselves, that creative energy, the snake if you will, can easily ascend to the brain and give rise to great thoughts, insights, and inspiration. But when we are angry or upset, that energy gets usurped and the snake's venom comes out of our eyes, our mouths, and yes, sometimes even our hands as physical violence."

"That's what it feels like when I am hurting Ellie," said Steve. "Like I am injecting poison into her and myself at the same time." I nodded my agreement and understanding.

"So, being aware of our arms and legs helps divert our attention elsewhere," Ellie interjected. "But what do we do after that? We can't just sit and feel our arms and legs when we have issues to deal with."

She had a good point, so I elaborated. "No, of course not. But if you try to address those issues at white heat, you will both get burned. With practice, it only takes a few seconds to get connected through sensing and feeling. If you are both in agreement to do it as a matter of course, the fire will die down to a manageable level almost at once."

"But suppose I am trying to doing this and Ellie has forgotten and says things that start to push my buttons? What then?" Steve was looking worried at the thought. "I don't know how long I could do this arms-and-legs thing without wanting to retaliate verbally."

"Then you need to do a certain little mental exercise at the same time that you are sensing and feeling the arms and the legs," I replied.

"A mental exercise?" queried Steve. "I thought we were supposed to be staying out of our heads?"

Counting to Stay Conscious

"Sometimes we may find that even though we are doing the sensing-and-feeling exercise, the person confronting us knows just how to push our mental buttons. This is especially dangerous if that individual knows us well. In such a case, the urge to lash out and fight back may be stronger than our will to stay nonreactive. What we implement is something to keep our thinking processes occupied so we don't go over the edge. We do a counting exercise."

"You mean like when we're making love and I'm trying not to ejaculate too soon and count baseball scores?" suggested Steve.

"We'll, that's one way of looking at it, I suppose." I had to smile, not just at what Steve had said, but how much more relaxed and willing to be vulnerable and funny he was allowing himself to be. "It is a similar principle. The body wants to have a spasmodic reaction and you are trying to control it. All sensation resides in the brain. When we reach orgasm, key points such as the pituitary and pineal glands activate and switch us into a mode where conscious intention is overridden by natural inclination. Counting baseball scores is a linear thinking process that keeps the intuitive functions of the brain on hold. We might say that negative emotional reactions, violent speech, and bad behavior are also intuitive. More accurately, they are instinctive bodily responses triggered by mental and emotional collisions in the psyche at a point when reason can no longer prevail to hold reactivity in check. So what we do to combat this is count mentally, a specific series of numbers. Like this. . . ."

I took a notepad and in large figures, wrote the following numerical sequence: one-two-three . . . two-three-four . . . three-four-five . . . four-five-six . . . five-six-seven . . . six-seven-eight . . . seven-eight-nine. "And so on," I added, holding up the pad and showing Steve and Ellie what I had written.

Then I asked them what they noticed about the sequence.

"You're counting in sets of three," said Ellie, "and each new sequence begins with the middle number of the preceding sequence."

"Exactly," I replied, "and what I would like you both to do is count that series of numbers mentally while I make up some negative verbal rap and run it on the two of you. But first, let's just drop out of our heads, go mentally down to our feet and then sense and feel the arms and legs."

We took a few minutes to do this together. Then I further suggested that even though they were going to count mentally, I wanted them to try and do it as if the counting were actually taking place in their torsos. To facilitate this I had them place one hand on the solar plexus and one over the naval. Then I told them to start counting mentally and just keep going, no matter what I said.

"Well, anyone one can see that the world is going to hell in a handbasket," I moaned, putting on a doleful expression. "Look at the situation in the Middle East. Can you see a way out of that? And what about global warming? Lately I have been so depressed I'm starting to think that maybe the fundamentalist Christians are right and these are the end times. I went to the dentist the other day and while he was working on a cavity the anaesthetic wore off and, man, I was in such pain. It was agony. I thought, this is what everlasting hell must be like—strapped in a dentist chair with no painkiller while the devil drills away throughout eternity!"

At this point Steve and Ellie both burst into gales of laughter.

"What?" I inquired beseechingly. "You don't believe me?"

"No. I mean, yes ... I'll believe you if that's what you want. But personally, I really don't give a you-know-what!" said Ellie, now wiping away tears of laughter. "I heard everything you said, but it was like listening to an idiot. I could see that it was just your stuff."

"And you were not going to take delivery of it, right?" I interjected.

"Exactly. It was like you were hypnotized by your own agenda and none of it had anything to do with my life. I was immune."

"But you did hear what I was saying?" I looked questioningly at Steve.

"And you probably could have answered me if I had asked you a question at any point, right?"

"Oh, sure," Steve replied. "But I would not have had any charge on it. It was like watching a computer printing out text. I just observed it all impersonally."

Counting to Count on Each Other

Next I had Steve and Ellie try counting while they played off each other. I got them to sit facing each other. Then I had Steve sense and feel, and mentally count, while Ellie verbally ran some issues by him that had been troubling her of late. Steve just sat there and actively listened. I was proud of him. There was no sign of anima showing up to possess him when Ellie said something that made one of Steve's past actions or attitudes seem wrong. He just looked solid, focused, and gathered in an attentive way. When Ellie had finished, I notice that she seemed very calm and was looking at him with admiration. Then it was Steve's turn.

I quickly helped Ellie get into a state of sensing and feeling. Then she began to count mentally while Steve brought to the surface things that had been bothering him. Ellie, too, remained completely nonreactive throughout. She just sat and listened and seemed to be enveloped in peace. When Steve had finished, I asked both of them how they felt.

"Calm," said Steve.

"Peaceful . . . focused," said Ellie. "I feel like myself."

"And you did hear everything you said to each other? It wasn't like you were tuning one another out?"

"Not at all." Ellie was looking at Steve with great warmth. "I actually felt closer to him when I was speaking because he didn't react. Before, I used to take his reaction as a plus for me. It was like I had power over him for a second. But when he stays calm like that, I don't want to have power over him."

"What do you want, then?" I asked gently.

"I just want to love him," said Ellie, her eyes shining. "And I want to make love to him."

"Let's go home, honey," said Steve, reaching for both her hands as they stood up.

"Before you go, there's just one thing." I was not quite done with them yet. "Which of each other's eyes are you looking into right now?"

"I'm looking into Steve's left eye," answered Ellie.

"And I'm looking into Ellie's left eye," said Steve.

"What do you see?" I asked.

The love coming from Steve was incredible as he said, "I see the person . . . no, more than that . . . I see the *being* I first fell in love with."

"And you, Ellie? Who are you seeing?"

"I am seeing the man I married." Ellie shone as she looked up into Steve's face. "I am seeing Steve. He's my husband and there is no barrier between us. It feels like we're home."

"Whenever there is a ripple, just look into each other's left eye. I will explain more about that at your next session. Now I think I need to let you go."

And off they went. It would take a lot of conscious daily work on their part to make permanent the breakthrough they had experienced that day. But they were on their way.

Anima and Animus on the Loose in the World

Mutual suspicion and even outright hostility between the sexes is all around us. Across the social spectrum, in personal relationships, the workplace, and even casual encounters with strangers, manifestations of gender imbalance disturb the social equilibrium. What I have drawn from Jungian psychology has helped me to balance Yin and Yang, masculine and feminine, within myself.

An ancient Taoist concept called the "inner smile" helps me to transform negative emotional energy into a usable positive force. Insight gained from this source further helps me neutralize potential friction I encounter in the course of my daily affairs.

By creating a highly charged state of energy in my internal organs, I am able to renew myself constantly without anyone knowing what I am doing. I am going to share this technique with you as we learn how to transform the lead of negative emotional energy into pure gold.

CHAPTER TEN

Transforming Negative Emotions with the Tao

Dealing with Anger—Yours and Other People's

Personal growth is often preceded by a perceptual shift—a change in attitude that allows a new point of view to emerge. If we can stay mentally flexible, we can adapt our outlook to deal with the ever-changing situations that confront us each day. To do this we need practical answers to one of life's most interesting conundrums: how to handle negative emotions and turn their potentially destructive energy into a positive force for good in the world. It is impossible to feel and experience any aspect of *I AM* consciousness when we allow ourselves to be possessed by rage, fear, or any other negative emotion. Our entire physical structure becomes disturbed. Running negative energy through our system burns up the fine substances the body produces so that it can vibrate in sync with higher intelligence.

According to the Taoists, when we are angry, the life energy, or Chi, in our liver has become too Yang and fiery. Our rage acts as a poison to this organ, which is directly related to the flow of our blood. We auto-intoxicate, even as we try to dump our toxic waste on someone else. It is illegal to take garbage and waste materials from one city or state and dump them in another. But we generally think nothing of dumping our negative states into other people. Vociferously expressing anger, whether through yelling and screaming or nasty comments, insults, and caustic remarks, is not just an act of verbal abuse toward others. Because it poisons us as much as those to whom our rage is directed, it is really a form of self-abuse and verbal throwing up. We suddenly come to a point where we can no longer bear the toxic overload our negative thoughts and emotional upheaval have

produced in our bodies. We sometimes discharge this through violent outbursts in which we surrender ownership of ourselves to an involuntary
process of mental, emotional, and physical expression.

Some therapeutic disciplines subscribe to the view that it is healthy
and even necessary to release pent-up anger through pounding on a pillow
or screaming at your parents while imagining they are standing in front of
you. What is taking place with such methods is a process of discharge, a
release of toxic internal energy that cannot be converted into a usable positive power. This may be helpful in chronic cases where someone is stuck,
particularly if it happens in a safe, therapist-directed environment. But
only in very few cases is it likely to create permanent healing because it is
discharge and not *transformation*.

Another point of view encourages us to express our anger, whenever
we feel it, with anyone who upsets us. This is considered a form of personal authenticity, a valid and natural right. But what happens to the energy
behind violent outer expression? Where does it go when released? When
we throw off our own toxic emotional waste onto others, we become responsible for making the recipients of it ill. Making others sick through mis-
management of our own dysfunction is a crime against not only society, but
also against ourselves. Sooner or later it will boomerang back onto us.

A Parental Bully Gets His Comeuppance

In 1841, Ralph Waldo Emerson wrote an essay, "Compensation," which
was his way of talking about the law of karma. This principle of cause and
effect, imported into mass Western culture in the sixties, is now common
parlance. When John Lennon's recording "Instant Karma" hit the charts
on both sides of the Atlantic, it programmed mainstream thinking with
an update on the Biblical idea that we reap what we sow. Isaac Newton
had it down too: For every action there is an equal and opposite reaction.
When we see what people get away with in life sometimes, we might wonder
whether the Karma Police are asleep on the job. Not always, however.
Sometimes the principle of "what goes around comes around" takes powerful forms.

I was once a guest in a wonderful palatial home owned by a charming woman who was living the good life with a sense that it was ordained. She told me that she had been married for almost thirty years to a man who was an absolute tyrant. Perpetually angry, he could not bear to see anyone else not upset. Every evening meal was ruined by his baiting of his wife and children. If he came home and found his family in a good mood, he would instantly reduce the children to tears and destroy any harmony in the home. One day he went to work and never came back. This man worked in construction and fell off a high building onto his head. What remains of his life he will now spend in a comatose, vegetative state. The insurance money the wife and family received has given them a materially rich lifestyle few people could imagine. Free from tyranny, they are a happy family at last.

A garage mechanic who worked on my car insisted on telling me how he loved to beat people up. He had apparently been in hundreds of fights and described in detail several of his battles. With self-righteous vindication and blue language, he drew pictures of himself straightening out those who dared to offend him. When I pressed him further for the reason he got into these scrapes, he declared that he enjoyed hurting people. He also told me that he was accident-prone and had been in many auto wrecks. His body was always being dented and dinged, battered and bruised by circumstances that "came out of nowhere" to inflict havoc upon it. I started to suggest that maybe some sort of retributive process of cause and effect could be operating in his life. But a look in his eyes signaled that pushing such a notion might make me his next victim, so I prudently let it drop.

We are personally responsible for our negative emotions and how we let them affect other people. Yet it is strange how empowering negative energy can be for a while. The filmed footage of the Nazi rallies Hitler led prior to World War II show masses of people on fire with enthusiasm for the ravings of a madman. With shining faces and eyes brimming with the light of inspiration, his followers are obviously experiencing tremendous positive uplift. They have behind them the power of a negative manifesting a righteous self-affirmation. Who has not experienced self-righteous indignation at some time? But be careful about expressing it. The negative energy you are throwing someone's way may backfire and return to you with redoubled force.

The Movie Star and the Gang of Six

Horror film actor Vincent Price told a tale of terror that actually happened to him once in Italy. He was walking through the streets back to his hotel after an evening dining with friends, when two young punks jostled into him. As they ran away, he instinctively felt for his wallet and discovered it was missing. Instantly enraged, Price charged after the thieves. At the bottom of the street they turned into an alleyway and, being in blind rage, the actor ran after them. There in the darkness, the two thieves turned on him. But they were not alone. The gang to which they belonged had been lurking up the alley and now, the original two had become six. Price went through an instant attitudinal change. From acting like a giant of self-righteous ferocity, he became a complete mouse, turned tail, and ran away—without his wallet.

Don Quixote and the Windmills of the Mind

Generally speaking, if one must attack, it is far better to do so obliquely, in a nondirect manner. The dotty old knight Don Quixote charged directly at windmills, thinking they were giants. His lance got stuck in their sails. He was swept off his horse and went spinning round and round with the flailing arms of his "adversary." Eventually he was flung to the ground with a bone- and armor-rattling crash. The windmills had the advantage of being rooted in the ground, the *real* world. Their whirling sails were *in front* of Don Quixote when he charged headlong at them in direct confrontation. If he had approached the windmills *obliquely,* from the back or side, he would not have been unhorsed.

The "giants" were simply products of an overheated imagination. When we get upset in a social situation, like Don Quixote, we too can start projecting giants and goblins, witches and demons onto other people. If we angrily attack these external phantasmagoric creations of our own mind, our temporary dementia is readily apparent to others. They may be momentarily scared by the horrible energy we are putting out, but they will not respect us. And we too may get unhorsed, thrown down to confront reality by the wild perceptual distortions of our irrationality. Remember too that your anger may actually feed the other person. It might make someone who is normally a mouse as strong as a lion. And that lion could eat *you!*

Not Suppression, But Transmutation

Suppression of negative emotions can be extremely harmful to our well-being. We need to find safe ways to *transmute* anger, fear, heartache, sadness, and depression into useful fuel for life. Fortunately, negative emotions can quite easily be turned into positive, usable energy. Almost all of the techniques you have been learning in this book help in this. Because they give the brain something to do other than simply free-wheel, they deactivate our automatic physical and emotional responses. Therefore they are proactive. They put us in the driver's seat of self-determinism on a freeway where most of the other drivers are on automatic pilot.

Because these techniques need to be implemented repeatedly in our daily lives, so they can take root and become second nature, the key points bear repeating. Every time we place our mental attention on our arms and legs, feet, hands, and so on, by sensing and feeling, we are enabling ourselves to induce a sensation of deep calmness in our bodies. This has a profound effect on our five major internal organs—lungs, kidneys, liver, heart, and spleen. The Taoists tell us that these organs are the instruments that generate the life energy of our emotions. They are directly connected with how we feel moment by moment throughout the day. Each organ is designed to work directly with a particular type of life energy (Chi), and the natural quality of the energy is always *positive.* When we are in the grip of negative emotions, we are in an *unnatural* state. Our organs are working with a fuel they were not designed to use.

Every day for the last twenty years, simple Taoist exercises have enabled me to easily discharge negative emotional energy from my body. I want to

share with you some of these time-tested techniques because they will facilitate for you a perceptual shift about what negative emotions really are.
They will also enable you to actually transform disturbed emotional energy
into a positive charge, in seconds. Let's begin by looking at a table that
shows the relation between what we feel emotionally and our major internal organs.

The Internal Organs' Emotional Energy

Positive Energy States	Negative Energy States
Lungs	
Courage and strength	Sadness, grief, depression
Kidneys	
Gentleness, will to advance	Fear
Liver	
Kindness, sense of self	Anger, aggression
Heart	
Love, joy, happiness, sincerity, honor	Arrogance, cruelty, impatience, violence, cruelty
Spleen	
Balance, fairness, compassion	Imbalance, worry

Transforming Negative Emotions

Here is an example of how negative emotional energy can grip us and
squander our life force. Let us assume you are driving along in your car in
a positive state of mind when suddenly someone cuts in front of you dan-
gerously. You honk involuntarily and the other driver gives you the finger.
Anger and resentment flares up inside and you are seized with an impulse
to charge after that person and retaliate. You step on the gas and give chase.
But as you draw closer to the other vehicle at an intersection, the light
changes and the car sails through while you are commanded by red to stop.
All you can do is sit there and fume. Your liver is on the fritz, literally boil-

ing over with hot, dry, angry, Yang energy. This affects your heart, which quickly fills with an arrogant sense of self-righteousness. You imagine the person who has offended you burning eternally in the traffic school of hell.

The offender is oblivious to your inner stewing—doesn't even know you exist. You, on the other hand, sit behind the wheel at the light auto-intoxicating yourself. Consider that your blood cells are constantly streaming through your liver as your circulation sends them whirling round and round in your body. Blood cells turn into fleshy tissue, the very substance of which our bodies are made. As these cells pass through the liver and pick up on our anger, they become impregnated with it. Keep on being angry and they will be making body tissue that has a built-in anger charge. Sometimes we meet people whose posture and facial characteristics reflect the inner toxicity of malfunctioning internal organs. They live in angry bodies that will eventually rebel with chronic ill health for having to tolerate such abuse.

The Taoists have several powerful techniques for discharging this kind of stuck energy before it can do too much damage. Naturally, to change anything, we have to be willing to recognize that we *are* in a negative state and be willing to do something about it. If we are in denial and prefer to blame someone else for our discomfort, there can be no transmutation. By taking responsibility for our own feelings, negative or positive, we place ourselves in a position of power over our own automatism. To react emotionally in an uncontrolled manner is to be run by our programming. By practicing a technique for transmutation when we see that we have become dysfunctional, we can quickly restore our body's "energy factory" to optimum production levels. We prevent emotional and mental shutdown. Our nuclear core remains centrally located and steady and we do not pollute the social environment by discharging our toxic waste into the atmosphere.

The *Smiling Down* Technique, Version One

This is a wonderful tool for keeping lungs, kidneys, liver, heart, and spleen working with the positive qualities of emotional energy. It is based on the ancient Taoist technique of the "inner smile." Although there are three methods of practice, the basic principles are the same for all three and can be applied to each situation.

The first method is to practice in private each day as part of a quiet time or regular meditation period. If you have not yet formed the habit of a morning sitting, I suggest you do so without delay. In daily life, one does not wish to get overdrawn at the bank and start bouncing checks. Similarly, we need to make sure that our "energy banks" of inner peace remain full and vital throughout the day. Otherwise, we may find ourselves running out of capital in the middle of the day. So get in the habit of at least ten minutes of silent communion with your own depths every morning before starting the day.

Begin by sitting in a comfortable position. I personally use a chair that enables me to sit upright with my back away from the back of it. The hands can rest comfortably on the lap and the feet should be flat on the floor to make a good "grounding" contact with the earth. This does not mean you have to be on the ground floor of a building or outside. One can ground from a high-rise or even in an airplane. It is more a question of intent, and the soles of the feet pointing toward the earth certainly helps in this regard.

Close your eyes and relax. Breathe normally and watch the breath for a few minutes to interiorize the mind. Next, put a slight smile on your face. If you don't feel like smiling, "assume a virtue if you have it not" . . . and smile anyway. Feel the positive state of mind that this act of intentionally smiling produces, as a warm sensation of comfort on the skin of your face. Now let the smile energy fill your entire head. Feel it in your mouth and your cheeks, on your tongue, and around your teeth. Let it migrate into your brain and let your brain cells drink in the smiling energy.

Smiling to the Throat and Lungs

After enjoying the sensations of happy smiling energy in your head for a few minutes, let your closed eyes direct it down into the throat. Feel your throat filling with the smiling energy. Let your thyroid gland and your vocal chords happily bathe in the warmth of your smile. The entire throat area just seems to relax and open up.

Now continue smiling from the throat down into the lungs. Smile with a sense of gratitude toward your lungs for all the work they do breathing for you. They are busy every moment of our life, working away on our behalf, usually unnoticed and unappreciated. Feel how they relax and expand as they receive your smiling energy. Every cell and pore of the lungs drink happily in recognition that you are in communion with them. The lungs seem to fill with a sense of courage and strength. This the normal state for healthy lungs.

Let your lungs rejoice in the smiling energy. Stay there as long as you wish and try to feel that the smile is filling your lungs with a sensation of strength, personal fortitude, and courage to accomplish life goals. Then extend the smiling energy you have gathered in your head, throat, and lungs into the heart.

You should spend at least 30 to 60 seconds immersed in deep attention on each organ as you are smiling down. Try not to get impatient and move on to the next organ until you have made a full connection with the preceding one. In our modern world of rush and panic, we are habituated to scurrying from one engagement, one meal, one task to the next at breakneck speed. Take your time.

Healing the Heart

Day after day our hearts beat to give us life, unacknowledged by us for their constant efforts. Now, as we let our closed eyes focus on the heart, we smile with deep thankfulness into the heart. See the heart open up like a red rose, to receive your loving, smiling recognition. As your attention settles into the heart, let feelings of love and happiness form inside it. Smile to your heart and feel it smile love and happiness back to you.

When you establish this connection, you will feel a sense of joy in your heart spreading throughout your body. Stay as long as you like in the heart and then move on to the liver.

Loving the Liver

This large organ is under the lower rib cage on the front right side of the body. Take the smiling energy you have gathered in head, throat, lungs, and heart, and smile it down into the liver.

The eyes have an outer and an inner directive capability. It helps to feel that your closed eyes are actually looking down through your body into the liver. Let your attention gather in the liver area and bathe it with the healing smiling energy. The negative state for the liver is when it is generating, or holding, anger within itself. Let us now apply the remedy to reverse that tendency by mentally generating the antidote, a feeling of *kindness* in the liver. As you smile this quality into the liver, be sure to feel kindness for yourself first of all. Then feel it for others—a nice general feeling of being kindly and well disposed to all.

The Kidneys

From the liver, direct the flow of smiling energy around to the small of your back and focus it on both your kidneys. The positive quality for the kidneys is *gentleness*. Fill your kidneys with the smiling energy of this virtue, as you let your smiling attention extend from your head and all the organs treated so far, to include your kidneys. One kidney is Yang and the other Yin—male and female, we might say. Smiling gently into the kidneys helps them both relax and come into balance with each other. Daily practice of this balancing act carries over into one's personal life. Men and women become more natural in their mode of social expression, rather than men sometimes acting effeminately or women behaving like men.

Now four of the five major organs have been treated to a nourishing feast of inner smiling energy. Bringing the spleen, which is the organ of balance, into awareness will complete the smiling down, version one process.

The Spleen

This is located under the left front lower rib cage, across the body from the liver.

As your attention extends from the kidneys and all the places in the body you have smiled into so far, try to feel that they are all connecting with and relating to the spleen. It doesn't matter that you may not know exactly what any of these organs look like. The main thing is that when you place your attention in any body area, you visualize the smiling energy in that area of the body as the quality of energy that organ is designed to run on. With the spleen we are projecting a balancing energy into the general vicinity of the spleen. As you mentally think "balance" into the spleen, notice how all the organs you have smiled into now feel to be *in balance with each other*. You feel to be in balance with yourself.

Smiling Down, Version Two

This variation on the technique works best after you have learned to heal your relationship with the internal organs using smiling down, version one, outlined above. Here too, you sit in silence. But instead of focusing mainly on the five major organs, once the smiling energy has been generated in the head, smile it through the entire body to the feet. You are passing a wave of loving energy through the throat and neck, onto and into the shoulders, down through the upper chest, solar plexus, stomach, abdomen, pelvic floor, and legs to the ground. You are feeling it move through the lungs and heart, liver, kidneys, and spleen, as well. But you are also aware of taking the smiling energy through the layers of skin, bloodstream, and all tissues. By the time you reach your feet, every cell of your body should be tingling with positive, live energy.

It is also very important to include your sexual organs in this flow of attention. Blockages and neglect of connection with this most powerful aspect of ourselves can produce multiple problems—physical, mental, and emotional. So be sure and smile into your genitals. Women should smile into their ovaries. If the ovaries have been removed, it is important to smile into them anyway, as if they are still there.

Amputees sometimes report that years after a limb has been removed, they can still feel the missing arm or leg. This phantom-limb effect happens because the physical body has an energetic counterpart, a double some-times referred to as the "astral" or "emotional" body. Exercises such as smil-ing down, or sensing and feeling, awaken our mental perception of this body of energy and can yield and almost tactile mental rapport with it. Daily practice of smiling through every physical organ and tissue gradually produces a continual sensed awareness of the second body as an energetic presence. The consciousness of the majority of people is trapped in, and limited to, the physical body they see and feel with their senses. This is a reality view of extremely limited perception. Those who hold to it have no clue that their sensate perceptions are limited because they have no com-parative experience of anything else.

Cultivating Consciousness in the Garden of Chi

The individual who cultivates a sensate awareness of a physical body, *and a second body made of the energy that vivifies the first,* has a supreme advan-tage over the one-dimensional type. The person who is plugged into the energy behind material creation is more apt to be in sync with a life that is nearer to the hidden forces that create the world around us. The circum-stances of such an individual's life start to unfold with an almost miracu-lous quality. The perception of reality is not limited to a world of material cause and effect. The "reality" of the material world becomes subordinate to a will and perception that has expanded beyond the "facts" of life. As we move up the staircase of evolution, we become free from the laws we were subordinate to previously. And we ourselves become a law governing that which we have just escaped. So, to have freedom and power we must expand—or atrophy.

No matter what physical limitations past situations have placed upon us, we can move toward freedom and renewal by smiling down. For exam-ple, if one has arthritis, one can smile into the affected area. This is the opposite of what normally happens when we are physically afflicted. Our first tendency is to hate the pain and try to get away from it. But in the act of smiling *into* the pain, something about the acceptance or acknowledgment that it exists can produce healing and, on occasion, instant relief.

I was once in the dentist chair when the anaesthetic began to wear off in the middle of prolonged drilling. Not wanting to have a second shot with its numbing mental fog aftereffect, I decided to smile into the pain. I focused with exact pinpoint accuracy at the spot where the drill was hitting the nerve—*and started to bliss out.* I could still feel the pain, but was in touch with a force of energy that was greater and seemed to have an insulating effect on the pain caused by the drill. The bliss got so intense that a huge smile started to cross my face. As it got wider and wider, the dentist, thinking that the pain was making me tighten up my face, asked me to relax my mouth. Little did he know that an "inner smile" was producing an altered state of consciousness while he performed his pain-inducing procedure—hence, the outer smile.

It follows from the foregoing that it is in our highest interest to develop a sensed awareness of the energetic results produced by the act of interior smiling. Combining this with sensing and feeling, and with self-remembering, enables us to manifest tremendous personal power. All the tools and techniques in this book are interconnected and interrelated. Doing one enhances the ability to do the others, and vice versa. There is no reason why one cannot be doing some aspect of these procedures all the time, assuming of course that one wishes to be conscious and not walk through life like an automaton.

Smiling Down, Version Three

Version three is for social situations. For example, while someone is speaking to us, we can be smiling down while listening. This puts us into a recharge mode so that we are easily gathering energy inwardly, while being outwardly attentive to the other person. Normally, when someone speaks to us, our minds free-associate based on our inferential understanding of the situation and what that person is saying to us. We may also experience a variety of subjective feelings—positive, negative, or confused. There is often a desire to jump in and grab the conversational ball as soon as the other person stops speaking. All this consumes energy. But if we smile down while listening, we stay relaxed and willing to listen, watching and waiting our turn to speak. When we do say something, we do not do so in an agitated manner, but with a measure of grace and focus.

I am smiling down all the time. (Even as I type these words, I am inwardly smiling.) There are few situations or circumstances that will not benefit from this procedure. Naturally, if one has suffered genuine loss or is experiencing major emotional pain, this needs to be acknowledged or perhaps treated therapeutically. When the natural recovery process starts, a genuine, heartfelt return to smiling down will help one return to normal quickly.

There are many circumstances in the course of a day when we can practice these techniques unbeknownst to anyone. Whether waiting for a red light to change or standing in line at the supermarket, one can always be "making a profit" from the radiance produced in one's inner world by this simple practice.

Smiling Down and Self-Remembering

To develop *I AM* consciousness, we must develop the knack of knowing who and what we are at all times, through self-remembering. Again, I must stress that this refers primarily to being connected to yourself at a soul level. Who and what you are in social definitions, while important, is secondary. If you can maintain connection with yourself at all times, your social self will find its right expression as a natural consequence.

Self-Remembering in Airports

Crowded public environments can be very useful for practicing heightened self-awareness. Airports are particularly useful because when we travel, the subconscious mind naturally unwinds. The flow of fresh impressions flushes out patterns of thought and reaction associated with our regular lives.

Travel today is fraught with the specter of international terrorism and we have to practically get undressed to board a plane. The potential for becoming irritated in an airport is high, in face of the surging crush of luggage-lugging bodies struggling toward check-in, the possibly rude attitude of individuals who scrutinize our tickets and ask inane questions of dubious necessity ("Did you pack your own bags?" "No, I hired Bag Packers Unlimited"), and finally the shoeless, arms-straight-out crucifixion stance as one is swept with an electronic phallic symbol, probing to see if one's body is wired to explode.

When a security checker asks me to extend my arms in an imitation of Christ, if I am sensing and feeling, I am more easily able to resist the temptation to say, "Father, forgive them for they know not what they do."

I always try to practice self-remembering as soon as I enter an airport. Putting myself in a state of reactive neutrality allows the intensity of energy generated by the heterogeneous activity in the terminal to fall upon my *essence* instead of my *personality*. Airports are places of flux and constant change—people are moving through life, they are going places. By sensing and feeling my arms and legs, I seem to pick up on the underlying current of transitional energy available in an airport at a deeper level than where potential annoyances exist. In other words, I can "eat" the energy of the place even while being subjected to major or minor annoyances.

I have found repeatedly that if I practice the above in any busy place that is alive with frenetic energy, a huge force of calm and certainty envelops me. It is as if the positive charge of energy in the environment, which is being obscured by the chaos, picks up on my practice and flies to me like iron filings to a magnet. This force wants to empower me. All I have to do is make myself available—first, by grounding the body, then by merging my human consciousness with the presence of a higher authority within myself: the *I* of *I AM*. Later I shall give you a very special technique to invoke the presence of *I AM* consistently.

While Eating, Avoid Negative Talk

Now let us explore a curious phenomenon that sometimes occurs when people eat in the company of others. If they are inclined to talk while eating, as the meal progresses, the quality of their conversational subject matter may turn negative.

Just as we breathe air to make our physical machinery turn over one more time, so should the act of ingesting food be a natural life-affirming action. Unfortunately, the enormous pressures and tensions of contemporary life make us tend to throw down our food in an unconscious manner. If we are allergic to our own bodies, as many people are, the act of eating becomes a double-bind process. We know we need to eat to keep going. But do we really want to be here? Do we like who we are? Are we pleased and excited about our prospective futures, or does tomorrow appear threatening, uncertain, and fearful? Most important, does eating stir the cells of our bodies into self-affirming vigor? Or does it activate negative cellular memories and unconscious states of allergy toward what one has made of oneself and life.

No Stress with My Curry, Please

While on a lecture tour, I was taken to an Indian restaurant by two gentlemen who were attached to the group hosting my presentation. We helped ourselves at an all-you-can-eat buffet and returned to our tables with sumptuously laden plates. We had hardly launched into the feast when the table conversation suddenly took a negative turn. Out of the blue, the gentleman on my right started talking about the horrors of the My Lai massacre during the Vietnam War.

What prompted this utterance escapes me now. But I remember the uneasy feeling that replaced the pleasant companionship that had prevailed prior to this shift. I put down my knife and fork and examined the speaker. Now that he had gone in this strange direction, my perception of him sharpened. I could clearly see that he was somewhat of a neurotic type, a factor I had not recognized before because I had been looking predominantly into his essence eye. As he saw me taking him in, the negative outpouring ground to a halt.

"This is a wonderful meal we have spread out before us," I said. "Might

I ask you to refrain from speaking about the horrors of war and other negative things while we eat?"

He caught himself at once and looked mortified. "Oh, I'm so sorry," he apologized. "I don't know what came over me."

"No need to apologize," I replied. "It happens. But negative conversation cancels out the value our body cells can receive from the process of eating."

Getting to the Positive

Notice that I addressed the problem at the Indian restaurant directly. I did not beat about the bush but came to the point right away. Out of our desire not to hurt other people's feelings, we often dance around verbally so much that they end up not knowing what it was exactly we wanted to bring to their attention. This does not mean we should go to the other extreme and preface a corrective suggestion with a phrase such as "Fred, I'm going to be brutally frank with you. . . ." As tactfully as possible, say the truth as it appears to you. And in a situation like the one described above, don't compromise. You are well within your rights to request that people behave in a positive way around you. When we are in a positive frame of mind and can hold it in the face of negative attitudes, we create an avenue by means of which others can exit from their delusions. We invite them to be more than they know they are. Here are a series of key elements that will help you to do this.

Bring Out the Best in Others

Begin by accepting people as they are. "Wouldn't it be wonderful if the world was more like thee and me" goes the old saying. Trying to change others by bullying, belittling, oppressing, directing, and/or criticizing them is a complete waste of time. Delivering "you" messages that tell other people they are wrong and you are right is equally futile. This does not mean that it is wrong to wish that other people would change their behavior in relation to us, especially if it is inimical to our well-being. This book is very much about getting others to change in relation to us, *but doing so by changing ourselves in relation to them!*

When you align yourself consciously with your body, mind, and emotions through the methods you are learning here, other people will automatically change in their actions and responses to you. By holding the field of coherence in and around yourself, you eliminate the propulsive desire to convert other people to your way of thinking. Your main aim is to stay focused and self-centered *no matter what.* In this manner, you silently invite other people to move beyond ego-driven conflict and align with their innate goodness, a quality they may have temporarily misplaced.

Compliment But Don't Flatter

We all like to feel that our best qualities are recognizable by others. A timely, well-placed compliment will often help people to shift into rapport with you. Criticism and fault-finding, on the other hand, tend to divide people. No one likes a character detective, someone who is always sniffing around looking for human weaknesses. Nevertheless, as you become more conscious through these practices, you *are* going to see the good, the bad, and the ugly of human behavior in a very clear way. Seeing it is one thing. "Telling it like it is," which is a cop-out phrase for being an opinionated jerk, is quite another. When you can clearly see other people's blind spots and weaknesses as simple, objective facts and feel no need to "let them have it," you will gain tremendous power.

The next stage of the game becomes even subtler. From a base of power, you may be able to gratify someone's ego without inflating it. Flattery is often based on recognition of a character flaw in someone that the deliverer tries to ignore by making the recipient blind to his or her own fault. *True* compliments, however, are a genuine recognition of an individual's *real* merit. They serve to reinforce natural self-confidence rather than inflate an ego.

Remember That Self-Interest Is a Prime Motivator

Generally speaking, we are motivated by our desire to create outcomes we think will enhance our lives. Knowing this, it is usually a good idea to focus on what other people want. Thus you can use *their* self-interest to sway them to go where you want *them* to go to serve *your* self-interest. This principle operates very much like Aikido. It takes into account the momentum of another individual's energy and quietly redirects it to the mutual advantage of both parties. The other person's self-interest consciously gets to be integrated into the human dynamic by you, the custodian of these principles. Most likely you will get what you want. And you will receive an influx of energy for self-remembering as a result of staying out of your head, sensing and feeling, and practicing divided attention during the social dynamic.

Try to find out what other people really want. If you impose what *you* think they want, they will feel frustrated. Many people don't really know what they want and they talk to find out for themselves what they are thinking, feeling, and seeking. This is especially true for women. Endeavor to see and hear the underlying subtext of any conversation to sense the underlying motivations. Desire is a prime motivator. If you can help people to get what they want, they will be naturally disposed to help you.

Be a Good Listener

Listen to people with full attention. While they are speaking, don't think about what you will say when they shut up. Do sensing-and-feeling awareness, or grounding in the earth. But don't let people go on and on forever and don't let attention hogs take you hostage. Many of us are in love with the sound of our own voice and once a "motor-mouth" gets started, it is sometimes hard to get a word in edgewise. Try not to interrupt, but look for the moment when the conversation provides you with a natural opportunity to take the ball. Then grab it and run with it and keep going until you are far away from the subject that fascinates them. Once on your own turf, you can call the shots.

Hold On to Self-Mastery

All people yearn for self-mastery and a sense that they are not at the mercy of others. When we make people feel inadequate, they will want to avoid us because we deprive them of a sense of personal power. But we can help them when we subliminally let them know the following:

> They cannot control us
> We do not wish to control them
> Together, the two of us will be able to access a space where we are both in control of ourselves.

Your self-mastery through nonreactivity is a great gift to others, because it uplifts and unifies those you encounter. They are able to align momentarily with *their* innate though forgotten potential for self-mastery through meeting you. On some level, you are giving them a temporary experience of emotional security. Lack of self-confidence engenders fear and further loss of self-confidence. When your self-mastery helps people to feel more emotionally secure, their increased self-confidence enhances *your* sense of emotional well-being. Perhaps the universe works on a principle of reciprocal maintenance or mutual nourishment, and we human beings feed off one another's thoughts, feelings, and states of energy. By staying in high-quality, cohesive states of self-connection, you ensure that when what you have been putting out comes back to you on the menu in the cosmic food chain, it will be a dish you can happily ingest.

Cultivate Dignity

This will increase your self-respect and earn the respect of others. Nine times out of ten, they will mirror you. Even if someone tries to undermine your dignity, keep it at all times. I clearly remember the great Welsh actor Richard Burton keeping his cool brilliantly on *The Dick Cavett Show* on PBS television back in the late 1970s. Cavett had Burton on five days in a row. It was obvious that a life of too much boozing and wild living had long since deprived the guest of the great vigor that had animated his early years of success. Nevertheless, it was fascinating to hear Burton rattling off great streams of poetry with his magnificent voice and recounting tales of show-biz life, both amusing and horrifying.

At one point Burton began to talk about the perils of alcoholism. He came from a family of coal miners in South Wales. Drinking was an omnipresent fact of life for the miners. It washed the coal dust from their throats and blunted the hard edge of the lives they led buried beneath the earth. Burton told of many roaring good times at the local pub. But then, as he got deeper into his discourse on the bottle, the Welsh bard in him came out and he poignantly said something to this effect about the downside of drinking.

> When the night is miserable and long and you're stuck in a motel in the middle of nowhere, in your drunken stupor the past rises up to torment you. You stare out the window watching the rain and see the faces of all those you have hurt through carelessness or indifference to their humanity. They haunt you like Caesar's ghost came to Brutus before the Battle of Philippi and you feel that you are the most wretched person on the face of the earth.

He paused for a moment and someone in the studio audience snickered, quite audibly and definitely on purpose. I am sure Burton heard it. But he did not bat an eyelid. He just kept on going, saying what he wanted to say. When he was done, he closed with these final words on alcoholism, which I clearly remember: "And I would like to assure you, on behalf of anyone who has ever suffered from this terrible disease, . . . it is no laughing matter."

I thought at the time, and still do, that Burton handled this with amazing dignity.

Here was some ill-mannered non-entity out in the audience, seizing an opportunity to have a go at a major public figure. Whatever personal failings Richard Burton may have had as a human being, he was an enormous talent. And he had certainly lived. Can we say the same of that individual in the audience who snickered? What type of people are so impotent that all they can do is throw mud at the carriage of a king as it goes past? We are all royalty and even a fallen king should be worthy of our respect.

Remembering this incident, I have always tried to keep my own dignity in the face of petty provocation. There is a saying: "If a fool calls me a fool I am none the worse for it, whereas he remains what he always was."

Try to keep your cool at all times and bear in mind that you are not going to get everyone you meet to replicate your emerging state of *I AM* consciousness. Christ couldn't do it and neither could Gandhi, who was killed by a madman. Jesus forgave his executioners and Gandhi forgave his killer, bowing to the God he saw in him as he sank to the ground. When we encounter those who would stamp out our joy and kill our consciousness with cruelty, negative remarks, and unpleasant behavior, we can still see God in them. Even if you have to give someone a metaphoric kick up their metaphysical backside, do it with forgiveness and with self-remembering. And keep your dignity.

CHAPTER ELEVEN

Awakening Identity in a World of Sleep

Change Yourself and Change the Dream

The world we touch and see is essentially an illusion. What else can we call the seemingly solid surfaces of tables and chairs, when in reality we know they are made of atoms and molecules? In a sense, our lives take place in a hologram of perceptions that have no more substance than a dream. Strangely, though, the dream seems changeable according to our understanding of it. If our *internal* perceptions of what life means are dense and gross, the life we experience *externally* will mirror the dullness of our insight. But if we have a refined sensibility of purpose, evolving an awareness of ourselves as souls *through self-effort,* what we experience within the hologram will reflect that. The natural order of the holographic substance of matter around us—"reality"—appears to be variable by our perception of it. Life shifts the way it responds to us materially according to our level of consciousness as we interface with it.

On several occasions, in altered states of awareness (such as when I got "zapped" by Mataji), I have clearly seen by direct experience that no one is actually "doing" anything. All that takes place in, around, and through us, as we journey through life, simply happens. And it happens in the same way that the sun rises, the stars shine, the wind blows, and the rain falls. The "reality" hologram is an automatic response system. When we are asleep in our own potentiality as vehicles for expanding consciousness and live as automatons, the world around us appears rigid, hard, and limited. As we open up to spiritual ideas, our perceptions change and the world as we have known it begins to change. It becomes fluid, flowing, and malleable. This shows us that matter is a manifestation of the formless spirit masquerading as form and as such it has the potential for infinite adaptability.

When we get this, not just as an idea, but as a direct, consciously experienced perception, the "reality," the doing that is being done through us that we see as our daily lives, happens at a new level of coherence and meaning. To repeat, as we change, the quality of what can be done in the world—*in, through, and around us*—starts to reflect the change in us. Life opens up in amazing new ways.

Sensing and Feeling the World As Your Larger Self

Once we've begun to feel our own bodies as energetic presence, we progress to sensing and feeling the same in trees, animals, cars, tables and chairs, the walls of the rooms we are in, and other people, as being alive with the essential underlying radiance of life itself. *That life is who and what we are!* When we connect directly with the *transpersonal* energy from which the *personal* world of our everyday relationships emerges, we bring *enlightening energy* into our interactions with other people. It doesn't matter if they are personally aware of it at the time or not. When we are in a self-remembered state, we are transmitting to the world and other people varying aspects of *the power of I AM consciousness.*

Just looking at someone while "holding the field" of power and presence will cause their souls to wake up for a moment and look back at you *through them. Enlightened personal interaction* is taking place, even as their habit-run, programmed selves sleep on in the collective trance that I saw holding my mother and sister in its grip years ago when Mataji awakened me.

Sometimes you may see a person's higher self, looking through the sleeping self and at you, watching while the sleeping personality continues to talk and move about in the same old patterns of behavior. Even if this only happens for a split second, you have changed the dream. Enlightened personal interaction appeared momentarily. The *I AM* in you looked at the *I AM* in that person. The individual before you started to experience self-remembering. If his or her personal self had been behaving badly just prior to that awakening moment, it would dry up. If he or she were ridiculing your interest in spirituality, the arguments would suddenly sound hollow and foolish. The person would move from an egotistic, separatist state toward an awareness of the unity of all life. This experience may be, for that person, the briefest burst of real consciousness.

Flashing the World Awake

When consciousness explodes in the cells of a human brain, even for a microsecond, sooner or later, the sleeping state of that individual is going to change. This is how the world will be remade—one person at a time, experiencing a higher reality. Through the real manifesting in the unreal, the hologram will eventually become more coherent. The quality of what can be done in, through and around us will collectively change our disenchantment about life into hopefulness. The world will always be a dream world. But by accessing higher consciousness, the supernal reality of our own being, the *I AM* that we are, *we access the power to change the dream.* We know what is real and from that knowing, we know how to change our human selves at will and by extension, *change the world.*

Stage One Awakening

When we first start to awaken, our personal experiences begin to reflect that change. We meet people of like mind. We are drawn to books that open us up still further. We start to have experiences of personal freedom from matter, and begin to know matter and ourselves directly, as different forms of energy.

Reading books and getting inspired by spiritual ideas, however, is simply *stage one* awakening. Certainly there is a rush of energy and a sense of liberation and life renewal in this phase, and this is natural and good. Should we not feel like rejoicing when we see that the bars of the prison that cage the human race exist only in minds that cannot directly see the illusory nature of the illusion? Because of this, in the beginning, we tend to tell everyone we meet that everything is an illusion. I know I did after my initial awakening.

Stage Two Awakening

After the first rush subsides, those who are successfully transitioning to higher consciousness enter the second phase. In the first stage there has been a huge download of information about consciousness and higher possibilities. The uplift that came from mentally grasping visionary possibilities created a high that is similar to being able to see Mt. Everest from the valley and imagining that one was already at the top, simply because one could see the peak. Actually getting up there requires tools and techniques that will rewire our body, mind, and emotional nature. We must go through these changes in order to withstand the enormous voltage that all three levels of spiritual awakening require. The techniques in this book empower us to transition successfully through the first three stages of awakening. They develop the will necessary to have the self-government of body, mind, and emotions that higher consciousness needs to express through us.

If we stay at the first level, eventually the exhilaration from the downpour of information in books and from various teachers dries up and we start to feel empty again. But by consciously establishing a daily routine of self-awareness inducements, such as sensing and feeling, self-remembering, and so on, the energy from stage one transitions to *stage two*. We then become capable of generating a high current of energy for ourselves and receive a transmission of spiritual power from the world around us. Matter starts to open up and reveal its inner essence as energy. As we become aware of this underlying reality through *directly sensed experience* (seeing the world and life made up of spiritual substance), our ability to know matter as an attribute of consciousness feeds into our body cells, which are also made of matter. They and we become more "energized" by life.

The more we see God in everything the more "godlike" we become. This is why spiritual people often seem more vibrant than the "matter is only matter" crowd, who stay where they are, unable to mentally transition into perceptions of higher possibilities. The lives of those who *have* transitioned become for those who cannot shift more and more incomprehensible. Moving up the ladder of consciousness in successive stages, we escape from the limitation of the laws that rule the realm beneath us. In stage two, we are learning to take command ourselves and be more fully in our bodily instruments in a conscious way. We are aware of ourselves more of the time, but can still fall back into the illusion on occasion.

Stage Three Awakening

After spending some weeks or months getting consciously connected with ourselves, we may start to become *conscious of consciousness itself.* An animal does not know that it is conscious. It exists but cannot stand off to one side and observe itself and say "this is me, I exist." A human being *can* do this. We are capable of being conscious that we are conscious. We *can* say "this is me, I exist." But when we are conscious of consciousness itself, we are beyond words and self-conceptualizing. This is the realm of pure feeling in which we experience our formless essence as a presence. We sense and feel a primal energy that permeates not only our own bodies, but those of everyone else and even the objects around us in the world "out there." We see *directly* that Maya, the great illusion, is made up of nothing *but* consciousness. The "reality" we give to the various aspects of the illusion we appear to be seeing around us is all in our heads!

When we put our hand on a tabletop and feel its solid surface, we are in touch with the last stop in a creative process coming out of the formless consciousness behind creation. As we touch matter, we are touching pure consciousness frozen into form within an *eternal living mind.* Becoming conscious of the all-permeating atmosphere of omnipresent consciousness manifesting as ourselves and in illusory creation around us is *stage three awakening.* This type of seeing does not happen all at once, nor when it first starts to manifest will it be there all the time. We have visits from it when we are in stage two, as well as visits *to* it. These become more frequent and last longer and can become more or less permanent the more conscious we become. Four things can hinder us on this journey:

Giving way to negative emotional energy and being possessed by it
Identifying with our reactions to the stuff people throw at us from
their personal confusion under the influence of Maya

Through worry and frustration, unnecessarily losing the energy it
takes to stay in the higher states for long periods
Inability to sustain and maintain a sense of personal identity when
faced with the self-hypnosis of limited consciousness that enslaves
millions and keeps the world in delusion

The principles and techniques in this book will enable you to stand
unshaken under the many pressures within and without. You can learn to
roam in the madness of the world like a giant of self-mastery, through
directive leadership of all your faculties of body, mind, and emotion. All it
takes is your willingness to actually do some work and go beyond this book
and all books to the next level, which is . . .

Stage Four Awakening: Seeing Truth Directly

In the first stage, books and teachers play an extremely important role.
They awaken interest in spiritual matters, speak directly to our awakening souls, and set our feet on the right path. They propel us forward and
if we successfully journey through the next two stages and enter the fourth,
these initial tools will have served their purpose and helped move us to a
"seeing" that is beyond words. No longer dependent on books and words
to know the truth about anything, we shall see it directly for ourselves.

There was a time when we had no words in our heads. As babies we saw
the essence of colors, flowers, the clouds, the sky, and people's faces, with
untrammeled perceptions. We experienced Plato's "seeing the thing in
itself" without overlaying onto it our projections based on past associa-
tions derived from similar objects and situations.

By the time we reach *stage four awakening,* we have learned to look at
anything we see and not go into our heads. We can *see without words* and
stop labeling, codifying, comparing, sorting through, filing and storing,
rectifying, judgment forming, rejecting, accepting, and all the other things
our inner mental idiots do to separate us from life.

G. I. Gurdjieff, the Rabelaisian Greek-Armenian teacher and notorious disturber of human complacency, once pounced on one of his students and said forcefully, *"All the time you are thinking, thinking! I am looking."*

Direct Seeing

Can you imagine just looking at things and seeing them without your brain churning out verbal commentary? Words are simply the labels we use to describe objects. They are not the "things in themselves" and yet they have taken over our lives. An individual who *sees directly* is not possessed by words. Truth is not perceived with the word-thinking mind but with the atoms. When you know something on a cellular level, you are in sync with the truth inherent in the atoms of the objects of your perceptions. Be it a tree, a flower, a brick wall, or a person, suddenly what you are seeing is alive with the energy that underlies all creation. You are *seeing* truth directly because you are vibrating with it in yourself and so you see it everywhere.

This "seeing of truth" can happen when you are talking to a person and there is confusion in the dynamic. Suddenly, without reasoning in the usual way, you see and know the truth of the situation exactly. And you are able to speak from that truth with a sense of unshakable certainty that clears up the confusion for everyone concerned.

Your personal clarity acts as a power that initiates momentary restoration to wholeness for people who are confused. Confusion arises from forgetting that *I AM* has become ourselves. Self-remembering restores us to memory of *I AM* as a conscious experience, to a greater or lesser degree, dependent on our skill in invoking it through practice. When we connect with it, confusion of personal identity ceases. Low self-esteem and the truth that comes from direct experience of oneself as a divine being cannot coexist. The greater power (true seeing) cancels out the negation of the lower power (perceptions of life based upon illusions), and by its silent presence, restores people to who they are—*I AM* manifesting as people with all the best qualities we human beings should embody as brothers and sisters.

Direct Action

Being able to enter into this state of dual awareness, that is, being fully human while infused with higher-power energy and presence as we deal with people, can trigger others into experiencing it as well. This process works through induction. One magnetic coil charges up another with the same current, until both are vibrating on a higher level. When we get into a state of *I AM* consciousness in the face of interpersonal difficulty, that state causes other individuals to *replicate our state*. To some degree, they feel the power and the presence of *I AM* in themselves and behavioral shifts can occur.

This is the essence of true leadership. We are enlightening through personal interaction with their "sleeping" personality-identified selves, as we charge up their mortal coil with a degree of presence. Sometimes we have to hold this field of higher consciousness while we deliver an "awakening shock" to someone who is behaving inappropriately toward us This does not require that we ourselves get verbally abusive. But it does mean *not being afraid to speak out when necessary in a direct, powerful, even forceful manner that brooks no opposition*. The double whammy of consciousness and speech directed to make a point is extremely powerful. No need to raise your voice and yell. It is often more effective to talk *under* someone who is incensed. They raise their voice and you lower yours in tone and volume, while speaking with a deadly calm and self-assurance. But if ever you do have to yell, be sure to practice sensing and feeling, divided attention and self-remembering. Then you will simply be playing a role, acting out to achieve a result with no malice, desire for revenge, or intent to wound.

The Magical Power of the Third Force

We don't need to get caught up emotionally in other people's dream, delusion, or upsets. We can seduce them with higher power. Let us suppose someone is mad at you and having an apoplectic fit in your face. You can still feel the reality of who that person is as presence behind the ludicrous behavior. And instead of letting yourself be manipulated into receiving the full brunt of his or her negativity, you can stand unshaken ("arms," "legs"). When the storm has passed by without upsetting you, there is a chance for that person to come around.

The highest outcomes we can have with people happen because the *third force*—function #3, the reconciling power—is present. Remember electron and proton? Two mutually contradictory forces are brought into harmony by a third, neutralizing element, the neutron. So it is with people. They are annoying each other with opposing viewpoints and then, suddenly, reconciliation happens. The more you practice the techniques you have been learning and fill yourself with presence, the more you will be able to embody the reconciling power. Balancing the positive and negative charges of electromagnetism in your body will create the third force in and around you. Eventually the felt result of this *I AM* consciousness can become so strong that everywhere you go, your balanced energy field automatically switches the confused human mechanisms you encounter into greater balance and harmony. You are creating a new world because you are demonstrating it yourself.

The more fully this *seeing* the world through *I AM* consciousness is embodied, the more it can touch and awaken the essential nature of anyone caught in the great cosmic dream of Maya who is receptive to awakening influences. When this truth manifests through us, it can bring order to social confusion and transform egotistical, ignorant behavior with a look. This *true seeing* can only manifest within our consciousness *when we are in a state of presence.*

Again, techniques such as sensing and feeling and divided attention move one in the direction of stage four awakening because they use the mind to scan the body. They act upon the mind like a Zen koan. Forced to stop being "logical"—thinking in established patterns—the mind switches into a different mode and produces pure (nonword thinking) consciousness that fills the body with presence. People who have gotten to stage four awakening can do this at will, anytime, anyplace, even in the midst of intense social pressure. Their sense of themselves is based primarily on being in this state and not upon external identity support systems. Thus they cannot be so easily shaken by others. They know *who* they are because they can experience *what* they are.

I Am, Therefore I Think—But Who Is It That I Think I Am?

The famous dictum of René Descartes, "I think, therefore I am," is a reversal of a more profound perception: We can reason only because *we are.* Therefore it is more accurate to state "I am, therefore I think." Unfortunately, as we develop a social self-identity while growing up, a necessary ingredient just to get through life, we become so identified with or obsessed with *who we think we are,* that eventually we start to believe we *are* who we think we are. Remember my definition of an egotist? (He thinks he is who he thinks he is.) However, if we can consciously develop an observational stance from a soul level toward our personality structure, we can enjoy playing our roles in the world without becoming swallowed up by them. We can mold our personalities to be anything we want them to be, much as an actor shapes a character to make it of engaging interest to the audience.

No one in the world can really play you but *you!* Why not go for it and give an award-winning performance as yourself by consciously acting out who and what you want to appear as in the world. *Just remember, it is only a part you are playing and behind the actor's mask (persona) is the real you— the I AM. Don't get lost in the role through overidentification, and have fun doing it.*

It's Time to Play ... (Drum Roll) the "What's in a Name" Game

Cary Grant was recently voted the most popular movie star of all time. But where did his amazingly suave personality come from? Grant started out in life as Archibald Leach and modeled the persona we recognize by copying British actor and stage personality Jack Hulbert. When Michael Caine was about to play his first major movie role, he realized that the name Maurice Micklewhite might not cut it on a marquee. He had already decided on Michael as the first name. When he passed a movie theater that was playing *The Caine Mutiny*, the light switched on and he took his second name from that.

A longtime Cary Grant fan (both originally being Cockneys), Caine finally got to meet his hero in London, while shooting a movie there himself. The company was filming in a hotel and as Caine turned down a corridor one morning on his way to the set, who should he see coming in the opposite direction but Cary Grant.

As Caine drew near to Grant, he pointed at him and said, "You're Cary Grant!"

"Yes," replied the actor (imagine the voice). "I know."

Which is a perfect Cary Grant line. Curiously, when asked during a television interview "Who is Cary Grant?" the actor could only reply ruefully, "I wish I knew."

Again the question of true self-identity proved illusive. Grant created himself based upon another actor he admired. Somehow his globally recognized personal style emerged from this, but it was really based on a facade he had created. In his later years, he took LSD more than sixty times in an attempt to find out who he really was. Being able to step back and observe his personality structure as if it were someone else awakened Grant's essence. He became more authentically connected to and identified with his "inner self" (essence). Finally, he was able to merge his essence with his acquired personality and make it highly authentic. By the time Cary Grant died, he had become the Cary Grant he had always wanted to be!

Jack Nicholson said he learned to kiss by watching people in the movies do it. John Wayne, a.k.a. Marion Morrison, learned to move like a cowboy by watching *his* idol, early western screen star Harry Carey, and was coached in his walk by character actor Paul Fix. Working with veteran stuntman and action director Yakima Cannutt helped develop the Wayne style, as did being molded for stardom by the great director John Ford.

We may not personally know the people we admire whose images have shaped our lives. But in the best sense, they can represent an ideal that supports development of our personality as we find our social feet. This type of "borrowing" falls in the realm of mentoring by proxy. Nor should the fact that none of us know who we are preclude deriving enjoyment from playing our role as the social self we later become, whatever the sources of influence. There is nothing wrong with this. We all learn from each other and a touch of *conscious imitation* can be better than simply *unconscious replication of unconscious people*. But we must make sure that we eventually become our own person with a powerful and valid social persona—a sense of *me* and *I* that is not prey to accidental evils and is under our own jurisdiction and control. From this our "true" image will arise. Instead of being ruled by *false personality* and its attendant insecurities, we shall express *true personality* as a natural reflection of the soul.

Image Can Be Important When It No Longer Needs to Be

The strange thing is, the less we place our dependency upon image, the more we can feel free to express and enjoy whatever image we choose to display at any given moment. To be bound and dependent upon the external impressions we create is too limiting. Having a deep connection with the core of our being and enjoying expressing the variety of personal attributes available to us can be immensely satisfying. But first we must be able to recognize which parts of us belong to the soul and which aspects are transitory.

Personal Identity: Who Is *I* and Who Is *Me?*

What is the sequence of perception that makes us conscious of our own existence?

First, we are aware of our physical bodies, through sensations and actions. In conjunction, we experience emotions through our feeling function. The mind, which observes these processes, tries to make sense of them and the world around us. But each of us intuits a certain "something" within that is more fundamental than our instruments of expression.

It is the sensed *I* of our own existence, the underlying reality of our own being. If we ask ourselves what is the nature of this *I*, it simply tells us "I Am That I Am"—that "It" exists on an impersonal level and because of this, *we* exist on the personal level, as a human extension of our own unknowable depths. The root cause of our existence is therefore, we might say, this *self of ourselves.* Few of us have direct access to the power of this *I*, even though it underlies all the rest of our consciousness.

Self-remembering induces the *I* to manifest through us, so that we can live from a place of great power and personal security. When this is fully accomplished, a marriage will have taken place between that which resides at the core of our being—the *I* of the *I AM*—and that which arises from the human personality expression we know as *me.*

When we are primarily connected with *I*, and secondarily our sense of *me*, the different aspects of our personal self naturally become more focused, coherent, creative, and stable. When we try to live *without* a sense of connection with the *I*, it is hard to consistently enjoy being *me.* In such a state, the many different aspects of our human complexity will have no self-governing reference point. Our personal stability then depends upon which part of us predominates psychologically at any given moment.

Most of us would like to be consistent in our self-expression toward others. We would also like to feel that we are capable of giving and receiving of ourselves in a dependable manner. Too often, our behavioral inconsistency interferes with our ability to be who we truly want to be in social situations. We cannot always produce the various aspects of the personal self, or *me*, with dependable integrity. Ever frozen when your picture was being taken?

But when the personal *me* aspect is governed and supported by the externalized power of the indwelling *I*, the alchemy of our personal charisma blossoms naturally. Thus our human insecurity and inconsistency become minimized and manageable. This is no mean feat in our terrifying age.

Finding the Beauty of *Me*

I believe that what we refer to as *me,* our personal self, is meant to be a rich expression of unique individuality. The ideal person would be many-hued with charming and intelligent variations on a theme of who and what he or she is in the great human drama. Such people would have easy access to any part of themselves at any given moment. But when uncontrollable expressions of the *me* run away with our best intentions, they leave us personally dumbfounded. Lacking a true north, a guiding center of gravity within ourselves, we can become emotionally and psychologically disassociated.

When disconnected from the center, the *me* aspects of ourselves may say and do things that the *I* would never dream of doing. This is why criminals often protest their innocence by repeatedly affirming "I didn't do it!" And they may be right. It was not their *I* that did it, but some small aspect of personal predisposition living in the suburbs of behavioral instinct that momentarily called itself "I." This imposter got into the driver's seat and acted out through the total personality with a momentary voice of authority, usurping the regency of the *I* of *I AM.*

Our crimes against one another are committed by coalitions of our personal psychology we cannot control. They can possess us temporarily. We *become* them, and later, other aspects of ourselves deny their actions. Unfortunately, sometimes all the other parts of us have to pay for the indiscretions of the foolish aspects of ourselves.

I represents the soul, spiritual values, and inner stability. Is it any wonder that we suffer from low self-esteem when *me* lets us down and fails to act before others in a manner consistent with our ideal self-regard. *Me* is like a kaleidoscope containing millions of personality fragments that life twists and turns into new patterns and shapes second by second. Trying to keep the personality stable by "fixing" in our consciousness those aspects of the *me* self we like and would prefer to manifest all the time before others, is impossible. Living with a sense of *me* separated from *I* compels us to actually *become,* temporarily, any of the random kaleidoscopic patterns of thought, feeling, and reaction that occur as life turns the wheel of circumstance. On the other hand, being centered in the *I* is like grasping the kaleidoscope with both hands. Then we can hold it firmly and look through it to observe the good, the bad, and the ugly in ourselves with objectivity.

This gives us the psychological *inner space* to observe and be consciously selective of which aspects of our personality kaleidoscope we wish to express before others. With practice, we can learn to predominantly externalize the truly noble aspects of ourselves and share this richness with others. When we learn to live, move, and have our being centered in *I,* it is *we ourselves* who turn the wheel and create the personality spectrum of *me* we offer to the world. The result is spontaneity, charisma, right thought, right action, charm, grace, intelligence, wit, ease of being, forthright but appropriate self-expression, a sense of invincibility, personal harmony, and peace.

The Secret Treasure of Spiritual Success

The jewel in the crown of spiritual development may well be the reclamation of our most precious, intimate, and human selves: the elevation of the *me* aspect to perfect functioning. By infusing the personality structure with the energy of higher consciousness, of *I AM,* we re-endow ourselves with what we had when we were babies and lost along the way: the absolute beauty of the *me* aspect raised to spiritual maturity in a state of marriage with the soul.

When we can enter such a state, either through grace or consciously directed self-inducement, we will be naturally empowered by a great sense of *personal well-being.* The intelligence that has shaped the universe will directly influence our actions. We shall move through life as if guided by invisible radar beams to the highest outcome for our good on a consistent basis. This same force will also *redirect* the actions of those individuals who would hinder our evolutionary progress and confound any obtuseness they may exhibit toward us. Living in *I AM* consciousness is the greatest protection, because it centers us in a state that is *beyond duality* when almost everyone we meet is living *in it!*

People align themselves with confused life outcomes because of egocentric motives. The root of their action is not pure. Those who think and act from such a state of unconsciousness will *dumfound themselves before us when we are aligned with I AM consciousness.* The consequences of such misguided actions by others often take a humorous form. Let me tell you of when I was a "village idiot" and the universe defended me from ridicule.

The Three Farmer Stooges

I was living on Anglesey, a beautiful island off the coast of North Wales, where I had spent a lot of time as a child. In 1972 I had returned to its glorious vistas, clean air, and peaceful atmosphere. I wanted to try and make a supercharged spiritual breakthrough into higher consciousness through meditation and fasting. Many wonderful states came to me as I struggled to extract myself from the self-limiting patterns of the past.

The local farmers, like most people who live close to the land, had a nose for anything or anyone who seemed a bit out of the ordinary. I soon became aware that I was the object of muttering and snickering among three men who worked on the farmlands where I lived in a mobile home. As I would pass them on my way to the local shops, often in a state of expanded awareness, they would exchange knowing looks and "nudge, nudge, wink, wink" at one another. I could just hear their Welsh accents saying:

"Look out, boy-o, 'ere he comes again."

"Bloody peculiar if you ask me."

"Nutty as a fruitcake."

Normally I would simply ignore them and walk on as if they were not there, while trying to keep my dignity. I had already had some practice runs at staying centered with these three. Once they had caught me performing a healing ritual while hugging a tree. This had not helped reassure them of my sanity. (Every evolving spiritual person knows that tree hugging to get healed is par for the course, right?) And their observations of me swinging my head from side to side, while drawing an imaginary black line across the sky from a visualized paintbrush attached to my nose and blinking at the sun, had probably not helped either. (I was doing the Bates eye re-education exercises … what's the big deal?) In every British shire (at least in novels), there is usually a village idiot. Well, these Welsh farmers had me on their list as the number one candidate for the local office.

One morning I left my trailer and headed for the farm to get some milk. But this was not an ordinary day since I was experiencing an altered state. It was a variation on the experience when I got zapped by Sri Mataji and saw everyone asleep. Experiences like these were starting to come by themselves and this one produced a sensation of being spread out in consciousness over a vast area in every direction. As I walked, I seemed to be moving over the periphery of my own expanded being as *I AM* consciousness. The trees, the sky, the blue ocean, and the distant mountains were all myself, as were the cows, the sheep, and even the three jolly farmers. Crossing a field, I saw them doing some work on the pathway up ahead. They were about to drive a thick wooden post into the ground, right in the middle of the small opening that led from one field to the next. Since this was the only exit, I would have to pass right through the midst of them as they labored on, while laughing at me among themselves.

As I drew nigh, one man was on his knees holding the post, another standing and holding it higher up. The third was preparing to swing a large mallet, to hammer the top of the post and drive it into the ground. As I drew near, the kneeling man saw me coming and made some smart remark to the other guy holding the post. He looked my way with a smirk. But as he did so, his distraction caused the post to move off center as the third man was swinging his mallet toward it with both hands. The mallet curved through the air with all the weight he could muster behind it. But instead of landing smack on top of the post, it bounced off the edge and hit the chap who was standing to hold it on the arm. He cursed and let go of the post, which then toppled over, taking the kneeling man with it. At the same time, the mallet swinger lost his balance and fell forward on top of his buddies. As the post toppled to the ground, all three of them joined it, sprawling about in a tableaux grotesque of writhing limbs and curses. Meanwhile, still blissed out of my noggin, I passed through this melee as if guided by invisible radar beams of cosmic intelligence and entered the next field unscathed.

I had not needed to personally defend myself. Attunement with higher forces led me through the midst of their intended mockery. They undid themselves and became the village idiots in a scene that could have been lifted from the Three Stooges. From this experience, I learned that there is a level of attunement where we don't need to defend ourselves in the conventional sense. When we are in tune with higher laws, those who would gainsay us simply align themselves with denser laws. The grossness of their behavior cannot touch us as they create for themselves a lesson from a universe that reflects their own density of perception.

The Marriage of *Me* and *I*

You can see from this true story that the greatest security we can have, in the face of antagonism and the inner and outer complexities of life, is to be consciously connected with an unchanging sense of self at the core of our being. Imagine a central column of magnetic power within your psyche, around which the whirlwind of your ever-changing thoughts, moods, feelings, and personal expressions can revolve. Would not such an inner identity serve as magnetic north to the wild compass point rotations of confusion and insecurity that plague the human ego?

Who does not long to be free from any automatic imposition upon our sense of freedom and self-determination by our ingrained habitual responses to life? And who does not wish to feel secure and effective in a world where personal and national insecurity is a phenomenon of epidemic proportions? Such freedom and security can only come to us when we can place our attention, at will, upon a real and permanent sense of *I* within ourselves? To reiterate, we might describe *I* as our *transpersonal* sense of self and *me* as the *personal self,* the human expression that makes us recognizable to the world at large, if not always to ourselves.

Everything you have been learning in this book helps to fuse the *I* and the *me* into a unified working whole. Sensing and feeling, divided attention, and self-remembering are practices that naturally move us toward a blending of the personal and transpersonal. Instead of soul and ego being at odds, a marriage is created between our spiritual and human selves. Each serves the other in a blend of mutually beneficial cooperation. In a world where the contentious aspects of human nature seem to be running wild, the power that comes from uniting *me* and *I* accelerates our evolutionary possibility.

The Tree of Life Is the Spine and the Brain

To effect the marriage of *me* and *I*, we must connect with the latter *first*. Then our personality will restructure itself around our perception of an unmistakable internal energy that we recognize as *I AM*—the underlying source of our very being.

This power continually pulsates in and around the central column of the spine, which acts as a lighting rod as it transmits energy from our sexuality to the brain and back down again. According to the Taoists, the entire cerebrospinal system is designed to receive and transmit the energy of the earth and the universe through the entire body and radiate it out into the world. From that perspective, the human body-mind organism can be seen as an apparatus created for the reception, generation, and processing of certain energetic substances that serve cosmological purposes.

Individuals who truly understand this, not as a mental concept, but feel the truth of it in the cells of their body, cannot be egotists. They know that their desires and ambitions, valid as they appear to be, pale to insignificance when they consciously allow themselves to become mobile transmitting stations for the Holy Spirit. They know that *I AM* is the doer of all actions and place the flow of divine energy through themselves as a first priority in their lives.

CHAPTER TWELVE

I AM and Self-Remembering

Way Back Then—When God Spoke Zen!

The name of God, as delivered to Western civilization through our Judeo-Christian heritage is I Am That I Am. What can a world that has "sold its soul for a mass of disconnected facts," to quote Carl Jung again, make of such an ambiguous statement? Obviously, it is over our information-stuffed heads. In her book *The History of God*, Karen Armstrong somewhat laughably declares that when Moses faced off with God on Mount Sinai and asked His name and got "I Am That I Am" for an answer, he was being told to mind his own business. If so, it is a strange God that would guide Moses through the blistering desert after being banished from Egypt, deliver a vision of Himself on a mountain, and then basically tell Moses to piss off. What Armstrong fails to grasp is the almost Zen koanlike nature of the statement "I Am That I Am." The rational mind can make nothing of it. Similarly, if we were to go on a Buddhist retreat and be told to stare at a blank wall for ten days, while asking ourselves over and over, "Does the dog have a Buddha nature?" our ordinary human intelligence would be unable to supply an answer. But out of striving to grasp the intellectually ungraspable, there might occur a breakdown of the ordinary logical mind that could create an altered state of consciousness, a direct perception of truth beyond "rationality."

The Transforming Power in Myth and Legend

Whether one sees the Old Testament as divine revelation or a collection of Jewish fairy stories, Moses' encounter with the burning bush is ripe for exciting metaphysical interpretation. Joseph Campbell's popular PBS television series *The Power of Myth* opened up many people to the notion that truth is not to be found in literal fact, but in the mythic dimensions contained in legend, folk tales, and fantastic stories. Let us look at the Mount Sinai close encounter with God from this perspective.

Moses sees a light high up on a holy mountain reputed to be the home of God and says, "I shall turn aside and see this wonder." *Turning aside means withdrawing from the affairs of ordinary, external activity, going within and having one's consciousness internalized, as in meditation.* He then climbs Sinai, the sacred mountain.

This "going up" represents ascension in consciousness. Arriving close to the summit, Moses sees that the light comes from a bush, burning with a fire that does not consume it. With his consciousness now interiorized, the personality of Moses and his ordinary sense of himself (his ego) are turned to face the inner light of his own divine being. He is experiencing "illumination," being internally ablaze with a fire of wisdom that does not consume what it burns around but produces "enlightenment"!

Sex on the Brain: Creative Energy and Higher Consciousness

Metaphysically, the burning bush represents the Tree of Life in the center of the physical body—the *real* mythic Garden of Eden. The human race has fallen out of conscious awareness of its true divine nature into the collective self-hypnosis of duality—the knowledge of "good" and "evil," the continual power play of opposing forces. The trunk of the Tree of Life is the spinal column and the branches and leaves the human brain, with its many functions of intelligence. The roots of the tree are at the base of the body, embedded in the tremendous latent creative power of human sexuality— the serpent in the Garden of Eden.

This power, sometimes referred to in esoteric systems as Kundalini, is largely responsible for the state of self-hypnosis we are in. When we are conscious of matter as the sole reality, Kundalini feeds into our imagination and makes us daydream about who we think we are and what we *imagine* the world to be. The serpent is coiled around the base of the tree, and at its root is our sexual energy. Though it can keep us asleep in imagination, we can also use its power to awaken from the trance of Maya.

To create an enlightened state of consciousness, sex energy must ascend to the top of the head, illuminating the atoms of the spine and brain with fire and light.

Sexual activity is not required to make this happen, although some Tantric practices can induce awakening in this way. But even a celibate mystic is drawing on the innate creative power of sexual energy when experiencing divine ecstasy. It is the raw fuel necessary for the transformation of consciousness.

Sex energy has been represented in many cultures as a snake or serpent power capable of giving knowledge. Images of Buddha sometimes show him with a snake coiled around his head. Some Egyptian gods are depicted with the head of a snake coming out of their heads at the point between the eyebrows. It is written of Moses, supposedly an ex-prince of Egypt, that he "lifted up the serpent in the wilderness," the desert of ordinary consciousness. He brought the serpent power of sex energy up to his brain and had a flash of illumination. Perhaps he learned something of this from the Egyptians, who probably got it from the Orient, where knowledge of the transforming potential of sex energy has been known for thousands of years?

We can only speculate, but let us assume that as his life force was drawn completely within, Moses contemplated the divine reality of his own true being, his personality having been laid aside with his shoes. His internal Tree of Life was "on fire" with "the light" of God that burns in the heart of every atom. Moses is seeing the God within himself and his personal self begins having a dialogue with *I AM*. A voice issues from the light and tells Moses that he is in communion with the God of his fathers, the God of Abraham, Isaac, and so on. This makes sense spiritually, because the spine and brain of every human being is a manifestation of this same One Light of Divine Intelligence. Abraham, Isaac, you, and I. Get beneath the skin and we are all made of the same eternal substance: I Am That I Am.

Anyone Here into Bondage?

The voice tells Moses that "It" has heard the cries of His children "which are in bondage by reason of their taskmasters." You will recall that Moses came to Sinai after being exiled from Egypt, where his people (the Jews) were hard-labor slaves.

For our purpose it doesn't matter that there is no historical Egyptian record that the Jews were ever in Egypt. We are pursuing the truth embedded in the myth. The symbolic value here is that all people who are enslaved by the collective illusions coming out of the consensus trance are *in bondage in Egypt.* They are making bricks out of mud and straw.

What a potent metaphor this is. Trapped in the perception of matter as matter, they see the world around them not as different patterns of energy, but as solids to be manipulated by egotistic human will. Driven by "taskmasters" of frustrated expectations and the pain of isolation from their own spiritual natures, their souls are restless. Their essential selves cry out for remembrance and deliverance from the bondage of limited self-awareness, whether their human personalities know of it or not. Even the soul of an atheist longs for freedom.

The voice of the inner light commands Moses to return to ordinary consciousness and material life (Egypt), go to Pharaoh (to ego consciousness), and demand that he "Let my people go!" From our unusual exploratory standpoint, the interpretation of "people" would be the thousands of sub-personalities, the "little I's" that make up who we are until we are governed by the real *I* of the *I AM.* As the impulse to awaken from the mass trance gets stronger and stronger, an "inner Moses" emerges in all of us.

A strong, God-directed part of ourselves stands up and demands of our Pharaoh-ego that it release its grip on the "children of Israel"—the multitude of undirected habits, thought patterns, and impulses that dwell in our consciousness—the many "people" that make up who we are. The soul demands of the ego, "Let my people go!"

The Power of *I AM* to Reorder the World

You will recall that in the legend, when Pharaoh finally releases the people and Moses leads them out into the desert toward the "promised-land," the mighty ruler regrets his decision and pursues the great migrating horde of people with his chariots.

Trapped with their backs to the Red Sea, Moses and his flock seem helpless as Pharaoh and his men rush upon them. But God sends a pillar of fire to bar their way. Then Moses stretches out his staff on the waters of the Red Sea and they part, famously, allowing the Children of Israel to cross safely. Once they are safely across, the pillar of fire holding back the Egyptians vanishes. No longer restrained, the charioteers of Pharaoh plunge into the miraculous pathway between the waters. They are drowned as the two walls of water collapse and the Red Sea returns to normal.

Great for Hollywood and Cecil B. De Mille but fantastic nonsense, one might be forgiven for saying. Yet British researchers have determined that if the story of Moses is real and not a myth, he would have been making his epic pilgrimage out of Egypt about the time a volcano erupted on the Mediterranean island now known as Santorini.

For weeks prior to the volcano's eruption, clouds of asphyxiating gas would have been flung high into the atmosphere, along with red mud. Winds could have blown noxious clouds toward Egypt, where red-earth-colored rain fell, turning the Nile to "blood." Aquatic life would die in the pollution, unleashing a "plague of frogs." After the volcano exploded, the "burning hail" that fell from the sky over Egypt was most likely red-hot pumice, likewise flung toward Egypt from Santorini.

As large chunks of the island finally sank beneath the sea, this created a tsunami-like effect. Water rushed in to fill the hole in the Mediterranean created by the volcano erupting and part of the island sinking. This pulled the waters of the Red Sea back, creating a safe passage to freedom for Moses and his followers. As they reached safety on the other side, a great sea wave rushed back toward the land and destroyed the pursuing Egyptians.

The British research team that put forward this proposition claimed this theory did nothing to diminish the extra-fantastic nature of these events. The miracle, they said, was that Moses was led by God to be in just the right place at just the right time.

Attunement with our destiny—being in the right place at the right time—can happen on a continuous basis as a result of going up our own "holy mountain" into higher consciousness and feeling the power and presence of *I AM* consciousness radiating within us. One does not need to hear voices and see one's brain and spine all light up. The greatest proof of God's presence is an all-pervading sense of peace, security, and strength that is greater than any difficulty external life can bring before us.

Fire Within—Truth Without

All truth seekers must come to a point when they *will* their own deliverance. We cannot grow unless we forsake bondage to old patterns and ways of relating to life based on the particular social sleep of the times. The language and imagery may change but the essential message is the same as it has always been. Awaken to live, or sleep to die in ignorance of who and what we truly are, never having really lived at all!

To awaken, we must cultivate a living experience of *I AM* through self-remembering. Then, backed up by the fire and light in our spine and brain, we must go out and experiment every day with truth, testing ourselves in the boiling cauldron of human activity. The question is this: Can we hold on to our divine connection with ourselves in the face of the madness? Are we able to not only stand unshaken amidst the crash of falling worlds, but can we also bring peace to those we encounter by staying connected with the reality beyond the illusion? You have the tools and the knowledge now to accomplish this. All that remains is your consent to do this work.

Our Tree of Life—the spine and rib cage—resembles an electromagnetic coil. Energy runs up and down in the human body constantly through this coil and floods the rest of the body (our Garden of Eden) with life. Individuals under the sway of Maya, the great illusion, have no sense of this. Their life force simply flows in and out of the brain, affirming that what is seen, tasted, touched, heard, and smelled is real. This is, as I said, the prime cause of the collective sociological self-hypnosis. Our life energy habitually flows out of the senses with such force that the objects we perceive consume our attention to a high degree. Under this spell, insufficient power remains within to feel our own energy at its source in the spine and brain. A powerful magnetic center must be generated within us to reverse the constant outgoing flow of energy through the senses.

We want to be focused energetically within to a degree *equal to the amount of energy going out.* Again, we are speaking of divided attention.

Divide Your Attention and Conquer

Through a constantly maintained *dual awareness* of life within ourselves *and* in the world around us, we can enable ourselves to actually *feel* the power of the universe in back of us. (For more details on the divided-attention exercise and other related techniques, see Chapter Eight.) This practice naturally helps magnetize the spine and brain and allows *I AM* to manifest as an inherent electrifying force in our daily affairs. It gives us sovereign power in a world of ego and the contentious clash of dominance-hungry personalities. Why? Because the *I AM* presence can be felt as a distinct vibratory sensation, emanating from the spine and radiating out all through the body and beyond.

Remember my previous definition of an egotist? This individual has *undivided attention*—and it is all upon himself! In such a case there can be no real sense of *I.* There is only the ever-changing shift of moods, desires, and personal insecurities. There is no real individuality. There is no *real I.*

Unlike such an individual, when we enter a state of divided attention while dealing with a dualistic external situation, *we experience a sense of personal unity.* Looking within and without at the same time, with equal attention, cancels out the usual sensed perception of the dualism of life—right-or-wrong, black-or-white. Dualism is the realm of the dilemma where irreconcilable differences are in a stand-off. Thinking in oppositions is the daily bread of the deluded mind, which has become addicted to dualistic perception. It can't get off the seesaw because it cannot see a higher possibility: the *reconciliation of opposites.*

A New World Order through *I AM* Consciousness

The opposite of peace is war. Neither can cancel out the other. Since the dawn of history, reasonable people have been trying to get rid of war by crying out for peace. Obviously, this does not work. What is needed is a third element. To create a new world of personal interaction, *the energy of reconciliation has to be present.* Any person who can feel, to some degree, some aspect of the presence and energy of *I AM,* particularly in a conflict situation, is introducing the reconciling force into the world. You and I cannot directly stop the various international conflicts that are raging. But when *I AM* is manifesting in your consciousness, your body cells (made of atoms, with their electrons, protons, and neutrons) are vibrating with the energy that balances opposites. By becoming a stable physical structure in a world that is atomically and anatomically out of whack, you are demonstrably manifesting the energy of the new world of personal interaction—right where you are. And you *are* changing the world because the world is made of atoms and you are part of the world.

The intelligence behind the scenes of the planet earth—whether God, the angels, extraterrestrial beings, or nature (your choice), whatever has caused us to appear in this world—must surely rejoice when human beings align with the truth of their existence. I know from my own experience that the more I align myself with that truth through self-remembering into higher consciousness *(I AM),* the more help I get *to do more of the same.* Life just opens up to show me more and more truth *(I AM)* everywhere.

We Were Born to Self-Remember ... But We Forget

Modern psychology overlooks the one factor that could open many doors to understanding the human psyche: that we human beings live in a state of *constant self-forgetfulness.* Watch people when a conversation starts and you will quickly notice how the interchange of words and feelings consumes the participants. Emotional reactions, political opinions, likes and dislikes, prejudices and predilections—all become mirrored in the animation of eyes, face, posture, body language, and tone of voice. Any sense of a governing body, a unique individuality, existing independently of what is being expressed, soon vanishes.

The moments in life we can vividly recall from memory, times when meaning was really present are generally proportionate to the degree of self-remembering we were in when the events first happened. In such cases, not only were we present physically at that particular time and place, we were *present to ourselves in that moment.*

Everyone experiences self-remembering from time to time. It is a natural faculty we have somehow misplaced in our evolutionary wanderings. But sometimes intense or highly meaningful situations can trigger us back into it. A few examples of this from my own life include:

Saying my wedding vows
The first time I held my children after their birth
The day I got divorced
Experiencing God as a direct reality
Entering various mystical states of consciousness
Looking into the eyes of my true love
The first time I flew in an airplane
When a madman tried to kill me
Hearing Gustav Mahler's Symphony #2 *(Resurrection)* while sitting
   in the front row, just a few feet from the Los Angeles
   Philharmonic

You will notice in this brief sampling that not all the triggering experiences were what we might term positive. Self-remembering can be precipitated by stress and shock and even conflict, as well as by positive circumstance. It is always characterized by a certain *vividness* of experience that can be recalled even years later with absolute clarity.

The following story relates how I was able to self-remember under stress by applying many of the techniques you have learned here. It also shows how I dealt with the shadow element and even used my own "dark side" to access a very high state of consciousness as I tried to create an enlightened personal interaction with someone during a tense situation.

Shadow Dancing at a Yoga Retreat

When I was performing *Forever Jung* in Florida in 1997, I was invited to stay at a nearby Yoga retreat. Sonia, the director, told me, after seeing the play, that she loved my work and would be honored if I would visit the retreat for three days as a guest. She added that on Friday, a few friends were invited over for dinner and suggested that perhaps I could give a little talk after the meal. I agreed and arrived at the retreat on Wednesday afternoon. The building was in a forest and the surrounding trees whispered gentle wind-borne messages to the blue sky and white Florida clouds, as they smiled their blessings down on the haven of peace.

But I soon discovered that all was not well in Yoga Land. The staff members were robed in the symbolic purity of white garments. But the darkness of their shadow selves lurked behind the facade of holy looks and affected spirituality. By Thursday I was noticing how irritated the staff could get with one another over trivial incidents. When one of them could not find a book she was looking for, she accusingly asked a colleague if she had taken it. A clash of denial and counter-accusation erupted and their habitually stuffed shadows filled the room with a crackling tension. When Sonia walked into the room, angry facial expressions turned to syrupy smiles as the two antagonists stuffed their shadows back inside their inner worlds.

On Friday morning, I got a phone call requiring me to change my weekend travel plans or risk losing several hundred dollars. I called a travel agent at once to rearrange my schedule, and was put on hold. While I was sitting there holding the phone, I saw Sonia bearing down on me, flapping her hands wildly as if to cut off my phone conversation. Placing my hand over the mouthpiece, I asked what was bothering her.

"John," she breathlessly declaimed, eyes wild with something akin to panic, "you can't tie up the phone lines like that. People may be trying to call for directions!"

"What people?" I asked guilelessly.

"The ones who are coming to hear you speak tonight."

"But I have an emergency. I must change my airline ticket at once."

It was as if I had never spoken. She repeated herself, now hovering over me like a righteous harpy. "You can't tie up the phone lines like that. People will be calling for directions!"

One of the things that pushes *my* buttons is when people repeat themselves to me, as if I'm too stupid to get it the first time. "What people?" I now repeated, taking a cue from her.

"We have thirty-five people coming to hear you speak and they are going to need directions. You have to get off the phone."

Thirty-five people? What happened to the "few friends" and a little after-dinner talk? It sounded like I was going to be giving a seminar. Since I was sitting and Sonia standing, she had a definite psychological advantage over me. I could feel my legs starting to shake a little as I tried to control a rising sense that I was being taken for a ride. (Later, I found out that the thirty-five "guests" were going to shell out $35 apiece for dinner and my talk.) Sonia could feel that I was getting a bit rattled and she plastered an expression of holy compassion across her face as she assaulted me with righteous healing balm.

"John, you're stressed out. You need to relax," she purred, drowning me in self-realization as she recovered her guru self. "Why don't you take time out and do some Yoga."

This invitation to stuff the shadow under a Yoga mat was the trigger I needed to turn this situation around. Sonia's comment was so delusional it made me *remember to remember myself.* My mind swept down to my feet and connected me with the earth's energy field, and I drew a tingling sensation of thick comfort up from my feet to the thighs. Then I stood up. Sonia and I were now going to see eye to eye. Or were we? I looked into her essence (left) eye and made no connection with it. It seemed inscrutably dull, almost blank. I tried the right eye, but connection there was physically blocked—a strategically placed curl of hair was hanging right in front of her personality eye, so that I could not see into the pupil. Ostensibly, Sonia had only one eye in operation—her essence eye, which seemed closed even though it was open.

What to do? For some reason I could not get the earth energy to move up from my legs into my body. Sonia and I were face to face, about six inches apart. Could it be that the close proximity of her energy field was affecting mine, so that I could not self-remember? I needed to create some space between us.

She began talking again about the need for people to call in for directions and as she did, I walked away from her in a semi-circular trajectory that ended with me facing her about eight feet away. Once I was out of proximity to Sonia's energy field, I was able to sense and feel every part of myself simultaneously. A great energetic wave of vibrant certainty gripped me. I felt incredibly peaceful and yet attentively poised to act in this interesting dynamic that had arisen.

As Sonia rattled on, I saw clearly that she was completely asleep, self-hypnotized by her particular agenda. She was in the trance I had seen my mother and sister in after Mataji had zapped me awake. Although Sonia was being negative, the naturally positive energy in the air was being electrified by her reactivity. Soon it would become negative unless I could "eat it" first. Suddenly, as I was self-remembering, all this positive energy flew across the room to me. It hit my already charged energy field with a megawatt impact, seemingly tripling the intensity of my consciousness, which began to expand, filling the entire room. This all happened in the twinkling of an eye but as the energy build-up climaxed, Sonia sensed something unusual was going on.

"Tell me what you are doing!" Her demand held a tone of uncertainty. For the first time since she accosted me, her truculent attitude was shaken as I simply held her gaze and felt the dynamic. She had gotten herself into a scenario in which the interplay between positive and negative energy was capable of producing the food of heightened awareness for both of us. But Sonia was out to lunch while lunch was being served. Finally, I answered her question in a low, steady voice.

"I'm building up my sense of personal power and presence at your expense!"

Her jaw dropped open and her one visible eye widened dramatically. "You're a very bad man!" she declared, stamping her foot.

"You're right," I agreed, as I started to advance upon her across the room. "I am a very bad man."

And Sonia turned and fled.

Eating the Force of the Dark Side

A huge force field of energy now surrounded me. It permeated my flesh, my mind, my entire being, while at the same time rooting me down into the earth. I felt absolutely invincible. Where had it come from so suddenly? What had generated such a huge field of power in, through, and around me?

The techniques I used to ground and self-remember had helped set the process in motion. But I had not behaved toward Sonia in a manner that might be called "good." I did not "make nice" with her but danced with her shadow in a direct, powerful manner. Aren't grace and presence supposed to descend upon us as reward for being "good" and behaving like a saint? I had played about with the underlying dynamic of the situation in a somewhat subversive manner. Why was I being rewarded with a surge of higher consciousness for being "bad"?

Obviously, my host and her cohorts adhered to the viewpoint that "goodness" and "holiness" bring about the saving grace of the Most High. This accounted for the white outfits of purity, the practiced smiles of righteousness, and the general atmosphere of forced relaxation that pervaded the retreat. But underneath the highly polished surface of imitation holiness, the shadow lurked and seethed in caverns of rejected discontent. When Sonia saw me "tying up the phone lines," her shadow went berserk. There is nothing like throwing money into the pot of an unstable paradigm to make it boil over. (Thirty-five people at $35 per head, remember. You don't need a calculator to figure out that someone was going to make a healthy bit of change from my visit and it wasn't me. Sonia did actually slip me a twenty-dollar bill as I was leaving the next day, "for expenses.")

Wholeness versus Goodness

Note that I did not say anything that could remotely be construed as a personal put-down of Sonia. I did not get angry or insult her. On the contrary, it was she who insulted me by calling me a "very bad man." And what did I do when she verbally attacked me? I *agreed* with her, saying, "yes, I am a very bad man." This is exactly the opposite of what normally happens. If someone insults us we attack and return the blow. Carl Jung once declared that he would "rather be whole than good." Wholeness means taking into account the shadow—ours and the other person's.

Knowing our own potential for cruel behavior allows us to control its expression. People who have to have an image of themselves as a "nice person" may find it hard to accept that they have a bad side. Nevertheless, an unrecognized and ungoverned shadow will still find ways to act out. In the case of the "nice person," it often manifests through passive-aggressive behavior.

Sonia normally controlled the retreat in a passive-aggressive manner and the staff members were in awe of her "holiness." Attempting to hide their own shadow and appear "holy" themselves, they constantly kowtowed to her. The sense of ego inflation this produced reinforced her natural tendency to deny her own shadow. In order to get her to see this and accept responsibility for her hidden dark side, it engineered the dynamic she encountered with me. Thus she had the opportunity to face her own shadow by projecting it my way. When I would not carry it for her, in her mind she turned me into a "very bad man." And when I agreed with her and said that I was indeed a very bad man, she had no place to go, and so she bolted.

But the really controversial element in this story is the statement "I'm building up my sense of power and presence at your expense." This was not 100 percent true. I was able to build up my power and presence *because* her behavior was compelling me to quickly go deep into sensed and felt experience of myself. If it had really been "at her expense," I would have been stealing something that belonged to her. All I did was magnetize my being in such a manner that the positive energy she was unable to absorb from the surrounding atmosphere at that moment flew to me and built up my energy field.

Do you doubt this is possible? If what I have just said made you go into your head, then for you no proof is possible. But if you try it for yourself and pull it off, you will know by *direct experience* that it is not only possible, but it is how the world works on a molecular level. When we interact with the minds of other human beings, we are in the wonderful world of human subjectivity. When you say "blue," other people free-associate with every shade of blue they ever experienced. If you get rattled because you sense they don't get your meaning, the atoms of your body fall out of harmony. Electron, proton, and neutron struggle to stay in balance and you feel stressed. But when you remember yourself, these three primal elements quickly realign and you feel harmonious and powered up again. You have "eaten" nuclear energy and the result is presence and power.

Had Sonia been in a stable frame of mind, she might have been able to absorb a positive charge from the friction of the moment. But her wild behavior made her body-mind-emotional vehicle unable to function as a useful instrument. As I walked away from her across the room and then turned to look at her, having reached a certain level of atomic coherence in my body through self-remembering, all the unused positive energy in the dynamic flew to me. She didn't want it . . . so I took it.

Expansion in the *I*

After Sonia had departed in her self-generated confusion, I went outside for a walk. I could feel my consciousness spread out over the entire area. My spirit seemed to pervade the trees in the forest surrounding the retreat. Even the buildings themselves were simply aspects of my own vast body of awareness, as were the white clouds and the watching blue vastness of the sky.

This is the deepest level of self-remembering. A sense of *I* is apprehended through direct experience as all-pervading and ever-existing. The center of this awareness, when active, is the brain and cerebrospinal axis. From it a subtle radiance, pouring out from it in every direction, gently carries the soul to the far horizons of consciousness. Miraculously, in this instance, this state had been precipitated for me by a social disruption, an attack by someone else's unintegrated shadow. I realized that this is why we are supposed to love our enemies and bless those who curse us. When we do, we can benefit from vast forces of transformational intelligence. We can be instantly healed, even before the unkind blow has landed.

This requires of us that we place self-remembering before negative, knee-jerk reaction. But it is well worth taking the time and effort to train ourselves to high levels of self-mastery over negative emotions. The goal is not simply to prevent people inflicting their misguided perceptions and attitudes upon us. The right kind of attention in moments of tension allows us to access high states of consciousness in which our real *I* emerges as the substratum of not only our intelligence and being, but of life itself.

Devils in Bottles and a Snake That Hissed

Having the wisdom and perspicacity to redirect one's shadow elements and those of others wisely is key in all of this. The Sufis say that angels know only one thing: how to be angels. Devils, on the other hand, know everything. The shadow knows everything about everyone and life in general. If we can get this to work for us instead in a positive, nondestructive, peacekeeping way, we have a magic helper.

King Solomon issued a command that all the genies were to be captured and put into bottles. That way they could be let out only when a situation arose that called for their particular talents. If we can get a grip on our shadow, *which we do by accepting that we ourselves are capable of anything,* then we can keep it in a psychological inner bottle and let it out consciously to serve our wits in a difficult situation.

Many people have useless, nonintegrated shadow elements. These unconscious aspects of personality sometimes act as irresponsible free agents that cross up their lives. Sonia is a fine example. My bottled genie, let loose with my permission, had fun dealing with her shadow on the loose. Without inflicting any personal harm on her, it helped me see what she was up to, and then went back in the bottle. I allowed myself to hiss, but not bite. The old holy man in the story of the snake that wouldn't hiss would doubtless have approved.

If I had once slipped and sought to inject venom into Sonia, the poison of ill will, to personally hurt her, then my genie would have turned on me and I would have suffered. *Motive is everything.* You can, and on occasion *must,* speak and act in a manner that confronts the delusional behavior of other people. This may be done directly or indirectly. Or, as I was able to in this case, by a combination of both manners. But in any event, when you are dealing with another person's shadow, you will need the help of your own dark side. Only the shadow knows the shadow. Get yours to help you so that you can be a good angel *and* a good devil—not an imitation angel and a bad devil.

A Warm Wrap with Sonia

I am pleased to report that there was a happy ending to my retreat visit. The little talk for the invited guests on Friday night went extremely well. As I was speaking, I could see Sonia's higher self watching me with intense interest. Her ego had received an awakening shock from our encounter and her personality had reordered itself. She seemed less attached to her role as the flawless leader and more personally authentic.

I saw this even more clearly the next morning as we stood in the doorway of the retreat to say good-bye. Gone was the lock of hair covering up her personality eye. There was a softness about her that had previously been obscured by her need to control. Although she would not be able to rationalize about what had happened to her, on a deep, wordless level, change had occurred and our souls knew truth had passed between us. Now the *I AM* was present, looking through her at me and me at her. We were both sensing a presence flowing between us now. As we shook hands, her ego struggled to make one last attempt to come across in a superior, "holier than thou" manner. But she could no longer do it. That which was awakening in her overrode the impulse to separate. Strange, is it not, that sometimes a negative dynamic is the very catalyst required to create a shift in consciousness and change behavioral patterns.

For a fleeting moment, that which is the same in both of us connected in recognition and reestablished enlightened personal interaction through *I AM*.

"You will come back, won't you?" asked Sonia with absolute authenticity. In that moment she looked extremely beautiful.

"Yes, of course," I said, taking both her hands in mine. "Anytime."

We smiled at each other, radiant with presence.

The Healing Gift of Self-Remembering

When we can hold the field of self-remembering in and around ourselves, we create a space for others to have a similar experience. Even though they may be self-hypnotized, forgetful, and asleep, if we self-remember for them, they can become self-remembered too for a moment. What a gift this can be to other people, and it is a choice we have in any situation. Shall we validate the illusion of Maya, the cosmic magic spell that divides the primal Oneness into fragments and limitations of temporal identity? Or stay in the energetic presence of our souls through self-remembering and "hold the field of unity" while dealing with the forces of separation in everyday social situations? Spiritually mature individuals know how to do this. They are willing to step out of false personality into an actual, sensed consciousness of the soul as divine presence, moment by moment throughout the day.

In the beginning we will go in and out of these states. One minute delusional, awake the next, and then back into sleep again. But by training ourselves over time, we can make the sleep periods less and less. Eventually, through self-remembering, we can become the true creators of our own destiny. The self-remembered life *is* life! The choice is ours: "To sleep perchance to dream" . . . or to awaken and live!

CHAPTER THIRTEEN

The World-Enlightening Power of *I AM*

Developing Conscious Will

It takes a strong yet relaxed willingness to practice the techniques that lead to self-remembering. Ordinary thinking is nothing more than the rapid streaming of a series of automatic synaptic connections running randomly across the cerebrum. This self-perpetuating brain activity we mistake for ourselves. But the brain is simply an organ through which the soul expresses itself as consciousness. To be able to observe the thoughts running through the brain as largely inaccurate cerebral cyber-chat puts one in a position of great power. Most people *become* what they are thinking, instantly and without realizing it. A millisecond of thought possesses the brain and the personality acts out the mental download as emotional impulses, attraction or aversion, loving or loathing, and so on. To go against this great stream of unconsciousness, we must *will* ourselves to step out of it and see what we take to be ourselves from a *self-observational* mode.

Only by separating from and *nonidentifying* with our programming can we effect a *rebirth* into autonomous self-government. We were born to have dominion over the equipment nature has provided for our souls to operate through. But we mistake the effect for the cause and, instead of claiming autonomy, become automatons. This is not pleasant news. People don't like to be told they are asleep and have little or no free will. But there is a great freedom to be had for the taking, once we realize and accept that the wages of sleep are self-limitation.

You are *not* your body, or your mind, or your emotions. They are simply the instruments of your soul's expression. Creating the dominion of *conscious will* over and above our body, mind, and emotional selves puts the house in order. *Real* will is an attribute of *I AM* and is developed by doing this work of reclaiming ourselves.

Eight Steps to Self-Reclamation

Here is a recap of some of the main principles we have covered so far. These follow each other as stepping stones in a logical path to reclaiming our true selves.

1. Willingness to Do the Work (Conscious Will)

In order to advance toward any goal, one must be willing to repeatedly practice and apply the principles required to attain the knowledge one wishes to acquire. We can drive our cars on the freeway because we learned how to operate them and studied the laws necessary to get a license. The same principle obtains here. If you want to successfully drive your body vehicle through the traffic snarls, detours, and chaos of the modern world, you must study how it works and learn to drive it properly. Remember that it has three operational aspects: the physical, emotional, and mental. When you can line up all three and get them to conform to your will to proceed as desired and intended, you and your soul can drive in the carpool lane. While others struggle to surmount the karmic mountains of global non-cooperation with the harmony of natural law, you will be in sync with the greater purposes of evolution. So do the work. Instead of just reading this book as a set of interesting ideas, apply what you have been exposed to in your daily life. The results will come by themselves.

2. Self-Observation

You are not your name and social identity. To be able to step to one side and see John or Alice, Fred or Anita, as if you were watching someone else, is liberating. When picking up a knife or fork from the table, brushing your teeth, or walking into a room, watch yourself from the outside as if your were looking at another person. Some people who have undergone a near-death experience report finding themselves outside their own body, looking down at it from the ceiling while it lies on a hospital operating table. Obviously, we don't want to be floating around in space while conducting our daily affairs. We want to be fully present, as the next step implies. But at the same time, we need to stay slightly detached and observational.

3. Becoming Body-Centered

If you have taken a good look at the world around you, having come so far in our explorations, I am sure you have seen for yourself how stuck in the head the human race has become. You will have noted the accordion-like wrinkling of foreheads when people try to squeeze information from their brains while speaking. Hearing the thin, high-pitched, tension-laden voices that arise not from the depths of the stomach but from the head, with an unpleasant nasal cavity resonance, will likewise have clued you in. The world of talking heads is all around us. By dropping down out of your head into your body you have a supreme advantage over those who are top-heavy with too much thinking. The power of a human being is in the body, not the head. The head contains the brain, which is the ultimate organ of perception. But the head needs the body to execute its plans and make its dreams come true. Stay body-centered, even while you move your awareness to the next step, sensing and feeling.

4. Sensing and Feeling

As I wrote this chapter, sitting at my computer, my hands flying over the keyboard, I practiced self-observation. I also scanned my body with my mind and held an attentive awareness of presence in my hands, feet, arms, legs, head, and torso simultaneously. I was practicing sensing and feeling. An atmosphere of presence seemed to pervade every part of my body. Fixing part of my attention upon it was no hindrance to the act of typing. In fact, the words flowed from brain to hand without an intervening analytical thought. The book appeared to be writing itself through me.

Playing tennis or golf, or doing any other activity, or holding any con-versation, the principle would be the same. Sensing and feeling makes us available to ourselves and available to the action of the moment. We participate as both the self-witnessing party and the instrument of action. Life is being done in and through us at a high degree of coherence. Try to hold the field of sensed and felt presence in every activity, both private and public. Soon it will become second nature and make being head-centered seem quite abnormal.

5. Nonidentifying and Nonreacting

This is closely related to self-observation. When we hear voices in our heads telling us self-limiting stories about ourselves and we believe them, we are identifying with internal delusions. When someone verbally attacks us and we get upset and respond in kind, we are both identified *and* reactive. We are being driven internally by external illusions. When we can separate from these types of reactive impulse as they arise within ourselves, we are *nonidentified*. Because we have stepped into the observational mode, we clearly see the turning gears and cogs in the psyche for the automated processes they really are. From such a space of nonreactivity, no reasonable person would say, "I am now going to behave like a reactive imbecile." By allowing possession by anger, or any other negative emotion to possess us, we are surrendering our autonomy to reactivity. In such moments we cease to exist as self-determining individuals.

This is not to say that we should not acknowledge to ourselves personal negative feelings—rage, jealousy, desire to wound, and so on. Denial and suppression are never healthy, but transmutation is. We can learn to accept that negative emotions are stirring within us, yet not feel compelled to surrender our personal autonomy to them. Whenever anger arises within me, as it does on occasion, I step to one side inwardly and say to myself, "Look what *it's* thinking now!" Then I sit back and watch the tales told by my version of Shakespeare's "idiot": thoughts "full of sound and fury signifying nothing" until they run out of steam. This principle can be applied to worry, fear, or any other disturbance of one's psychological equilibrium. When we can *see* it, we are not it! We are that which is doing the looking!

And a great peace can descend upon us. When we identify with our rubbish, we become it and will be swept away into reactivity. Step back from reaction into nonidentification and save masses of energy for sensing and feeling and self-remembering and deep peace.

6. Seeing Eye to Eye

The importance of knowing which eye to look into during interactions with others cannot be overemphasized. To actually see and connect with someone else's essence is a great blessing, to them and to yourself. Being able to see someone's egocentric baloney coming at you from the personality eye and not buy into it is also a gift. People in the grip of their mechanical programming are powerless. But when we silently resist their temporary malfunctioning, through a look that signals to *their* soul that *our* soul knows they are behaving in a delusional manner, we extend to them a chance to come out of the madness, if only for a moment.

Certainly it takes courage to stand unfazed by the unpleasant energy that can roll off a person who is angry and venting. It also requires nerve to face down sarcasm or meanness with a quick look into the personality eye. But with a few successes in the field under your belt, you will start to enjoy those inevitable moments in life when people act out their stuff in front of you. For two reasons: first, you will feel an instant increase in power as you are backed up by the higher intelligence just behind the surface appearances of life and, second, you will be helping others by holding up a mirror before their conscience.

I strongly suggest you read over the chapters dealing with the eyes and start implementing the information there at once. Those who have attended my workshops and learned about the eyes often call or email me with their success stories. Perhaps it has been a bullying boss at work or a nagging family member. Or a rude stranger who was dealt with from a new perspective. Once one actually experiences the remarkable changes in interpersonal action, reaction, and interaction, as a result of consciously implemented *seeing,* a new course in life is set. To go back to the unconscious way of blundering through each social situation by chance then seems ridiculous.

So let us not be afraid to look the world in *both* eyes and challenge all we meet to wake up, by staying awake ourselves to the best of our ability at all times. And as we look out through our eyes upon creation, remember also to keep an equal amount of awareness upon yourself as the one who is looking. This, of course, is accomplished by practicing divided attention.

7. Divided Attention

The goal here is to keep as much energy flowing inward toward the center of our physical being—the spine and the brain—as we have flowing outward through the senses. Otherwise, we shall fixate on the barrage of external impressions bombarding our senses and be captured by the world outside ourselves. Our attention is easily held outwardly when we become fascinated with something or someone. This can sometimes be an asset, as when, for example, a concert pianist rips through a Rachmaninoff piano concerto flawlessly, becoming one with the piano, conductor, and orchestra. But what if the musician forgets to be present to him- or herself in the moment? And what if the necessary sense of gathered self-attention, required to remain not only present, but a few mental milliseconds ahead of the score, is lost? Obviously, disaster could ensue.

Maintaining divided attention also enables us to read the coded subtext behind human behavior in response to us. If we are out of tune with ourselves, we may get paranoid when people start looking cross-eyed our way. When we are in tune, however, we will be able to decipher the unconscious messages being delivered to us through those we must interact with. We can then adjust our speech, mannerisms, and behavior to get into alignment with the best outcome for ourselves in any situation. Those who are capable of picking up subtle cues from the unconscious will instantly and intuitively sense that we are back on track and respond positively. They will move of their own volition to get into alignment with us. They will know subliminally, unless they wish to remain stuck, that it is in their best

interest to harmonize with our intention because we have moved into consciousness. We actually *lead* them out of the ego-driven trance of Maya.
Not by verbal argument or forceful domination of their personalities, but
by moving out of the illusion ourselves. We teach through conscious example by becoming and demonstrating the energy of consciousness.

Inveterate egotists and willful abusers of social behavior will disenfranchise themselves from the beneficent energy that radiates from an individual who is maintaining a state of divided attention. If they start to get
angry, rude, or insulting toward someone in the divided state, the energy
behind the attacker's hostility can serve to propel their supposed victim
into high consciousness. The lower is compelled to feed the higher if the
higher stays conscious through the practices in this book. To remember
oneself is to become a spiritual aristocrat and claim one's power as a Prince
or Princess of the Universe. We are all servants of life, willing or not. But
when we wake up and remember ourselves in the illusion, life then serves
us even as we serve life.

8. Self-Remembering

Only the self-remembered can be said to be truly alive, for if we cannot
remember ourselves, who or what is there in us to know that we actually
are alive? It is a scary proposition to contemplate that who we think we are
is largely a fiction. But it can also be highly liberating. We need strong
incentives to initiate long-lasting behavioral changes. As social animals, we
humans possess an innate cunning when it comes to self-deception. How
else can we explain away the fact that death is only a stopped heartbeat
away as we hurtle down the freeway at seventy-plus miles per hour? Perhaps
a certain amount of self-deception is necessary just to get by. But what
excuse can there be for not wanting to be fully conscious of our own existence? If we truly realized how precious life is and that this planet is a
school, to which we have come to reclaim awareness of our divine origins
under difficult conditions, we would not waste a second.

The True You and Personal Greatness

How many years have already slipped by while we were absent from our lives? Where has our sensed connection of presence within our bodies been? What have our minds been fixated upon, minute by minute, day by day? Usually anything and everything *but* staying in connection with the core reality of our essential being. We have substituted this for the constant narcissism and insecurity of the imaginary self, which we have assumed ourselves to be. Identification with the insecurities of *false personality* has usurped our *true personality* as expression and extension of the soul. Lost in the shuffle is the ability to be not just either a spiritual being or a sleeping-walking automaton, but *how to be personally great!* Who would not wish to have and express the true personality we were born to give to the world? Such a perfect expression can only come about when the human and divine in us are balanced in equal measure.

We have all known moments of what it feels like to be our personal best self. Without those scattered jewels of being with the truth of ourselves on the most personal level, life would be unbearable. Perhaps it was when we first fell in love and were filled with hope and noble dreams, as we aspired to make a better life for ourselves and our beloved one. Or when we first held our newborn child and glowed inwardly with a pride that was free from all vanity, because it was instigated by the unconditional love of one precious life for another.

At such times, when remembrance of the essential goodness of life itself *and of ourselves* is present, even the most subversive elements buried in our darker sides seem manageable. Self-remembering is not simply re-identification with the transpersonal, higher consciousness and the soul. It is ultimately inclusive of the best aspects of our most precious human selves, living in concordant harmony with the very worst.

Again, we are faced with a paradox. How can the best of us coexist with the worst? Are they not mutually incompatible? On the contrary, as long as we live in this world of duality, they are mutually inescapable! That which we most dislike and fear in ourselves, our shadow nature, is an essential ingredient for growth. The dark, hidden side of creation causes us to generate sufficient self-propulsion to rise above its influence and seek freedom. As the growing shoot struggles from the darkness of the earth that surrounds its genetic state, to eventually burst forth into the light, so too must we push against the ground of our own ignorance and reach for the sky.

If we hate that within and around us that we consider dark or even evil, we will be divided against ourselves. By accepting and embracing the darkness as a necessary component of life, even as an aspect of God's will, we can find freedom from its limiting power. The self-remembered soul knows that only consciously connected awareness with that which is absolutely real within us can help us withstand the chaos of duality. By merging our human identity with "I Am That I Am," the divine core of individual life, we stand at a moving point of balance between the light and the dark sides of human nature. When we are self-remembered, we have become self-conscious—we are fully aware of our own existence. We are truly alive!

Creating *I AM* Consciousness

Long ago, the great yogis of ancient India developed particular strategies for cultivating and invoking the consciousness of *I AM*. Although little known and understood today even in the East, these practices are still vital and usable by us in the West. Their power works magnificently when combined with the techniques you have been learning in this book.

Through constant repetition of certain rhythmic patterns of words that echo "I Am That I Am," we can put ourselves into a state of oneness with *I AM*, which is implied by the words. In order to be truly effective, these mantras and affirmation statements must be performed with body, mind, and emotions fully engaged at the same time. Done simply from the head, as is usually the case with word repetitions, they remain nothing more than words. Executed while practicing sensing and feeling, divided attention, and self-remembering, they can change both *inner* and *outer* world.

The "I Am I" Technique

To induce awareness of the *I AM,* we simply set up a constant stream of repeated, rhythmic *mental* verbal patterns based around such phrases as "I Am I, I Am, I, I Am I, I Am I, I, I!" Or simply "I, I, I, I, I" or "I Am, I Am," over and over. This is not done out loud, *but mentally with full-body sensed and felt awareness.* We keep repeating these word patterns over and over again, not with our attention in the head, but as if the words are forming and vibrating in every part of the body simultaneously. This presupposes that we have already trained ourselves in the art of dropping out of our heads and can center into the body at will.

These rhythmic repetitions can be done at various speeds, from fast to slow or medium. In the beginning you will be able to get the pattern going for a few minutes and then lose it, as you become caught up in some other mental or physical activity. Eventually, you can train yourself to do the repetitions more or less constantly. One might ask how it is possible to execute normal functions such as driving a car, writing a letter, or conversing with other people while executing this technique?

When we fall in love we cannot stop thinking about the object of our affections. Night and day, he or she is on our mind. The first thought of the day is usually of that person, as is the last one at night. Strangely, while so romantically influenced, we often function *better* than at any other time. Under the intensity of our affections and attractions, our faculties are brought into heightened focus because, first, we are being energized by love and, second, we are revolving our consciousness around *that which we take to be the source of our love.*

In actual fact, the beloved person is *not* the source, but the *external trigger* that activates our own capacity to feel and experience love. The ultimate source of that experience is the *I AM* within ourselves *and* in the other person. Two *I AM*-nesses are vibrating together and producing a state of oneness. This triggers a sympathetic resonance in the surrounding atmosphere. The *I AM* in the various objects of creation (the heart of every atom) starts to sympathetically resonate in sync with what is now alive and vibrating in us and in our beloved. Thus, even when we are separated from our lover by distance, the world around us seems to sing with harmony. You have heard the expression "When you're in love, the whole world is Jewish"— or Muslim, English, or American. When the *I AM* is active as presence in us, we seek and find it everywhere.

It follows then, that if we could put ourselves into such a highly empathetic state with creation, *at will*, then we might find creation reordering itself around our intention and mirroring our internally sensed divinity everywhere we go.

Daily Practice Brings Results

Cultivating a daily habit of sitting for five or ten minutes and doing *I AM* repetitions after practicing the sensing-and-feeling exercise is a great way to start reprogramming the body and mind. I never begin my day, answer the phone, speak to or interact with another person, until after I have fully immersed myself in higher consciousness. In the beginning, I had to make a relaxed effort to keep my mind entirely focused on, say, my left foot for sixty seconds, before moving to the right foot or drawing my attention of the presence up my leg to the knee. Sometimes I would actually have to say mentally "left foot, left foot," as if the words were forming not in my head but actually in my foot. Then I would work my way through each body part doing the same, "right hand, right hand," and so on. But now, as soon as I place my attention on any body part, there is an electromagnetic tingling sensation of energy there; a thick, flesh-permeating presence will gather there.

After getting sensationally connected, we then focus on any body part and say "I" to it. For example, with the mind in the left foot, mentally say "left foot" a few times. Then switch to placing *I* awareness in the left foot, and say "I, I, I" and so on while focusing completely there. Then move to the calves, thighs, hands, arms, and beyond, in sequence, doing the same. Once a sensation of *I* in the arms and legs has been established, one can then feel it in the head by sensing and feeling first the face and then the entire head, repeating "I, I, I, . . ." mentally in and around the head with conscious awareness.

Be sure not to lose what you have gathered in the arms and legs when you do this, so you do not get stuck in the head again. When you can feel arms, legs, and head equally, drop down into the throat, upper chest, solar plexus, stomach, and abdomen in sequence, repeating the procedure of sensing and feeling and chanting "I, I, . . ." or "I Am, I Am, . . ." in each area. End by dissolving all these separately sensed, felt, and chanted areas of the body into one whole-body awareness. Chant over and over, "I, I, I, . . ." or "I Am , I Am, . . . ," as if sitting in a huge sphere of energy that encases your body from head to foot. Then rise and get on with your day, trying to hold on to this global awareness of *I AM* and presence. If you lose it in activity, remember to remember yourself and it will come back to you. Eventually, you will be able to stay in a self-remembered state even in the midst of the most exacting activity, as I learned in Florida, one evening in 1998.

High Consciousness = High Performance Skills

While waiting to perform *Forever Jung* at the Maitland Civic Center in Orlando, Florida, I was sitting by the lake outside the building, some forty-five minutes before the performance. The sun was setting and its low angle caused myriad sparkles of light to dance off the ripples on the water's surface. Standing in the reeds at the edge of the lake, near where I sat on the grass, was a heron. It was so still that I had been there for ten minutes before I saw it. Suddenly, its neck arched and its head shot down into the lake, caught a fish, pulled back out of the water, swallowed the fish, and returned to its original position of perfect immobility. The whole scenario, the sunset on the water, and the perfect attunement with nature displayed by the heron put me into an altered state. The evening air became drunk with bliss and I entered the observing *I* mode. I then "watched" as my body got to its feet and started to walk around the lake.

None of the passersby noticed anything out of the ordinary. But again, I could see them as sleepwalkers in a dream, moving through life oblivious to the bliss that surrounded them. With the play about to start in fifteen minutes, *I* watched John Maxwell return to the theater, get into costume, clip on the remote microphone, converse with the stage crew, and walk out as the curtain went up to begin the play.

For the next two hours, this observing *I* watched the twenty characters and scenes from Jung's life unfold on stage in one of the most vivid and real performances ever. Afterward I greeted people who had stayed behind to offer words of appreciation. A Hindu couple, perhaps in their mid-fifties, approached me. The woman took both my hands in hers and gazed up with rapturous tear-washed eyes into my eyes.

"Oh, Doctor Jung," she said emotionally, "it was so beautiful, so inspiring." What struck me as unusual about this incident was that Indian women generally avoid physical contact with strangers and here she was holding both my hands. Also, the play had been performed while I was in the "observer" mode. But apparently the characters presented on stage had been so real that she thought I *was* "Doctor Jung"!

From this we may deduce that being in a self-observing "witness" mode is not only not incapacitating, it can actually help us to attain peak performance levels. It is also clear that self-observation in the manner described and self-remembering are closely related, and the former can precipitate the latter. Note too that in the incident by the lake, I did not actually do anything to trigger the experience. It simply happened without an act of conscious will on my part. But the groundwork had been laid by my regular practice of the life-changing techniques that prepared my body and brain to host such an experience.

Apparently, we are caught in a Catch-22 whereby we have to develop conscious will to get to those moments in time where no will at all is involved in being where we wanted to get. It is as if we must climb the tower of knowing by self-effort, but can only fly into space from it by letting go.

We Are All Actors in the Holographic Cinema of Life

Sir Laurence Olivier said that appearing before an audience is like lion taming. One false move, one lapse of attention on your part, and they will have your leg off. They want to applaud you for being professional enough to evade this. But at the same time they want to see you fall. Our social lives are largely improvisational theater. We never know what the next scene will be or who we shall be required to act (interact) with. If we play our parts well, we can pass safely through the various dramas that come our way and may even thrive. The trick is to avoid being undone by bad actors, scene-snatching egotists who will steal our lines and our lives and try to make us stumble and look ridiculous before our peers.

Don't let them do it. Be strong! Be brave! Look those scenery-chewing vagabonds in the eye of your choice and say inwardly, "I'm not taking delivery of that," and then speak your truth. You don't need to wound or harm them. But you must not be like the snake that was afraid to hiss. When the circumstances call for it, by all means let them have it! You can even roar like a lion at times. Just remember to remember yourself and be a *conscious actor* when you do it. Then there will be no malice behind your actions. You will simply be clearing a space in which truth can reorder itself and manifest more clearly in your life and the lives of those around you.

A higher intelligence is active in the world at all times. Experiences such as the one I had in Florida are given to show it in operation so that we can further align ourselves with its beneficence. I have taken the time to describe my experience of it in that particular instance because I was required to perform a regular job while simultaneously maintaining a heightened state of awareness. Far from being incapacitating, such states can and must give rise to our ability to execute our tasks in the world with excellence.

By demonstrating the power of the soul in action, we confound those who would ridicule and seek to devalue spirituality. Even a gross materialist cannot argue successfully against a life that is lived well. If our soul aspirations cause us to appear ungrounded, flaky, irresponsible, or just plain weird to other people, Utopia for the Planet Earth will remain a dream.

We need to have our feet firmly planted on the ground while our far-reaching consciousness probes the stars for the energy and vision that make us feel at home in the universe. The vastness of space is *not* empty. It is pervaded in every direction by a substance we on earth know and recognize as love. This magnetic power is pulling us back into the Godhead from which all else has sprung. At the same time it is pouring through us into the world to heal it with a visionary, energetic transmission of human possibility. To align ourselves with this love requires enormous courage, because we are living in a world filled with people who have failed to connect with life, *even within themselves.* Therefore love and its associative spiritual values have been trampled upon for centuries while cynicism and interpersonal cruelty have prevailed.

You and I have not only a right, we also have a *duty,* to protect ourselves from the tyranny of minds that worship the illusory delusion of separateness. Only by living in the energy that comes from lives filled with spirit, can we demonstrate the power of love over the ego-driven pride of minds that try to live in separation from the Eternal Good.

G. I. Gurdjieff described love as "knowing and understanding enough to be able to aid someone else in doing something necessary for himself, even when that person is not conscious of the need and might work against you. Only in this sense is love real and worthy of the name."

Having read this book, you now have the means at your disposal to help other people in the manner described above—even if they are "not conscious of the need and might work against you." Through the application of what you now know from reading this book, you are, and will be, creating a new world of enlightened personal interaction. Every time you look into the eyes of other people while you self-remember, you will see the Divine in those people, even if they are "working against" themselves. And for a moment, they may remember themselves too. *I AM* will be present and the hypnotic sleep of Maya's spell undone by the awakening touch of *that which is true seeing itself* in another human being.

May you ever grow in courage, strength, and wisdom as you venture out to play your part in the evolutionary struggle of our times. Shakespeare did not quite get it right. "All the world" is not a stage—it's a holographic movie theater! We are all winging our way through the play we call life as best we can, improvising as we go. When you have to appear in a dramatic scene that requires you to make others aware of your personal value and spiritual power, do so with joy and peace in your soul. We are never alone. There is always back-up from *I AM,* which we have been sent here to represent. And the presence of *I AM* can be invoked in all our affairs through self-remembering. Then the waters of the duality of life will part before us and we shall pass safely through all the difficulties that come our way.

And while you are out there in the madness, trying to remember yourself, remember too that everything we see is simply an illusion, a play of atoms masquerading as the screen of solid matter we call reality. On that screen, God is playing Hollywood with a cast of billions. Play your part well . . . and I'll see you in the movies!

Recommended Reading

In Search of the Miraculous by P. D. Ouspensky, 1949 and 2001. An essential overview of the life and teachings of G. I. Gurdjieff through conversations with this enigmatic teacher. Contains much information on shifts in self-perception required to awaken from the collective trance. An uncompromising look at the automatism that runs the human race and the difficult position we are in on the planet Earth. Not for the faint-hearted or mentally lazy.

Waking Up by Charles Tart, 1986 and 2001. An easier entry into the collective sleep phenomenon likening the human brain to the hard drive of a computer and life experience to the software. Contains some useful exercises, including Gurdjieff's "sensing and feeling" technique.

The Gurdjieff Work by Kathleen Speeth, 1989. A small volume outlining all the basic Gurdjieff principles with illustrations. Explains the law of three and seven and other ideas in simple, direct terms. Also gives an overview of various Gurdjieff groups. Warns about self-appointed teachers who claim lineage from the man himself and have developed a cultlike atmosphere around themselves.

Awaken Healing Light of the Tao by Mantak and Maneewan Chia, 1993. A sweeping overview of the Taoist approach to developing one's Chi with a view to being able to make the body able to trigger high states of consciousness without becoming personally unbalanced. Extremely useful for Westerners interested in balanced personal evolution.

Taoist Secrets of Love: Cultivating Male Sexual Energy by Mantak Chia, 1984. In-depth coverage of all aspects of refining sexual energy and using it to open up new cellular territory in the brain and feed it with the most powerful awakening energy available to us. Beautifully written with drawings, diagrams, and specific techniques.

Memories, Dreams, and Reflections by C. G. Jung, 1961, 1962, 1963, and 1989. This "inner autobiography" is an essential read for all who wish to understand their psychological nature. Jung's personal experiences have a universal appeal and his story can have a healing effect upon the open-minded reader.

Autobiography of a Yogi by Paramahansa Yogananda, 1946, 1974, and 1998. The first teacher from India to come to America (in 1927) and stay for decades, Yogananda's account of his extraordinary encounters with advanced souls during his search for illumination rings with rare authenticity. Beatle George Harrison was highly enamored of this teacher and his book, claiming that "when I read it I knew it was the truth." Contains many accounts of exalted states of consciousness that inspire the reader to seek the same.

Hypnotism and Mysticism of India by Ormond McGill, 1979. Known as "the Dean of American Hypnotists," McGill tells of his travels in India seeking the truth behind such phenomena as the Indian rope trick and other seemingly miraculous events. What he came across instead is knowledge of how the *I AM* consciousness is behind the power to command all phenomena of nature to bend to our true desires. A fascinating text with many techniques.

How to Win Any Argument Without Raising Your Voice, Losing Your Cool, or Coming to Blows by Robert Mayer, 2005. Full of street-smart savvy about how to get along with people, Mayer offers a nonconfrontational approach that has an Aikido-like sensibility to sway people into harmony with us. Larry King calls Mayer "a lawyer's lawyer"; this entertaining, fun book enables readers to employ his real-world negotiation and persuasion tactics while implementing the heightened-awareness exercises.

Science and the Akashic Field: An Integral Theory of Everything by Ervin Laszlo, 2004. This widely acclaimed overview of the latest scientific insights into how the universe appears to be what it is creates a marriage of ancient wisdom with modern intelligence. The author explains in direct, comprehensible scientific terms how we are all connected to everything and reinforces the practical implications of *I AM* consciousness. There is no escape from the underlying oneness of creation and for those who need scientific theory to be convinced to make the leap to hyper-reality, here it is.

Consciousness Speaks by Ramesh S. Balsekar, 1993. Nondualism is a state of consciousness in which the play of opposites that appear to predominate everywhere in "reality" is canceled out by direct perception of unity.

Balsekar is a major proponent of the view that "everything simply happens" and that nobody is doing or can do anything. Disturbing, yes! But also very much in line with the Gurdjieff view of life. Learning to simply let everything happen in, through, and around us without interference by ordinary minds is the essence of truth.

Waking the Tiger by Peter Levine, 1997. A world-renowned expert on recovering from trauma makes a valid case for recovering our "sensed/felt" connection with our bodies and emotions. This enormously popular book gives hope and vision that we can and must heal from the traumatic effects of life through reconnection with self.

Brain Lock: Free Yourself from Obsessive-Compulsive Behavior by Jeffery M. Schwartz, 1997. Want to get rid of those ridiculous, rubbishy thoughts that parasitically invade your brain? If Howard Hughes had had this book he might not have become a hand-washing recluse. The stories of people obsessing that ketchup bottles contain blood or going out in the night to scrub car battery acid leaks from neighbors' driveways may seem like hilarious black comedy. But these folks are out there with us on the freeway and the same impulses lurk in our brains. Schwartz prescribes a four-step program to nip obsessive thinking in the bud and be free of our inner idiots.

Change Your Brain, Change Your Life: The Breakthrough Program for Conquering Anxiety, Depression, Obsessiveness, Anger, and Impulsiveness by Daniel G. Amen, M.D., 1999. Scare your teenagers straight with horrifying brain-scan pictures showing how drugs and booze punch holes in the surface of the brain and shrivel it up. Also learn how to reprogram your brain and heal it so that it functions optimally to achieve a supra-normalcy of function.

The Invisible Partners: How the Male and Female in Each of Us Affects Our Relationships by John A. Sanford, 1980. Despite being an unlikely blend of Jungian psychologist and Episcopalian minister, Sanford manages to nail the phenomenon of every man having a female side and every woman an inner man, and how these archetypal forces can act out through us to interfere with our relationships. A highly practical psychological guide to finding personal balance and wholeness in this time of gender identity confusion.

About the Author

Originally from North Wales, John Maxwell Taylor is known internationally for his twenty-character, one-man play, *Forever Jung,* based on the life of pioneering Swiss psychologist Carl Gustav Jung. In 1996 Taylor received the prestigious Gradiva Award in the Best Actor category for his portrayal of Jung from the National Association for the Advancement of Psychoanalysis in New York. His other theater works include *Faustorama: The Metaphysical Musical* and *Crazy Wisdom,* a musical on the life of Russian mystic and philosopher G. I. Gurdjieff. In addition to Jung and Gurdjieff, Taylor has been influenced by the work of Paramahansa Yogananda and Taoist master Mantak Chia.

As a pioneering European rock star in the sixties, Taylor with his bands opened for The Beatles and The Rolling Stones in Paris, and performed for Queen Elizabeth and family on the Royal Variety Show at the London Palladium. For the last ten years he has led workshops in personal and spiritual transformation throughout the United States. He lives in Encinitas, California.

Learn more about John Maxwell Taylor at
www.worldtransformations.com